William Walker Wilkins

Political Ballads of the Seventeenth and Eighteenth Centuries

Vol. 1

William Walker Wilkins

Political Ballads of the Seventeenth and Eighteenth Centuries
Vol. 1

ISBN/EAN: 9783744776646

Printed in Europe, USA, Canada, Australia, Japan

Cover: Foto ©Thomas Meinert / pixelio.de

More available books at **www.hansebooks.com**

POLITICAL BALLADS

OF THE

SEVENTEENTH AND EIGHTEENTH CENTURIES

ANNOTATED

BY W. WALKER WILKINS

"*More solid things do not show the complexion of the times so well as Ballads and Libels*"—Selden's Table-Talk

In Two Vols.

VOLUME THE FIRST

LONDON
LONGMAN, GREEN, LONGMAN, AND ROBERTS
MDCCCLX

PREFACE.

NEARLY one hundred and fifty years have elapsed since the last *Collection of State Poems* was published. And that collection, which was comprised originally in two, but afterwards augmented to four volumes, relates only to a period of our history extending over little more than half a century—namely, from the usurpation of Cromwell to the accession of Queen Anne. But for the fact that the volumes in question are "by various hands," and therefore represent more fully than any others the satirical wit of the limited period to which they refer, they would scarcely deserve a passing notice, so very partial and inaccurate are the contents of them. They contain, moreover, few *political ballads*, properly so called; but consist almost entirely of long and insipid "poems," chiefly from the pens of Buckingham, Rochester, and other exalted personages, who exercised in their day considerable influence about the Court, and in the government of the country, and who, rather as an exercise of a supposed necessary accomplishment than from any baser motive, occasionally amused themselves with ridiculing the foibles of majesty, and exposing the intrigues of their rivals for his confidence. Such writers are manifestly no exponents of the *popular mind:* the vast majority of their compositions have long since fallen into neglect, almost oblivion, and are never likely again to interest, much less influence, any class of readers.

Whilst every other department of literature has been thoroughly explored, amplified, and variously illustrated, our modern Political Songs and Ballads — the best popular illustrations of history — constitute the solitary exception to the general rule. Two causes in particular may be assigned for the singular indifference with which such compositions have been hitherto treated. In the first place, they are so diffusely scattered as to render hopeless any attempt by a single individual to make, if such a thing were desirable, an entire collection of them, or indeed any approximation to it; and secondly, their rarely possessing any literary merit.

There are, however, few compositions more

interesting in themselves, or that offer more valuable material to the historical inquirer, than these ephemeral productions. Referring to an age less fastidious in its tastes and expressions than our own, too many of them, it cannot be denied, are not only faulty in construction, but also objectionable in matter. Yet these are not the only *criteria* by which they should be judged. The ordinary rules of criticism, indeed, do not apply to them. They are the emphatic songs of a liberty-loving people; they contain the out-pourings of unconquerable spirits, the unequivocal sentiments of resolute men; in a word, they are the rude but most expressive monuments of the great political struggles in which our jealous ancestors were engaged; and on that account they merit, if not our critical admiration, at all events deliverance from absolute oblivion. In the absence of these artless effusions, our social history would be incomplete. They exhibit as well the manners as the feelings of past generations. The student, by looking narrowly into them, may oftentimes be enabled to deduce most important conclusions respecting the origin and issue of former insurrections and factions; just in the same manner as the geologist, who, detecting on the surface of the sedimentary rock the latent impressions of some primeval storm, or the footprints of races long extinct, determines the course of the one and the character of the other.

"The popular songs of a nation (remarks an able writer on Political Literature) constitute one of the most palpable manifestations of its political feelings and sympathies; and this is more strikingly the case, if other legitimate channels for the expression of public sentiment be choked or dried up by the repressive hand of power. The song-writer is an ubiquitous and privileged character. He pursues his avocation in the family circle, in the workshop, in the tavern, at the gay festival, in the squalid alley, in the barrack-room, and in the mess-room of the sailor. His strains are hearty, bold, and genial; the embodiment of thought, emotion, and melody. The popular song is easy, simple, and born of the incidents of the day. It is the intellectual personification of the feelings and opinions of a people. It is the delight of the multitude, the joy and solace of the many. It laughs in derision at despotic power, lightens the social burdens of life, and inspires the patriot with hope. Of the popular satirical song much has been written, but nothing definitely settled. There is a schism among critics on its nature and character. It is a compound of delicate essences and incommunicable graces which bids defiance to definition. But we know that popular songs must be the energetic and faithful transcripts of general experience and feelings. Their necessary characteristics are fancy, passion, dramatic effect, rapidity, and pathos. They are not transferable; the popular satire and humour of one country cannot be adequately relished by another; nor, in the same country, are such productions so influential on public opinion in subsequent periods of its history, as when they first appeared. Time blunts the instrument, and deadens the national perceptions of the witty and ridiculous."

The real value and importance of such ephemeral productions may be best discerned in the volumes of the late Lord Macaulay, the only native historian who has thought them worthy of his particular study and use. It is no disparagement to the literary fame of that distinguished writer, to affirm that they have imparted to his pages a vitality which the profoundest knowledge of the principles of human action, combined with the greatest erudition and the higheft defcriptive powers, could never have effected without them. It was from thefe long-neglected picture-writings of great hiftorical fcenes, and of the celebrated individuals who are crowded in them —" in their habit as they lived "— that he derived fo much of his wonderfully minute knowledge of all that related to the ftirring times of the feventeenth and eighteenth centuries. To thefe defpifed and inexhauftible fources of information, he was principally indebted for his life-like delineations of character; for his defcriptions of popular commotions; and, not unfrequently, for his knowledge of the motives by which public men were actuated, at particular conjunctures, in their conduct.

The admirable ufe made of them by Lord Macaulay, in his hiftorical fragment and effays, has fuggefted the idea of collecting and republifhing the following fpecimens. They have been gleaned from exceedingly rare (not a few, I believe, *unique*) fingle-fheets and broadfides, old manufcripts, and contemporary journals, in the national and other libraries. A few have been extracted from very fcarce volumes, which were publifhed at the clofe of the feventeenth or early in the eighteenth century; and fewer ftill have been derived from more modern books, in order to give a greater completeness to the series. Thus by far the larger portion will be entirely new to the generality of readers.

In my selection of the Ballads I have been guided (so far, that is, as the limited means at my disposal would admit) by a desire to reproduce such only as are particularly characteristic or illustrative of the periods to which they respectively refer; and, at the same time are not unfitted to meet the general eye. Licentiousness, unfortunately, as every literary antiquary knows, is the rule rather than the exception with this class of popular compositions.

It is almost unnecessary to state that the names of the various parties alluded to in these pages are rarely to be found in the original broadsides, or in the early volumes whence they have been obtained. Sometimes names of individuals have been omitted altogether, at others their initials only have been given, for reasons too obvious to mention. In restoring them (which was by no means the least onerous part of my editorial labours), without the usual distinguishing brackets, I have been led to do so simply to avoid fatiguing the eye of the reader, and disfiguring almost every page with very needless additions. As a guarantee, however, for accuracy in thefe important refpects, I beg to affure the reader that, in every doubtful inftance, I have never relied exclufively upon my own judgment, but invariably have fought that of fome literary friend better qualified than myfelf to folve the difficulty. I feel confident, therefore, that no error of the kind referred to will be detected in the following pages.

My original intention was to include in the prefent collection the moft celebrated political ballads referring to the reigns of the laft two Georges; but finding my prefcribed limits would not admit of anything like juftice being done to them, I have been reluctantly compelled to abandon that part of my fcheme. Should, however, the prefent feries happily meet with the approbation of the public, I fhall furnifh with pleafure the remaining inftalment, in the fhape of an additional volume.

London, October, 1860.

CONTENTS

OF

THE FIRST VOLUME.

CHARLES I.

A. D.		PAGE
1641.	The Organ's Echo	3
	On the Army marching from London . . .	7
1643.	When the King enjoys his own again	10
1644.	A Prognoſtication on Will Laud, late Archbiſhop of Canterbury	13
1646.	A Mad World, my Maſters	19
	The New Litany	23
1647.	The Parliament	28
	The Anarchie, or the Bleſſed Reformation ſince 1640	32
	On his Majeſty coming to Holmby . . .	38
	The Members' Juſtification	40
	The Cryes of Weſtminſter	43
	I Thank You Twice	54
	Prattle Your Pleaſure (under the Roſe) . .	57
	The Old Proteſtant's Litany	59
	The Cities Welcome to Colonel Rich and Colonel Baxter	65
1648.	The Puritan	71

THE COMMONWEALTH.

A.D.		PAGE
1649.	A Coffin for King Charles, a Crown for Cromwell, and a Pit for the People	79
	The Dominion of the Sword	89
	A Salt Tear	91
	The State's New Coin	95
1652.	Upon the General Pardon paſſed by the Rump	96
1653.	The Houſe out of Doors	100
	The Parliament Routed	105
	The Sale of Rebellion's Houſe-hold Stuff	111
	A Chriſtmas Song	117
1654.	A Jolt on Michaelmas Day	121
1655.	A Free Parliament Litany	125
1657.	The Protecting Brewer	132
	A Ballad	135
1659.	A New Ballad to an Old Tune	138
1660.	Win at Firſt, and Loſe at Laſt	144

CHARLES II.

1660.	The Noble Progreſs	153
	A Ballad	159
	The Cavalier's Complaint	162
	An Echo to the Cavalier's Complaint	165
1661.	A Turn-coat of the Times	167
1663.	The Old Cloak	173
1666.	Clarendon's Houſe Warming	177
1674.	On the Lord Mayor and Court of Aldermen preſenting the King and the Duke of York with a Copy of their Freedom	185
1676.	The Hiſtory of Inſipids	190

THE FIRST VOLUME.

A.D.		PAGE
1678.	The Geneva Ballad	203
	Titus Telltroth	207
	Information	213
1679.	On the Lord Chancellor's Speech to Parliament	216
	A New Satirical Ballad of the Licentiousness of the Times	219
	Geneva and Rome ; or, the Zeal of both boiling over	224
1680.	The Loyal Tories Delight	227
1679.	The King's Vows	231
1683.	The Loyal Sheriffs of London and Middlesex, upon their Election	236
	London's Lamentation for the Loss of their Charter	241
	Vienna's Triumph	245
	Dagon's Fall	249

JAMES II.

1687.	A Short Litany	255
1688.	The Advice	258
	The Catholic Ballad	261
1687.	The True Protestant Litany	268
1688.	Private Occurrences	270
	Lilli Burlero	275
	A New Song of an Orange	279

POLITICAL BALLADS

CHARLES I.

THE ORGAN'S ECHO.

(To the tune of the Cathedral Service.)

[Southey, the ableft apologift of Laud, ftates that libels and ballads againft the Archbifhop "were hawked and fung through ftreets, and caricatures exhibited, in which he was reprefented as caged, or chained to a poft; and with fuch things the rabble made fport at taverns and alehoufes, being as drunk with malice as with the liquor they fwilled in." This is doubtlefs one of the ballads referred to. The original broadfide whence it is copied is furmounted with a rude woodcut of the unfortunate Archbifhop bound to a poft, with a pair of expanded wings on his fhoulders, fignificant of his defire to efcape. "Neile of Winchefter and Laud of London (fays Carlyle) were a frightfully ceremonial pair of bifhops; the fountain they of innumerable tendencies to papiftry and the old clothes of Babylon." In juftice, however, to the memory of the Archbifhop, it fhould be added that whilft his great reverence for antiquity and fondnefs for the pomps and ceremonies of religion expofed him to the hatred and perfecution of the fanatical Puritans, his jealous guardianfhip of the interefts of the Church of England rendered him equally obnoxious to the Papal Court, where his judicial murder was regarded as more likely to advance than retard the Roman Catholic caufe in this country.]

*EMENTO MORI,*
I'll tell you a ftrange ftory,
Will make you all forry,
For our old friend William;
   Alas, poor William.

As he was in his bravery,
And thought to bring us all in slavery,
The Parliament found out his knavery,
And so fell William;
    Alas, poor William.

His pope-like domineering,
And some other tricks appearing,
Provoked Sir Edward Deering*,
To blame the old prelate;
    Alas, poor prelate.

Some say he was in hope,
To bring England again to th' Pope;
But now he's in danger of an axe or a rope;
Farewell old Canterbury;
    Alas, poor Canterbury.

There's another of the same litter,
Whose breech cannot choose but twitter,
He was against all goodness so bitter,
'Twas the Bishop of Ely.†
    Alas, poor Ely.

---

* Alluding to Sir Edward's speech in Parliament (Session 1640) on the government of the Church, in which he accused Laud and other prelates of obtruding new canon laws upon the laity, after the fashion of Rome.

† Dr. Matthew Wren, previously Bishop of Norwich, but now of Ely, who was deprived 5th July, 1641, and committed to the Tower for "high misdemeanours" in the last mentioned diocese.

And all the reſt of that lordly crew,
Their great inſolencies are like to rue,
As ſoon as Parliament their lives do view,
Come down, brave prelates;
    Alas, poor prelates.

You know likewiſe in this two or three year,
Many a one for Lamb* paid very dear,
But now he begins to ſtink for fear;
Therefore take heed Doctor Lamb;
    Alas, poor Doctor Lamb.

Then there is alſo one Doctor Duck†,
The proverb ſays, *What's worſe than ill luck;*
We hope the Parliament his feathers will pluck,
For being ſo buſy, Doctor Duck;
    Alas, poor Doctor Duck.

Deans and Chapters with their retinue,
Are not like long for to continue,
They have ſo abuſed their great revenue;
That down muſt ceremonies;
    Alas, popiſh ceremonies.

---

* Dr. Lamb, a high churchman, and preacher of St. Mary Hall, in Oxford; he ſurvived the Rebellion, and died (1664) rector of St. Andrew's, Holborn.

† Dr. Arthur Duck, Chancellor of Wells and London. He was one of the "ſuffering" clergy, and died 1648.

Ecclesiastical courts are down too, they say,
England may be glad of that happy day,
They have, of late, borne such a great sway,
That farewell those poor proctors ;
    Alas, poor proctors.

And now the papists are at their wits ends,
To see the downfall of so many friends,
But they shall all rue it ere the Parliament ends,
Believe it, Roman Catholics ;
    Alas, poor Catholics.

There is another that hardly thrives,
Which many men of life deprives,
He was in Newgate for having two wives,
It is the young hangman ;
    Alas, poor hangman.*

---

* Whether Derrick or Brandon is here referred to matters nothing; the fact of associating such a functionary with prelates and deans is characteristic of the period.

ON THE ARMY MARCHING FROM LONDON.

[The Parliament adjourned itfelf on the 3rd and reaffembled on the 20th September, 1641. In that interval all claffes were greatly agitated by the movements of the Royalifts, whom they feared might furprife the capital. To fecure their own perfons from infult, as well as to reftrain thofe who fecretly fympathifed with the King, the Parliament demanded a guard from the Earl of Effex, before the Army fet forth, which was immediately granted. The ballad —a royalift's effufion —ridicules the pretenfions and fears of the Parliamentary leaders.]

OME tell me what you lack,
  That the knaves in a pack,
 You will not fee forthcoming:
  Love you treafon fo well,
  That you'll neither buy nor fell,
 But keep a noife with your drumming.

  What do you guard,
  With your watch and ward,
 Your own ware or wife's thing?
  If up come the blades,
  Down go all your trades,
 They'll not leave you a dead or a live thing.

What do your prophets fay?
When will come that very day,
That all your money fhall be paid in?
Great Strafford he is dead*,
You have cut off his head,
And the Bifhops are all laid in.†

Yet ftill you grow poor,
As any common w——,
That long hath been without her jading;
None will come and buy,
You may learn to fwear and lie,
As you were wont to do with your trading.

Yet ftill I do find,
There's fomething in the wind,
That long hath been a-framing;
O that is flat and plain,
The Parliament muft reign,
And you'll have a king by naming.

---

* The earl fuffered 12th May, 1641.

† The prelates here alluded to were thofe who, at the inftigation of Williams, Archbifhop of York, forwarded a declaration to the Lords, complaining that they were unable to travel in fafety to their places in Parliament, and at the fame time protefting againft the validity of any refolutions, &c., paffed in their abfence. For this prelatical declaration, eleven of its fubfcribers, including the Archbifhop, were, by a vote of the Lower Houfe, committed to the Tower, and charged with *high treafon!*

We may fee how they can,
From a woman take a man,
If fo they pleafe to declare him;
But let them take heed,
For the King is king indeed,
And the foldiers cannot fpare him.

Is it nothing, do you think,
Twenty-four in a clink,
Kings to make up his fucceffion:
Befides you have as good,
Three princes of his blood,
And three kingdoms in poffeffion.

His virtues to ye,
Something, too, fhould be,
If that you could amend them;
But inftead of chafte and juft,
You'll have cruelty & luft.—
Marry, another King Harry God fend you!

WHEN THE KING ENJOYS HIS OWN AGAIN.

BY MARTIN PARKER.

[There are several verſions of this celebrated ballad extant; this is the original one. Ritſon included it in his *Collection of Ancient Songs*, but was unaware of the fact that Martin Parker (who he deſcribes as a mere Grub Street ſcribbler and great ballad-monger of Charles the Firſt's time) was the author of it. In reference to it, he remarks: "It is with particular pleaſure that the editor is enabled to reſtore to the public the original words of the moſt famous and popular air ever heard of in this country. Invented to ſupport the declining intereſt of the royal martyr, it ſerved afterwards with more ſucceſs to keep up the ſpirits of the Cavaliers, and promote the reſtoration of his ſon; an event it was employed to celebrate all over the kingdom. At the Revolution [of 1688] it of courſe became an inherent of the exiled family, whoſe cauſe it never deſerted."]

HAT Booker* can prognoſticate,
  Concerning kings or kingdoms' fate?
 I think myſelf to be as wiſe
 As he that gazeth on the ſkies:

---

* Booker, Pond, Rivers, Swallow, Dove, and Dade, whoſe names occur in this and the following ſtanza, were the moſt famous aſtrologers and almanac makers in the ſeventeenth century.

My skill goes beyond,
The depth of a Pond,
Or Rivers in the greatest rain;
Whereby I can tell,
All things will be well,
When the king enjoys his own again.

There's neither Swallow, Dove, nor Dade,
Can soar more high, nor deeper wade;
Nor show a reason from the stars,
What causeth peace or civil wars:
The man in the moon
May wear out his shoon,
By running after Charles his wain;
But all's to no end,
For the times will not mend,
Till the king enjoys his own again.

Though for a time we see Whitehall
With cobwebs hanging on the wall,
Instead of silk and silver brave,
Which formerly it used to have;
With rich perfume
In every room,
Delightful to that princely train,
Which again you shall see,
When the time it shall be,
That the king enjoys his own again.

Full forty years the royal crown
    Hath been his father's and his own;
And is there any one but he,
    That in the fame fhould fharer be?
        For who better may
        The fceptre fway,
    Than he that hath fuch right to reign?
        Then let's hope for a peace,
        For the wars will not ceafe,
Till the king enjoys his own again.

Till then upon Ararat's hill
    My Hope fhall caft her anchor ftill,
Until I fee fome peaceful dove
    Bring home the branch I dearly love:
        Then will I wait,
        Till the waters abate,
    Which now difturb my troubled brain,
        Elfe never rejoice,
        Till I hear the voice,
That the king enjoys his own again.

A PROGNOSTICATION ON WILL LAUD, LATE ARCHBISHOP OF CANTERBURY,

WRITTEN A.D. 1641, WHICH ACCORDINGLY IS COME TO PASS.

[The date of this ballad is 1644, and was probably written shortly after the fate of the Archbishop was made known. His trial lasted from the 12th March, 1643-4, to the 29th July, 1644. The bill of attainder against him was passed on the 4th January, 1644-5, and he suffered on Tower Hill with great firmness on the 10th of the same month.]

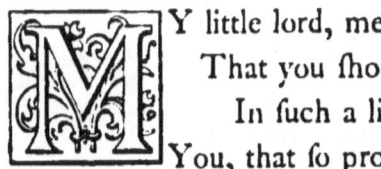

MY little lord, methinks 'tis strange,
 That you should suffer such a change,
  In such a little space.
You, that so proudly t'other day,
 Did rule the king, and country sway,
  Must budge to 'nother place.

Remember now from whence you came,
 And that your grandsires of your name,
  Were dressers of old cloth.*

---

* The Archbishop's father was a clothier at Reading.

Go, bid the dead men bring their shears,
And dress your coat to save your ears,
   Or pawn your head for both.

The wind shakes cedars that are tall,
An haughty mind must have a fall,
   You are but low I see;
And good it had been for you still,
If both your body, mind, and will,
   In equal shape should be.

The king by heark'ning to your charms,
Hugg'd our destruction in his arms,
   And gates to foes did ope;
Your staff would strike his sceptre down,
Your mitre would o'ertop the crown,
   If you should be a Pope.

But you that did so firmly stand,
To bring in Popery in this land,
   Have miss'd your hellish aim;
Your saints fall down, your angels fly,
Your crosses on yourself do lie,
   Your craft will be your shame.

We scorn that Popes with crozier staves,
Mitres, or keys, should make us slaves,
   And to their feet to bend:

The Pope and his malicious crew,
We hope to handle all, like you,
    And bring them to an end.

The filenc'd clergy, void of fear,
In your damnation will bear fhare,
    And fpeak their mind at large :
Your cheefe-cake cap and magpie gown,
That make fuch ftrife in ev'ry town,
    Muft now defray your charge.

Within this fix years fix ears have
Been cropt off worthy men and grave,
    For fpeaking what was true ;
But if your fubtle head and ears
Can fatisfy thofe fix of theirs,
    Expect but what's your due.

Poor people that have felt your rod,
Yield *laud* to the devil *, praise to God,
    For freeing them from thrall ;
Your little *grace*, for want of grace,
Muft lofe your patriarchal place,
    And have no grace at all.

---

* Armftrong, the king's jefter, once afked permiffion of his Majefty to fay grace at dinner, when the Archbifhop was prefent, which requeft being granted him, he exclaimed "All praife to the Lord, and little *laud* to the devil!" a witticifm that was never forgotten by the vulgar in the times of the Rebellion.

Your white lawn sleeves that were the wings
Whereon you soared to lofty things,
    Must be your fins to swim ;
Th' Archbishop's *see* by Thames must go,
With him unto the Tower below,
    There to be rack'd like him.

Your oath cuts deep, your lies hurt sore,
Your *canons* made Scot's cannons roar,
    But now I hope you'll find,
That there are cannons in the Tower,
Will quickly batter down your power,
    And sink your haughty mind.

The Commonalty have made a vow,
No oath, no canons to allow,
    No Bishop's *Common Prayer;*
No lazy prelates that shall spend
Such great revenues to no end,
    But virtue to impair.

Dumb dogs that wallow in such store,
That would suffice above a score,
    Pastors of upright will ;
Now they'll make all the bishops teach,
And you must in the pulpit preach,
    That stands on Tower Hill.

When the young lads to you did come,
You knew their meaning by the drum,
   You had better yielded then *;
Your head and body then might have
One death, one burial, and one grave,
   By boys—but two by men.

But you that by your judgments clear
Will make five quarters in a year,
   And hang them on the gates
That head shall stand upon the bridge,
When your's shall under Traitor's trudge,
   And smile on your miss'd pates.

The little *Wren*† that soar'd so high
Thought on his wings away to fly,
   Like *Finch* ‡, I know not whither;
But now the subtle whirly-*Wind-*
Debanke § hath left the bird behind,
   You two must flock together.

---

* Five hundred London apprentices marched to Lambeth Palace to seize him; but the Archbishop, being apprised of their design, effected his escape. One of the ringleaders, a tailor, was hung for this attempt.

† See ante, p. 4.

‡ Lord-Keeper Finch, who, to save his life, fled beyond sea, and did not return till the Restoration.

§ Sir Francis Windebanke, Secretary of State, and (says Whitelock) "a great intimate of Archbishop Laud, having been questioned

A bishop's head, a deputy's breast,
A *Finch's* tongue, a *Wren* from 's nest,
   Will set the Devil on foot;
He's like to have a dainty dish,
At once both flesh and fowl and fish,
   And *Duck* and *Lamb* to boot.

But this I say, that your lewd life
Did fill both Church and State with strife,
   And trample on the Crown;
Like a bless'd martyr you will die,
For Church's good; she rises high,
   When such as you fall down.

---

for reprieving Jesuits and priests, and suspected of worse matters, to prevent any farther trial, he escaped into France [1640], where he remained to his death (as is reported) a professed papist."

A MAD WORLD, MY MASTERS.

[This ballad illustrates the confusion of the times by expoſing the various expedients of the Commons to make themſelves feared. In a ſimilar ſpirit, Marchmont Needham wrote, a few months later, in his *Mercurius Pragmaticus:*

"O goodly kirk that we have got
  Of Loudon's information;
What thanks we owe unto the Scot
  For our bleſt Reformation!

The Crown and Sceptre out of date,
  The Mitre low doth lie;
While we are govern'd by a ſtate,
  And hug Democracy.

We have no King, we are all kings,
  And each doth do his pleaſure;
And therefore 'tis we act ſuch things,
  And ſin beyond all meaſure.

When we have toil'd ourſelves in vain,
  For to be rulers all,
We muſt entreat our Soveraign
  For to be Principal!"]

E have a King and yet no king,
  For he hath loſt his power;
For 'gainſt his will his ſubjects are
  Impriſon'd in the Tower.

We had ſome laws (but now no laws)
  By which he held his crown;

And we had eſtates and liberties,
    But now they're voted down.

We had religion, but of late,
    That's beaten down with clubs;
Whilſt that profaneneſs authoriſ'd
    Is belch'd forth in tubs.

We were free ſubjects born, but now
    We are by force made ſlaves,
By ſome whom we did count our friends,
    But in the end prov'd knaves.

And now to ſuch a grievous height
    Are our misfortunes grown,
That our eſtates are took away,
    By tricks before ne'er known.

For there are agents ſent abroad
    Moſt humbly for to crave
Our alms; but if they are deny'd,
    And of us nothing have;

Then by a vote *ex tempore*
    We are to priſon ſent,
Mark'd with the name of enemy,
    To King and Parliament:

And during our imprisonment,
  Their lawless bulls do thunder,
A licence to their soldiers,
  Our houses for to plunder:

And if their hounds do chance to smell
  A man whose fortunes are
Of some account, whose purse is full,
  Which now is somewhat rare;

A *monster* now *delinquent** term'd,
  He is declar'd to be,
And that his lands, as well as goods,
  Sequester'd ought to be.

As if our prisons were too good,
  He is to Yarmouth sent,
By virtue of a warrant from
  The King and Parliament.

Thus in our royal sovereign's name,
  And eke his power infus'd,
And by the virtue of the same,
  He and all his abus'd.

---

* Those who had been most noted for their adherence to the maxims of the Court or the principles of Laud were voted *delinquents*, and thereby kept in awe by the Commons, who, according as they conducted themselves towards that irresponsible body, could prosecute or leave them unmolested.

For by this means his caftles now
    Are in the power of thofe,
Who treach'roufly with might and main,
    Do ftrive him to depofe.

Arife, therefore, brave Britifh men,
    Fight for your King and State,
Againft thofe trait'rous men that ftrive,
    This realm to ruinate.

'Tis Pym, 'tis Pym*, and his colleagues,
    That did our woe engender;
Nought but their lives can end our woes,
    And us in fafety render.

---

* John Pym, the noted parliamentarian, who died in 1643.

THE NEW LITANY.

[Satirical pieces in the form of a Litany originated, and were very common, in the times of the Rebellion. They were so constructed to give additional annoyance to the Puritans and Presbyterians, whose rabid opposition to all established forms, whether in matters pertaining to religion or the state, was invariably based on a plea of conscience. The *New Litany* exposes the tyranny and hypocrisy of the now "omnipotent" Parliament.]

FROM an extempore prayer and a godly ditty,
From the churlish government of a city,
From the power of a country committee *,
    Libera nos, Domine.

From the Turk, the Pope, and the Scottish nation †,
From being govern'd by proclamation ‡,
And from an old Protestant, quite out of fashion,
    Libera, &c.

---

* During the war, the discretionary powers of the Country Committees were excused from a plea of necessity; but the nation was reduced to despair when it saw neither end put to their duration nor bounds to their authority. These committees could sequester, fine, imprison, and corporally punish, without law or remedy.

† The Scots, who had been summoned to the aid of the Parliament, committed depredations upon friend and foe alike.

‡ The King had prohibited, by proclamation (17th Oct. 1643), all commerce with London and other quarters of the Parliamentary forces.

From meddling with those that are out of our reaches,
From a fighting priest, and a soldier that preaches,
From an ignoramus that writes, and a woman that teaches,
      Libera, &c.

From the doctrine of deposing of a king,
From the *Directory**, or any such thing,
From a fine new marriage without a ring,
      Libera, &c.

From a city that yields at the first summons,
From plund'ring goods, either man or woman's,
Or having to do with the House of Commons,
      Libera, &c.

From a stumbling horse that tumbles o'er and o'er,
From ushering a lady or walking before,
From an English-Irish Rebel †, newly come o'er,
      Libera, &c.

---

* The *Directory* for the public worship of God, agreed upon by the Assembly of Divines at Westminster, 1644, which was substituted for the book of *Common Prayer*. Of that famous Synod, Marchmont Needham, when a Royalist, wrote:
  "Only one text may 'scape their hands,
   Since they have ta'en such pains:
  To lay their lords in iron bands,
  And bind their kings in chains!"

† The Earl of Thomond, who, when Lord Forbes was despatched to Munster, was (says Ludlow) "unwilling to oppose the English interest, and no less to make the (Irish) rebels his enemies, chose to withdraw himself into England." Though he bore offices under the Cromwells, yet he professed all loyalty to the Stuarts.

From compounding, or hanging in a filken altar,
From oaths and covenants, and being pounded in a mortar,
From contributions, or free-quarter,
        Libera, &c.

From mouldy bread, and mufty beer,
From a holiday's faft and a Friday's cheer,
From a brother-hood, and a fhe-cavalier *,
        Libera, &c.

From Nick Neuter, for you, and for you,
From Thomas Turn-coat, that will never prove true,
From a reverend Rabbi that's worfe than a Jew,
        Libera, &c.

From a Country-Juftice that ftill looks big,
From fwallowing up the Italian fig,
Or learning of the Scottifh jig,
        Libera, &c.

From being taken in a difguife,
From believing of the printed lies,
From the Devil and from the Excife †,
        Libera, &c.

---

 * Alluding, probably, to the warlike lady Anne, wife of Sir Wm. Ingleby, of Ripley, Yorkfhire, who accompanied her hufband throughout the civil war.

 † The excife was one of the principal and moft obnoxious taxes levied by the Long Parliament. It was firft introduced in 1643, by

From a broken pate with a pint pot,
For fighting for I know not what,
And from a friend as falſe as a Scot,
>> *Libera, &c.*

From one that ſpeaks no ſenſe, yet talks all that he can,
From an old woman and a Parliament man,
From an Anabaptiſt and a Preſbyter man,
>> *Libera, &c.*

From Iriſh rebels and Welſh hubbub-men,
From Independents and their tub-men,
From ſheriffs' bailiffs, and their club-men,
>> *Libera, &c.*

From one that cares not what he ſaith,
From truſting one that never payeth,
From a private preacher and a public faith,
>> *Libera, &c.*

From a vapouring horſe and a Roundhead in buff,
From roaring Jack Cavee, with money little enough,
From beads and ſuch idolatrous ſtuff,
>> *Libera, &c.*

Pym, who (according to Marchmont Needham) borrowed the idea from Holland :
> "Free-quarter is a tedious thing,
>   And ſo is the excife;
> None can deliver us but the King
>   From this d—d Dutch device."

From holydays, and all that's holy,
From May-poles and fiddlers, and all that's jolly,
From Latin or learning, since that is folly,

       Libera, &c.

And now to make an end of all,
I wish the Roundheads had a fall,
Or else were hanged in Goldsmiths' Hall*,
 Amen.
       Benedicat Dominus.

* Where the Royalists compounded for their estates.

THE PARLIAMENT.

BY J? CLEVELAND.

[This is one of the bitterest fatires of John Cleveland (the firft writer of eminence who efpoufed the Royal caufe), and is aimed againft the Long Parliament, which met on the 3rd November, 1640. Its doings are thus fummed up by Butler, in one of his earlieft effufions : —

> "The Saints in mafquerade would have us
> Sit quietly whilft they enflave us;
> And, what is worfe, by lies and cants,
> Would trick us to believe 'em faints;
> And though by fines and fequeftration
> They've pillaged and deftroy'd the nation,
> Yet ftill they bawl for *Reformation*!"]

OST Gracious and Omnipotent,
And Everlafting Parliament,
Whofe Power and Majefty
Are greater than all kings by odds;
And to account you lefs than gods,
Muft needs be blafphemy.

Mofes and Aaron ne'er did do
More wonder than is wrought by you,
For England's Ifrael;
But though the Red Sea we have paft,
If you to Canaan bring 's at laft,
If't not a miracle — ?

In six years space you have done more
Than all the Parliaments before ;
You have quite done the work.
The King, the Cavalier, and Pope,
You have o'erthrown, and next we hope,
You will confound the Turk.

By you we have deliverance,
From the design of Spain and France,
Ormond, Montrose, the Danes;
You, aided by our brethren Scots,
Defeated have malignant plots,
And brought your sword to Cain's.

What wholesome laws you have ordain'd,
Whereby our property's maintained,
'Gainst those would us undo ;
So that our fortunes and our lives,
Nay, what is dearer, our own wives,
Are wholly kept by you.

Oh! what a flourishing Church and State,
Have we enjoy'd e'er since you sate,
With a glorious king (God save him !) :
Have you now made his Majesty,
Had he the grace but to comply,
And do as you would have him !

Your *Directory** how to pray
By the Spirit shows the perfect way;
In zeal you have abolisht
The Dagon of the *Common Prayer*,
And next we see you will take care,
That Churches be demolisht.

A multitude in every trade
Of painful preachers you have made,
Learn'd by Revelation;
Cambridge and Oxford made poor preachers,
Each shop affordeth better teachers —
O blessed Reformation!

Your godly wisdom hath found out,
The true religion, without doubt;
For sure among so many,
We have five hundred at the least,
Is not the Gospel much increast?
All must be pure if any.

Could you have done more piously
Than sell Church lands† the king to buy,
And stop the City's plenty?

---

* See ante, p. 24.
† Episcopacy was abolished by ordinance 9th Nov. 1646, and a Commission appointed in the following year to proceed with the sale of the bishops' lands.

Paying the *Scots Church-militant*,
That the new Gospel helpt to plant,
God knows they are poor saints!

Because th' Apostle's creed is lame,
Th' Assembly doth a better frame,
Which saves us all with ease;
Provided still we have the grace
To believe th' House in the first place,
Our works be what they please.

'Tis strange your power and holiness
Can't the Irish devils dispossess *,
His end is very stout:
But tho' you do so often pray,
And ev'ry month keep fasting day †,
You cannot cast them out.

---

* Ireland was not finally subjugated by the Parliament till the year 1650.

† At the outbreak of the Rebellion a public fast was appointed by Parliament for the last Wednesday of every month; but shortly after the death of the king the observation of it was annulled by proclamation (23rd April, 1649).

THE ANARCHIE, OR THE BLESSED RE-FORMATION SINCE 1640.

BEING A NEW CAROL WHEREIN THE PEOPLE EXPRESS THEIR THANKS AND PRAY FOR THE REFORMERS.

To be faid or fung of all the well-affected of the kingdom of England and dominion of Wales, before they eat any plum-broth at Chriftmas.

To a rare new tune.

[Written by a loyalift about the period when Charles I. began to defpair of fuccefs in England, and meditated throwing himfelf into the arms of the Scotch, which he did in the fpring of the year 1647. A curious broadfide of the day, entitled *The Mournfull Cryes of many thoufand poore Tradefmen, who are ready to famifh through the Decay of Trade; or, the warning Teares of the Oppreffed*, contains a moft lamentable account of the then ftate of the country, and more particularly of the City, as well as an expofure of the hot contentions between the various parliamentary fections, and the cupidity of all. "O yee Parliament men, heare our dying cry, *Settle the Commonwealth! Settle the Commonwealth!* ftrive not who fhall be greateft untill you bee all confounded!"]

NOW that, thanks to the Powers below,
We have e'en done our do,
    The mitre is down,
    And fo is the crown,
And with them the coronet too;

Come clowns, and come boys,
Come hober-de-hoys,
   Come females of each degree;
Stretch your throats, bring in your votes,
And make good the Anarchie.
 And thus it shall go, says Alice,
 Nay, thus it shall go, says Amy;
  Nay, thus it shall go, says Taffy, I trow,
  Nay, thus it shall go, says Jamy.

Ah! but the truth, good people all,
The truth is such a thing,
For it would undo, both Church and State too,
And cut the throat of our King;
 Yet not the Spirit, nor the new light,
  Can make this point so clear,
  But thou must bring out, thou deified rout,
   What thing the truth is, and where.
Speak Abraham, speak Kester, speak Judith, speak Hester,
 Speak tag and rag, short coat and long;
Truth's the spell made us rebel,
 And murder and plunder, ding-dong.
  Sure I have the truth, says Numph;
  Nay, I ha' the truth, says Clemme;
  Nay, I ha' the truth, says Reverend Ruth;
  Nay, I ha' the truth, says Nem.

Well, let the truth be where it will,
We're sure all else is our's;

VOL. I.   D

Yet thefe divifions in our religions,
May chance abate our pow'rs:
    Then let's agree on fome one way,
        It fkills not much how true;
    Take Prynne* and his clubs, or Say* and his tubs,
        Or any fect, old or new;
The Devil's i' th' pack, if choice you can lack,
    We're fourfcore religions ftrong,
Take your choice, the major voice
    Shall carry it, right or wrong:
        Then we'll be of this, fays Megg;
        Nay, we'll be of that, fays Tibb;
        Nay, we'll be all, fays pitiful Paul;
        Nay, we'll be of none, fays Gibb.

Neighbours and friends, pray one word more,
There's fomething yet behind;
And wife though you be, you do not well fee,
In which door fits the wind.
    As for poor Religion, to fpeak right,
        And in the Houfe's fenfe,
    The matter's all one to have any or none,
        If 'twere not for the pretence:
But herein doth lurk the key of the work,
    Even to difpofe of the crown,

---

* The celebrated Wm. Prynne and Lord Say and Sele, the latter of whom was at one time as ftaunch a republican as the other was a Puritan.

Dexteroufly, and as may be
  For your behoof in our own.
    Then let's ha' King Charles, fays George;
    Nay, let's have his fon, fays Hugh;
    Nay, let's ha' none, fays jabbering John;
    Nay, let's be all kings, fays Prue.

Oh! we fhall have (if we go on
In plunder, excife, and blood)
But few folks and poor to dominion o'er,
And that will not be fo good:
  Then let's refolve on fome new way,
    Some new and happy courfe;
  The country's grown fad, the city born mad,
    And both Houfes are worfe.
The Synod has writ, the General hath —
  And both to like purpofe too;
Religion, laws, the truth, the Caufe,
  Are talkt of, but nothing we do.
    Come, come, fhall 's ha' peace, fays Nell;
    No, no, but we won't, fays Madge;
    But I fay we will, fays fiery-faced Phill;
    We will and we won't, fays Hadge.

Thus from the rout who can expect
Ought but divifion;
Since Unity doth with Monarchy,
Begin and end in One.

If then when all is thought their own,
  And lies at their beheſt;
Theſe popular pates reap nought but debates,
  From that many Round-headed beaſt.
Come Royaliſts then, do you play the men,
  And Cavaliers give the word;
Now let's ſee, at what you would be,
  And whether you can accord.
    A health to King Charles, ſays Tom;
    Up with it, ſays Ralph, like a man;
    God bleſs him, ſays Doll; and raiſe him, ſays Moll;
    And ſend him his own, ſays Nan.

Now for thoſe prudent Things that ſit
Without end, and to none;
And their committees, that towns and cities
Fill with confuſion;
  For the bold troops of ſectaries,
    The Scots and their partakers;
  Our new Britiſh States, Col Burges * and his mates,
    The Covenant and its makers:
For all theſe we'll pray, and in ſuch a way,
  As if it might granted be;
Jack and Gill, and Mat and Will,
  And all the world would agree.

---

* Dr. Cornelius Burges, lecturer at Paul's, London; at one time chaplain to Charles I., and afterwards a zealous penſionary of the Parliament.

A p—x take them all, fays Befs;
And a plague, too, fays Margery;
The Devil, fays Dick; and his dam, too, fays Nick;
Amen, and Amen, fay I.

☞ It is defired that the knights and burgeffes would take efpecial care to fend down full numbers hereof to their refpective counties and boroughs, for which they have ferved apprenticefhip, that all the people may rejoice as one man for their freedom.

UPON HIS MAJESTY'S COMING TO HOLMBY.

[This ballad was written after Charles I. was fold and delivered to the Englifh Commiffioners by the Scotch, and conveyed by the former to Holmby Houfe, Northamptonfhire, en route for Newmarket (16th Feb. 1647.)]

HOLD out, brave Charles, and thou fhalt win the field,
Thou canft not lofe thyfelf, unlefs thou yield
On fuch conditions as will force thy hand
To give away thy fceptre, crown, and land;
And what is worfe to hazard by thy fall,
To lofe a greater crown more worth than all.

Thy poor diftreffed Cavaliers rejoiced,
To hear thy Royal refolution voiced,
And are content far more poor to be
Than yet they are, fo it reflects from thee:
Thou art our Sovereign ftill, in fpite of hate,
Our zeal is to thy *perfon*, not thy *ftate*.

We are not so ambitious to desire
Our drooping fortunes to be mounted higher,
And thou so great a monarch, to our grief,
Must sue unto thy subjects for relief:
    And when they set, and long debate about it,
    Must either stay their time, or go without it.

No, sacred Prince, thy friends esteem thee more
In thy distresses than ere they did before;
And though their wings be clipt, their wishes fly
To Heaven by millions for a fresh supply:
    That as thy cause was so betrayed by *men*,
    It may by *angels* be restored agen.

THE MEMBERS' JUSTIFICATION.

[On the 23rd June, 1647, the army prefented itfelf before Weftminfter, and charged with high treafon Denzil, Holles, Glyn, Waller, and eight more of the leading Prefbyterians, and infifted upon their being expelled the Houfe. The obnoxious members accordingly withdrew; and the greater number of them, fufpecting the intentions of their opponents, quitted the kingdom, and fought a refuge in Holland and elfewhere.]

EN HOLLIS is a gallant man,
    And was for them too crafty;
    What he pretended for the king,
    Was for the members' fafety.
Sir Stapleton's * a firm brave boy,
    Although his fpoufe is courtly,
He went to York, and labor's loft,
    He could not bring Frank Wortley.†
The Parliament hath fitten clofe,
    As ere did knight in faddle;
For they have fitten full fix years,
    And now their eggs prove addle.

---

* Sir Philip Stapleton, M.P. for Heydon, Yorkfhire. He was one of thofe that fled, and died of the plague fhortly afterwards at Calais.

† Sir F. Wortley, Bart. of Wortley, Yorkfhire, a ftout Royalift, then a prifoner in the Tower.

Brave Fairfax did himself besiege
  Poor Frank, and him hath undone,
Yet lost more men in taking him,
  Than he did taking London:
Now whither is Will Waller gone?*
  To sea with Prince-Elector;
Will he forsake his lady so,
  And leave her no protector?
    The Parliament, &c.

Jack Maynard † is a loyal blade,
  Yet blind as any beetle;
He purchases the bishops' lands,
  Yet scarce can see Paul's steeple.
Both Glyn and Harlow ‡ are for Wales,
  And Lewis § for his madams;
These Britons will not change their bloods
  With Noah's, or scarce with Adam's.
    The Parliament, &c.

---

* Sir William Waller, the well-known Parliament general; he was one of those who fled his country.

† Sir John Maynard, with Jo. Glynn, M.P. for Caernarvon, Serjeant-at-arms, and Recorder of London, remained behind. They were both committed to the Tower, on the charge of high treason, in the following September.

‡ Col. Edw. Harley (not Harlow), M.P. for Herefordshire, and brother to Sir Robt. Harley.

§ Sir Wm. Lewis, M.P. for Petersfield, Hants. He fled over sea.

Clotworthy * is a zealous man,
  Yet hath his purse well lined;
So hath Wat Long† yet he's, we know,
  Religiously inclined:
But Nichols ‡ is for Pluto's court,
  In inquest of his father,
Or his uncle Pym, there he found,
  Stroud, Hampden, Pym, together.
    The Parliament, &c.

These three have Pluto's Mercury sent,
  And wonder they prove such men,
To make three kingdoms one poor State,
  And do it worse than Dutchmen.
Their Synod § now sits in great fear,
  And so does Jack Presbyter ‖,
That we shall have a king again,
  And once more see a mitre.
    Yet they have sitten wondrous close,
      As ere did knight in saddle,
    For they have sitten full seven years,
      And now their eggs prove addle.

---

* Sir John Clotworthy also passed out of the kingdom. He it was who framed the charge against the unfortunate Earl of Strafford. He was one of the Commissioners to treat with the over-bearing army.

† Walter Long, M.P. for Bath; he accompanied Hollis and Sir P. Stapleton to France.

‡ Anthony Nichols, M.P. for Bossiney, Cornwall; he was arrested while attempting to put to sea.

§ The Synod for the Suppression of Blasphemies, &c.

‖ The proverbial name of the Presbyterian party.

THE CRYES OF WESTMINSTER;

Or a Whole Pack of Parliamentary Knavery Opened and Set to Sale.

[This fcurrilous broadfide was publifhed 22nd Feb., 1647, when the Parliament, having finally triumphed over the King, and fecured him in the Ifle of Wight, difgufted the moderate party by ftrictly prohibiting (17th Jan.) all communication with him. As a palliation of their conduct they publifhed their famous Declaration (15th Feb.), which afterwards ferved as a model for the impeachment of Charles in their High Court of Juftice. At no period during the Rebellion were fo many ballads and pamphlets publifhed againft the dominant powers as at this. In vain the Parliament ordered them to be burned by the hand of the common hangman, and offered rewards for the difcovery of their authors. *The Cryes of Weftminfter*, which was included, doubtlefs, amongft thofe juft referred to, is abfolutely decent compared with *The Parliament's Ten Commandments, A New Teftament of our Lords and Saviours the Houfe of Commons*, &c. &c.]

OME, cuftomers, come : Pray fee what you lack,
Here's Parliament wares of all forts in my pack.

Who buys any Parliament Privileges —
   My new Privileges?

'Twill teach you many pretty things,
And raise you above gods and kings.
> *These are the cryes of Westminster,*
> *That are heard both far and near,*
> > *But a while, I pray, stand by,*
> > *And you shall hear another cry.*

Who buys the Parliament's Declaration against
  the King? New, new, new.
'Twill surely unblind your eyes,
That you may read a hundred lies.
> *Thus goe the cryes of Westminster, &c.*

Buy a new Ordinance to repair Churches:
A new Ordinance: New, new, new.
The Achans now restore the pledge,
To save their saintships' sacrilege.
> *Thus goe the cryes of Westminster, &c.*

Buy a new Ordinance of the Commons
 against stage-players *: *New-lye* printed, and
New-lye come forth.
Saints now alone must *act* for riches,
The plot outsmells old Atkins' † breeches.
> *Thus goe the cryes of Westminster, &c.*

---

* On 22nd Jan., 1647, all stage-plays were suppressed "for the future," and the mayor and other magistrates ordered "to take down all boxes and seats" in the theatres.

† Sir John Atkins, the puritanic alderman (and subsequently lord mayor) of London. Few of his contemporaries were more severely "balladed" than this unfortunate individual.

Buy a new Ordinance of the Commons. That none
   shall make any more Addresses* to the King, or
   receive any Message from him, upon pain of
   High-treason, Imprisonment, Death, or Plun-
   dering: But when these shall swing in a string,
   true subjects will obey their King.
Challoner, Mildmay, Martin, Veine,
Are fitting of their crowns to reigne.
        Thus goe the cryes of Westminster, &c.

Buy a new plot, found out by Sir John Wray †,
   to blow up the Thames, or the city to betray,
   'tis as true as all the rest, before ne'er known by
   man or beast.
'Twill keep you still in jealousies and fears,
And set you altogether by the ears.
        Thus goe the cryes of Westminster, &c.

---

* 17th Jan., 1647. "Resolved, &c. By the Lords and Commons assembled in Parliament, that the person or persons that shall make breach of this order [*i.e.* by addressing the King] shall incur the penalty of high treason."

† Sir John Wray, of Glentworth, Bart., who made himself extremely ridiculous by his constant fear of plots by the Jesuits and others. The satirist here probably alludes to the baronet's characteristic conduct about this time, when an overcrowded bench in the House suddenly gave way with a loud crash, and precipitated several members to the floor, and Sir John, by shouting out that "*he smelt gunpowder,*" added greatly to the confusion of the scene.

Buy the four Bills sent by the Parliament
   from Selden * and my Lady Kent; after long de-
   bate of this blessed Parliament; who buys
   the Four bills here.† Great Charles he will
   not betray his trust unto such as they; his honor's still intire, his conscience tried nine times
   i' th' fire, the Devil give all his foes their hire
   and raise them toward Heaven above a halter
   higher.
Let all the people say, Amen,
For we shall ne'er have peace till then.
   Thus goe the cryes of Westminster, &c.

Who buys any bishops' houses, or their
   goods, books, house-hold stuff or hoods; here
   are good pasture grounds, corn, hay, and grass
   in all our rounds, if it be not good the Devil confounds. Amen.
May all the trees to gibbets turn,
Or firing make to hang or burn.
   Thus goe the cryes of Westminster, &c.

---

* The learned John Selden, solicitor and steward of the Earl of Kent, whose lady was a great patron of literature and learning, and therefore the friend of Selden.

† The four bills proposed for the King's assent, namely, those relating to the Great Seal, Honours and Titles, Abolition of Episcopacy, and Declarations and Proclamations against the Parliament.

Have you any old arrears for the army, I'll
  give you tickets for 'em; have you any fubfidies,
  poll-money, loans, or contributions; have
  you any plate, horfe, or arms, old bodkins
  or thimbles, or wedding-rings *, have ye any:
  Have you any more Irifh adventures for fale of
  lands †, or a trick for one meal a-week. City
  Loans have you any; or Affeffments for the
  Scotts; have you any Five-and twenty parts,
  weekly or monthly affeffments for Effex, Fairfax, Manchefter's, the Scots, or Irifh army. Free-
  quarter have you any. Have you any of his
  Majefty's Revenue to fell, old fequeftrations
  or plunder; have you any more Excife, or For-
  tification money, or fines for delinquents,

---

* The women were zealous contributors to the Parliamentary caufe, and poured into the common treafury of war (1647) their ear-rings, filver fpoons, thimbles and bodkins; " infomuch (fays May, *Parl. Hift.*) that it was a common jeer of men difaffected to the Caufe to call it the Thimble and Bodkin Army." So Butler:—

> " Women, who were our firft apoftles,
>   Without whofe aid w' had all been loft elfe;
>   Women, that left no ftone unturn'd
>   In which *The Caufe* might be concern'd,
>   Brought in their children's fpoons and whiftles
>   To purchafe fwords, carbines, and piftols."
>   *Hudi.* Part II. c. ii.

† Alluding to the fale of the rebels' lands in Ireland.

compofitions, &c., or a new Ordinance for 400,000*l.* the month.
This is our *liberty* for to pay
The faints that now King Charles betray.
> *Thus goe the cryes of Weftminfter,*
> *That are heard both far and near,*
> *For a while I pray ftand by,*
> *And you will hear another cry.*

The Second Part.

(To the same tune.)

MY new Articles of Faith*, who buys the Parliament's New Faith? You may fee by their WORKS, they are worfe than Jews or Turks; let their faith be what it will, their religion is to kill.
> *Thus goe the cryes, &c.*

Who buys any Parliament jugglings of the neweft fafhion? *Hocus Pocus* never fhew'd more to cheat the nation, here is a

---

* The *Confeffion of Faith* fet forth by the Affembly of Divines, and confirmed by an ordinance of Parliament.

trick, by Martin's ring, shall suddenly depose
a king ; Tom * shews you a pretty trick also,
and at New-Market and St. Albans tells us
what he means to doe : Trusty Thomas thus
keeps his promise with his king ; grace forsake him, Devil take him, may all such false
knaves swing.
Thus goe the cryes, &c.

Who buys the army's proposals† ; custo-
mers pray draw near, the Devil in his pack
had ne'er such gear; Here's Cromwell's mas-
ter-piece, 'twill blind your eyes, and fill
your head with fifteen-hundred lyes.
Thus goe the cryes, &c.

Here's a fine Order, was the like ever seen,
shall murder all that love their King or
Queen, a knot of such traitorous

---

* Sir Thos. Fairfax, who (11th Feb. 1647) met the King on his way to Holmby, and discoursed with him on public affairs. Charles having observed, after the interview, "that the General was a man of honour, and kept his word with him," the royalists hastily concluded that Fairfax had promised to restore the King, despite the opposition of the Independents.

† Referring to the many proposals for disbanding the army, now that the war had terminated in the defeat and captivity of the King. The army, however, refused to disband until it had received the long arrears of pay due to it, as well as an indemnity for all acts done during the late struggles.

VOL. I.   E

Regicides were furely never feen, as Challoner, Mildmay, Martin, and Veine, all Parliament kings, that over us reigne : They are
all glutted with their fellow-fubjects' blood,
and yet pretend their good, but pray let it
be underftood, for all Burley's * blood, before
Jenkins † fhall die, a hundred thoufand in the
City of London will try, to make Martin, and
all fuch rogues to fly.
> *Thefe be the cryes of London town,*
> *Some go up ftreet, fome goes down,*
> But a while I pray ftand by,
> And you will hear another cry.

A new Ordinance, pray come and buy,
 to eftablifh the Prefbytery ‡ ; what Religion

---

* Capt. Burley, who was hung for attempting to refcue the King whilft a prifoner in Carifbrook Caftle.

† David Jenkins, one of the Welfh judges, who was charged with high treafon for publifhing his *Lex Terræ* (1647), in which he denied the authority and expofed the tyranny of the Long Parliament :
> " Thofe who have writ for the King, the good King,
>   Be it rhyme or reafon,
>   If they pleafe but to look
>   Through Jenkins's book,
>   They'll hardly find it treafon."
>   *Sir Francis Wortley.*

‡ Alluding to the ordinance, paffed by both Houfes in January, for dividing the kingdom into " diftinct claffical prefbyteries," and " congregational elderfhips."

next, puts me beyond my text? If this won't
please you, fee another, pray Sir try, for I
have a hundred more here in my pack for
you to buy.
 Thefe be the cryes, &c

Who buys a new Order, to new dip the
 King's ships, and to their eternal fames,
 give them all new names; the Parliament's
 ships forsooth; the *Royal Sovereign* must
 be the *Royal Traitor*, the *Prince*, the Parliament *Pinck*, and the whole Fleet the Parliament's navy. O brave Pirates! whither
 are ye bound, let cross winds toss you,
 whilst you all are drown'd.
  Thus to the world they make it known,
  Crown, sceptre, ships, and ALL's your own.
  Thefe be the cryes, &c.

Who buys a new petition from Taunton,
 that the Devil brought the last great wind,
 and the traitors now vaunt on. New, new,
 new; but as false as God is true, and so ye
 juggling devils all adieu.
  Thus goe the cryes, &c.

An Execration to all that hate King Charles.

AY God forsake ye, may the Devil take ye, may disease eat up your bones, consume your rotten members, may the palsie shake your hands and heads, and bloody visions haunt your beds; all Egypt's plagues, and two times more, wait on you all at either door; may all your wives turn arrant jades, and you live upon their trades; may the gout be in your toes, and no end be to your woes; may no surgeon hear your moans, and all your joys be sighs and groans; may the running of the reins, or the quinzy seize your brains; may the toothache and the fever, to plague you still do their endeavour; may the strangullion be your best friend, and ne'er forsake you till your end; may you be the People's scorn, and curse the hour that you were born; May Bedlam or Bridewell be all the house you have to dwell; may your children's children beg from door to door, and all their kindred, may they still be poor; may a guilty conscience still affright ye, and no earthly joys delight ye; may you have aches in

your rotten bones, gravel in your kid-
neys, as well as ſtones ; may your daughters
turn out bad, and their fathers go
clean mad ; may they never ſleep in quiet,
and fear poiſon in their diet ; may they
never ſorrow lack, and ſo the Pedlar ſhuts
his Pack. Only when they die ('cauſe they
were never true), when that their ſouls depart, Devil claim thy due !

  Printed in a Hollow-tree for the good of the State.
     [22nd Feb. 1647.]

I THANK YOU TWICE;

OR,

THE CITY COURTING THEIR OWN RUIN,
THANK THE PARLIAMENT TWICE FOR THEIR TREBLE UNDOING.

[This broadfide was publifhed, according to Thomafon, on the 21ft Auguft, 1647. It expofes the arbitrary meafures of the Long Parliament.]

HE hierarchy is out of date ;
Our monarchy was fick of late ;
But now 'tis grown an excellent ftate :
    Oh, God a-mercy, Parliament !

The teachers knew not what to fay ;
The 'prentices have leave to play* ;
The people have all forgotten to pray :
    Still, God a-mercy, Parliament !

---

* All the old feftive days having been abolifhed by the fanatical Puritans, the London apprentices beftirred themfelves, in the year 1647, and clamoured loudly for the reftitution of their time-honoured rights. This movement refulted in the publication of an Ordinance by which the fecond Tuefday in every month was appointed to be kept generally as a holiday.

The Roundhead and the Cavalier
Have fought it out almoſt ſeven year,
And yet, methinks, they are never the near:
    Oh, God, &c.

The gentry are ſequeſtered all;
Our wives you find at Goldſmith Hall,
For there they meet with the devil and all *:
    Still, God, &c.

The Parliament are grown to that height,
They care not a pin what his Majeſty faith;
And they pay all their debts with the public faith;
    Oh, God, &c.

Though all we have here is brought to nought,
In Ireland we have whole lordſhips bought †,
There we ſhall one day be rich, 'tis thought:
    Still, God, &c.

---

 * Alluding to the diſtreſſing ſcenes that were daily witneſſed in Goldſmiths' Hall, where the Committee of Sequeſtration ſat, and the wives and widows, with their children, of the unfortunate royaliſts were aſſembled, and petitioned "the Saints" in vain for a portion of the property of which the latter had deſpoiled them.

 † The rebels' lands in Ireland were confiſcated and put to ſale at low rates, as an inducement to the Engliſh to ſettle in that country.

We muft forfake our father and mother,
And for the ftate undo our own brother,
And never leave murthering one another:
>> Oh, God, &c.

Now the King is caught, and the devil is dead;
Fairfax muft be difbanded *,
Or elfe he may chance be Hotham-ed.†
>> Still, God, &c.

They have made King Charles a glorious king;
He was told, long ago, of fuch a thing;
Now he and his fubjects have reafon to fing
>> Oh, God a-mercy, Parliament!

---

* Parliament had juft voted the difbanding of the army.
† Sir John Hotham and his fon were executed in January, 1645, for correfponding with the King relative to the furrender of Hull to the latter.

PRATTLE YOUR PLEASURE
(UNDER THE ROSE).

[This farcastic song against the irresponsible Parliament is subscribed "Mr. Finis," and dated "Mr. An. Dom. 1647." Whilst it expoſes the peculative doings of the Parliamentary Committees, it teſtifies at the ſame time how completely the people were cowed into ſubmiſſion and ſilence by the ſword.]

HERE is an old proverb which all the world knows,
Anything may be ſpoke, if 't be under the roſe.
Then now let us ſpeak, whilſt we are in the hint,
Of the ſtate of the land, and th' enormities in 't.

Under the roſe be it ſpoke, there is a number of knaves,
More than ever were known in a ſtate before;
But I hope that their miſchiefs have digg'd their own graves,
And we'll never truſt knaves for their ſakes any more.

Under the roſe be it ſpoken, the City's an aſs
So long to the public to let their gold run,
To keep the King out; but 'tis now come to paſs,
I am ſure they will loſe, whoſoever has won.

Under the rofe be it fpoken, there's a company of men,
Trainbands* they are call'd — a plague confound 'em —
And when they are waiting at Weftminfter Hall,
May their wives be beguil'd and begat with child all!

Under the rofe be it fpoken, there's a damn'd committee,
Sits in hell (Goldfmith's Hall †) in the midft of the City,
Only to fequefter the poor Cavaliers —
The Devil take their fouls, and the hangman their ears.

Under the rofe be it fpoke, if you do not repent
Of that horrible fin, your pure Parliament;
Pray ftay till Sir Thomas ‡ doth bring in the King,
Then Derrick § may chance have 'em all in a ftring.

Under the rofe be it fpoke, let the Synod now leave
To wreft the whole Scripture, how fouls to deceive;
For all they have fpoke or taught will ne'er fave 'em,
Unlefs they will leave that fault, hell's fure to have 'em!

---

* The trainbands of the City had been drawn out to fupport the Prefbyterian intereft.
† The Committee of Sequeftration fat in Goldfiniths' Hall.
‡ Vide note, p. 49.
§ The common hangman.

THE OLD PROTESTANT'S LITANY.

AGAINST ALL SECTARIES
AND THEIR DEFENDANTS,
BOTH PRESBYTERIANS
AND INDEPENDENTS.

[The imprint of this broadside intimates that it was publifhed in "the year of Hope, 1647," and Thomafon, the collector, has added the precife date, namely, the 7th of September. The clofe of this memorable year was fpent in intrigue and negociation. The Prefby- terians, fupported by the Covenanters, were ftruggling to eftablifh an oligarchical afcendancy in themfelves againft the increafing influence of the Independents. Charles fecretly correfponded, in turn, with the two former factions, and indulged hopes of uniting them to the Irifh Catholics, whom he contemplated bringing over to his affiftance. The King's duplicity loft him the confidence of all. The Independents, by means of the army, having obtained the maftery over the Prefbyterians, fhortly afterwards proceeded to remove the only remaining obftacle to their entire fupremacy. The ballad illuftrates the confufion arifing from fo many conflicting interefts in the State.]

THAT thou wilt be pleaf'd to grant our requefts,
And quite to deftroy all the vipers' nefts,
That England and her true religion molefts
   Te rogamus audi nos.

That thou wilt be pleaf'd to cenfure with pity
The prefent eftate of our once famous city;
Let her ftill be govern'd by men juft and witty;
   Te rogamus, &c.

That thou wilt be pleas'd to confider the Tower,
And all other prifons in the Parliament's power,
Where King Charles his friends find their welcome but
    four;

                Te rogamus, &c.

That thou wilt be pleas'd to look on the grief
Of the King's old fervants, and fend them relief,
Reftore to the Yeomen o' th' Guard chines of beef;

                Te rogamus, &c.

That thou wilt be pleas'd very quickly to bring
Unto his juft rights our fo much wrong'd King,
That he may be happy in everything;

                Te rogamus, &c.

That Whitehall may fhine in its priftine luftre,
That the Parliament may make a general mufter,
That knaves may be punifh'd by men who are jufter;

                Te rogamus, &c.

That now the dog-days are fully expir'd,
That thofe curfed curs, which our patience have tired,
May fuffer what is by true juftice required;

                Te rogamus, &c.

That thou wilt be pleaf'd to incline conqu'ring Thomas *
(Who now hath both City and Tower gotten from us)
That he may be juft in performing his promife;
Te rogamus, &c.

That our hopeful Prince and our gracious Queen
(Whom we here in England long time have not feen)
May foon be reftor'd to what they have been;
Te rogamus, &c.

That the reft of the Royal iffue may be
From their Parliamentary guardians fet free†,
And be kept according to their high degree;
Te rogamus, &c.

That our ancient Liturgy may be reftor'd,
That the organs (by fectaries fo much abhorr'd)
May found divine praifes, according to the Word;
Te rogamus, &c.

That the ring in marriage, the crofs at the font,
Which the Devil and the Roundheads so much affront,
May be uf'd again, as before they were wont;
Te rogamus, &c.

---

* Sir Thomas Fairfax entered London, at the head of the army, 6th Auguft, 1647, and was appointed Governor of the Tower. Both the Parliament and City were now completely at the mercy of his troops, who, on the day following their entry, wantonly damaged many of the public buildings, &c.

† The royal children were at this time under the Duke of Northumberland's care at Sion Houfe; it had not yet been propofed to apprentice the Princefs Elizabeth to a button-maker.

That Episcopacy, us'd in its right kind,
In England once more entertainment may find,
That Scots and lewd factions may go down the wind;
     Te rogamus, &c.

That thou wilt be pleas'd again to restore
All things in due order, as they were before,
That the Church and the State may be vex'd no more;
     Te rogamus, &c.

That all the King's friends may enjoy their estates,
And not be kept, as they have been, at low rates,
That the poor may find comfort again at their gates;
     Te rogamus, &c.

That thou wilt all our oppressions remove,
And grant us firm faith and hope, join'd with true love,
Convert or confound all which virtue reprove;
     Te rogamus, &c.

That all peevish Sects that would live uncontroll'd,
And will not be govern'd as all subjects should,
T' New England may pack*, or live quiet i' th' Old;
     Te rogamus, &c.

---

* Charles' subjects, as well as himself, had occasion to regret that the leading Puritans were not suffered to depart, according to their desire, for New England, before the breaking out of the civil war. Of the many satirical songs of the period, referring to the " religious

That gracious King Charles, with his children and wife,
Who long time have suffer'd thro' this civil strife,
May end with high honour this natural life;
    Te rogamus, &c.

That they who have seiz'd on honest men's treasure *,
Only for their loyalty to God and to Cæsar,
May in time convenient find measure for measure;
    Te rogamus, &c.

---

liberty" enjoyed by the emigrants to that colony, the following is, perhaps, unsurpassed for its sarcasm and wit :—

 New England is preparing a-pace,
 To entertain King Pym, with his grace,
 And Isaac before shall carry the mace:
  For Roundheads Old Nick stand up now!

 No surplice, nor no organs there,
 Shall ever offend the eye or the ear;
 But a spiritual preach, with a three-hours pray'r;
  For Roundheads, &c.

 All things in zeal shall there be carried,
 Without any porredge read over the buried,
 No crossing of infants, nor rings for the married:
  For Roundheads, &c.

 The swearer there shall punish'd be still,
 But drunkenness private be counted no ill,
 Yet both kinds of lying as much as you will:
  For Roundheads, &c.

 Blow winds, hoist sails, and let us begone,
 But be sure we take our plunder along,
 That Charles may find little when as he doth come.
  For Roundheads, &c.

* The sum of 300,000*l.* raised upon the estates of the Royalists, was appropriated exclusively to their own use by the parliamentary committees at this period.

That thou all thefe bleffings upon us wilt fend,
We are no *Independents*, on Thee we depend,
And as we believe, from all harm us defend;

Te rogamus, &c.

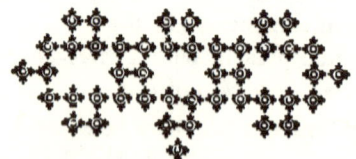

THE CITIES WELCOME TO COLONEL RICH AND COLONEL BAXTER,

WITH THEIR SOLEMN INVITATION TO THE SAINTED COMMANDERS OF THE ARMY, TO COME AND QUARTER AMONGST THEM.

[Compoſed when Fairfax, having reduced all the King's garriſons, returned in triumph to London, with part of his army, and took up his quarters at Whitehall.]

IF we may dare to ſay
    That you moſt welcome are,
    Moſt holy, holy colonels,
    Great Moguls of the war:
Our bleſſed Parliament,
Moſt wiſely for you ſent,
Your forces near to draw
For to keep us in awe.

For we are ſure to be
    Your vaſſals and your ſlaves,
    And 'tis but juſtice, we confeſs,
    That knaves ſhould ſtoop to knaves:

We were the firſt that ſtrove,
Such was our zealous love;
We are the laſt ſhall ſmart,
But you ſhall bear a part.

Therefore come with fife and drum,
    Ye army that are fainted;
And quarter here amongſt us,
    We long to be acquainted:
Oh 't will be very brave
Free-quarter here to have;
Each houſe turn'd to an inn,
What wonders then begin?

Hewſon, we have been to thee,   Col. Hewson,
    Ere now obliged much,   a shoemaker.
For ſhoes which thou haſt ſold us,
    Therefore we ſhall not grutch.
Pride, thee we ſhall not jeer,   Col. Pride, some-
Thou ever brought 's good beer,   time a drayman.
Meaſure thou didſt allow,
We'd liquor thee, I vow.

Okey, thou haſt ere now,   Col. Okey, a
    Before we were ſuch noddies,   tailor.
Although thou ſtoleſt half in half,
    Made garments for our bodies.

Staines, pray thou be not mist,   *Staines, a cozen-*
Who art an alchymist;   *ing alchymist.*
When we have spent our store,
Thy stone will help to more.

Watson, thee I long to see,   *Watson, a*
   By God, and by the Hallowes,   *clipper.*
We are glad that for embating coin,
   Thou lately 'scap'st the gallows.
Come, Lambert, there's a crew   *Lambert, a*
Would be baptized anew;   *dipper.*
Come with thy troops to town,
Help maids and wives to drown.

Oliver, we thee prefer,   *King Cromwell.*
   To guide these boys unto us,
Thou art the king of our new state,
   And worthy to undo us.
Thy nose and fiery face,
Speak thee a babe of grace,
And most regenerate,
As sack did e'er create.

There's no such thing as Charles our King,
   We here renounce him ever;
We'll have no king but thee, sweet Noll,
   Or Tom *, that glorious feather:

---

* Sir Thomas (afterwards Lord) Fairfax, Commander-in-chief of the Parliamentary Forces.

Our houses we'll prepare
For thy brave men of war,
Our wives we will adorn—
He's happy wears the horn.

Don't you believe we will deceive
　　Our truſt, or the leaſt harm you;
Or that we will a riſing make,
　　And then by force diſarm you:
Or that when as you ſleep,
We'll on your faces peep;
And for to gain your coats,
Moſt wiſely cut your throats.

You cannot ſure but be ſecure
　　'Mongſt us that firſt did raiſe you;
Who have allow'd you conſtant pay,
　　And evermore did praiſe you:
Do you not fear to venter
Amongſt us for to enter;
You know the Danes thriv'd well
Until the diſmal knell.*

　　Alas, you know the caſe is ſo,
　　　　We now muſt be content
　　To ſmart for our baſe follies;
　　　　Our truſty Parliament

---

* Alluding to the general maſſacre of the Danes by order of Ethelred II., 13th November, 1002.

(And you) have jointly now agreed
To prey on all we have;
But yet, by God, we'll break the rod,
And fight, our goods to fave.

The Scottifh nation are out of fafhion,
    You have no farther need,
But Jocky is refolved
    To come on this fide Tweed:
They'll now not be content
To have their money* fent;
They'll come themfelves and ftrain,
And then come back again.

But firft, thofe men accurft
    That have abuf'd their King,
They mean to call to an account
    For their good governing:
Say muft no longer rule,
Nor Martin, that fame mule;
And all the holy flock
Muft tafte the chopping block.

Whitehall now, I know not how,
    Is topfy-turvy turn'd;
The thimble-makers' † bonny-boys
    . Have private manfions fcorn'd:

---

* The purchafe-money of King Charles, namely, 200,000*l.*
† Vide p. 47.

King's houſes only be
Fit for our ſoldiery;
Parliament, army, all
Are Kings in general.

Come then, dear brethren,
   And fortify the city;
All that is in't we know is yours,
   Yet pray ſhow us ſome pity:
Or rather be ſo wiſe
To follow this advice,
Keep yourſelves where you are,
For we your mart ſhall mar.

THE PURITAN.

BY JOHN CLEVELAND.

[This ballad has been fometimes attributed to Samuel Butler, but it is to be found in the earlieft editions of the poetical works of John Cleveland, who no doubt was the real author of it. The ignorance, vulgarity, fanaticifm, and, above all, the ridiculous appearance of the Puritan preachers, were fertile themes for the wits of the age. Lucy Hutchinfon, in the life of her hufband, the Colonel, obferves: "Every ftage, and every table, and every puppet-play, belched forth profane fcoffs upon the Puritans; the drunkards made them their fongs; and all fiddlers and mimics learned to abufe them, as finding it the moft gameful way of fooling." Butler's "Roundhead" is quite as characteriftic as Cleveland's "Puritan," and well worth repetition,—at leaft, the firft four ftanzas of it :—

> What creature's that, with his fhort hairs,
> His little band, and huge long ears,
>   That this new faith hath founded?
> The faints themfelves were never fuch,
> The prelates ne'er ruled half fo much;
>   O! fuch a rogue's a Roundhead.
>
> What's he that doth the bifhops hate,
> And counts their calling reprobate,
>   'Caufe by the Pope propounded;
> And thinks a zealous cobbler better
> Than learned Ufher in every letter?
>   O! fuch a rogue's a Roundhead.

What's he that doth *high-treaſon* ſay
As often as his *aye* and *nay*,
   And wiſh the King confounded;
And dares maintain that Mr. Pim
Is fitter for a crown than him?
   O! ſuch a rogue's a Roundhead.

What's he that, if he chance to hear
A little piece of *Common-Prayer*,
   Doth think his conſcience wounded;
Will go five miles to preach and pray,
And meet a ſiſter by the way?
   O! ſuch a rogue's a Roundhead.]

ITH face and faſhion to be known,
   For one of ſure election;
   With eyes all white, and many a groan,
   With neck aſide to draw in tone,
With harp in 's noſe, or he is none:
   See a new Teacher of the town—
O the Town, O the Town's new Teacher!

With pate cut ſhorter than the brow*,
With little ruff ſtarch'd, you know how,
With cloak like Paul, no cape I trow,
With ſurplice none; but lately now
With hands to thump, no knees to bow:
   See a new Teacher, &c.

---

* The reaſon commonly aſſigned by the Puritans for cutting their hair ſhorter than their ears was, "becauſe long hair hindered the ſound of the word from entering into the heart"!

With coz'ning cough, and hollow cheek,
To get new gatherings every week,
With paltry change of *and* to *eke*,
With fome fmall Hebrew, and no Greek,
To find out words, when ftuff's to feek :
 See a new Teacher, &c.

With fhop-board breeding and intrufion,
With fome outlandifh inftitution,
With Urfine's catechifm * to mufe on,
With Syftem's method for confufion,
With grounds ftrong laid of mere illufion :
 See a new Teacher, &c.

With rites indifferent all damned,
And made unlawful, if commanded,
Good works of Popery down banded,
And moral laws from him eftranged,
Except the Sabbath ftill unchanged† :
 See a new Teacher, &c.

---

 * An allufion to the celebrated Zachary Urfinus' Lectures on the Catechifm, entitled *The Summe of the Chriftian Religion*, tranflated by Henry Parry in 1587, a work that was greatly efteemed and very popular in the seventeenth century.
 † So Marchmont Needham :—
  We are, the learned Synod fays,
   The Church of England's *nurfe* ;
  Who make them keep the Sabbath days,
   And all the week to curfe !

With speech unthought, quick revelation,
With boldness in predestination,
With threats of absolute damnation,
Yet *Yea* and *Nay* hath some salvation,
For his own tribe, not every nation*:
  See a new Teacher, &c.

With after licenfe cast a crown,
When Bishop new had put him down;
With tricks call'd repetition,
And doctrine newly brought to town,
Of teaching men to hang and drown:
  See a new Teacher, &c.

With flesh-provision to keep Lent,
With shelves of sweetmeats often spent,
Which new maid bought, old lady sent,
Though, to be saved, a poor present;
Yet legacies assure the event:
  See a new Teacher, &c.

---

* Sir William Dugdale, in his *Short View of the late Troubles in England*, gives the following specimen of a prayer offered at Southampton by a Puritan:—" Bless the King, O Lord, mollify his heart that delighteth in blood; open his eyes that he may see that the blood of saints is dear in thy sight. He is fallen from faith in thee, and become an enemy to the Church: Is it not he that has sinned, and done evil indeed? but as for these sheep [the Puritans] what have they done? Let thy hand, we pray thee, O Lord our God, be upon *him*, and on his father's house; *but not on thy people, that they shall be plagued.*"

With troops expecting him at th' door,
That would hear sermons, and no more ;
With noting tools, and sighs great store,
With bibles great to turn them o'er,
While he wrests places by the score :
  See a new Teacher, &c.

With running text, the nam'd forsaken,
With *for* and *but*, both by sense shaken,
Cheap doctrines forc'd, wild uses taken,
Both sometimes one by mark mistaken,
With anything to any shapen:
  See a new Teacher, &c.

With new wrought caps, against the canon,
For taking cold, tho' sure he have none ;
A sermon's end, where he began one,
A new hour long, when's glass had run one,
New use, new points, new notes to stand on :
  See a new Teacher, &c.

COMMONWEALTH

A COFFIN FOR KING CHARLES;
A CROWN FOR CROMWELL;
AND A PIT FOR THE PEOPLE.

To the tune of " Fain I would."

[This curious ballad was compofed when the diffolution of the Monarchy was completed. It is dated the 23rd April (1649), or juft about the period when the felf-conftituted " keepers of the liberties of England " declared it high treafon to proclaim or otherwife acknowledge Charles the Second. The ballad exhibits throughout the reactionary feeling that took place in the public mind upon beholding the tragical fate of the King.]

I.
Cromwell on the Throne.

SO, fo, the deed is done,
 the royal head is fevered,
As I meant when I firft begun
 and ftrongly have endeavoured.
Now Charles the I. is tumbled down,
 the Second, I do not fear;
I grafp the fceptre, wear the crown,
 nor for Jehovah care.

2.
King Charles in his Coffin.

Think'ſt thou, baſe ſlave, though in my grave
 like other men I lie,
My ſparkling fame and Royal name
 can (as thou wiſheſt) die?
Know, caitif, in my ſon I live
 (the Black Prince * call'd by ſome),
And he ſhall ample vengeance give
 to thoſe that did my doom.

3.
The People in the Pit.

Suppreſt, depreſt, involv'd in woes,
 great Charles, thy People be
Baſely deceiv'd with ſpecious ſhows
 by thoſe that murther'd thee.
We are enſlav'd to Tyrants' heſts,
 who have our freedom won:
Our fainting hope now only reſts
 on thy ſucceeding ſon.

4.
Cromwell on the Throne.

Baſe vulgar! know the more you ſtir,
 the more your woes increaſe,

---

* Owing to the ſwarthineſs of his complexion. Charles II. is alſo deſcribed in other contemporary ballads and tracts as reſembling, both in his perſon and features, King Henry VIII.

Your rashness will your hopes deter,
   'tis we must give you peace.
Black Charles a traitor is proclaim'd
   unto our dignity;
He dies (if e'er by us he's gain'd)
   without all remedy.

5.
King Charles in his Coffin.

Thrice perjur'd villain! didst not thou
   and thy degenerate train,
By mankind's Saviour's body vow
   to me thy sovereign,
To make me the most glorious king
   that e'er o'er England reign'd;
That me and mine in everything
   by you should be maintain'd?

6.
The People in the Pit.

Sweet Prince! O let us pardon crave
   of thy beloved shade,
'Tis we that brought thee to the grave,
   thou wert by us betray'd.
We did believe 'twas reformation
   these monsters did desire;
Not knowing that thy degradation
   and death should be our hire.

7.
Cromwell on the Throne.

Ye fick-brained fools! whofe wit does lie
    in your fmall guts ; could you
Imagine our confpiracy
    did claim no other due,
But for to fpend our deareft bloods
    to make rafcallions flee ?
No, we fought for your lives and goods,
    and for a monarchy.

8.
King Charles in his Coffin.

But there's a Thunderer above,
    who, tho' he winks awhile,
Is not with your black deeds in love —
    he hates your damned guile.
And though a time you perch upon
    the top of Fortune's wheel,
You fhortly unto Acharon
    (drunk with your crimes) fhall reel.

9.
The People in the Pit.

Meanwhile (thou glory of the earth)
    we languifhing do die :
Excife doth give free-quarter birth
    while foldiers multiply.

Our lives we forfeit every day,
    our money cuts our throats;
The laws are taken clean away
    or shrunk to traitors' votes.

10.

Cromwell on the Throne.

Like patient mules resolve to bear
    whate'er we shall impose;
Your lives and goods you need not fear,
    we'll prove your friends, not foes.
We (the *Elected* ones) must guide
    a thousand years this land;
You must be props unto our pride,
    and slaves to our command.

11.

King Charles in his Coffin.

But you may fail of your fair hopes
    if Fates propitious be,
And yield your loathed lives in ropes
    to vengeance and to me.
When as the Swedes and Irish join,
    the Cumbrian and the Scot
Do with the Danes and French combine,
    then look unto your lot.

12.
The People in the Pit.

Our wrongs have arm'd us with such strength,
  so sad is our condition,
That could we hope that now at length
  we might find intermission,
And have but half we had before,
  ere these mechanics swayed;
To our revenge, knee-deep in gore,
  we would not fear to wade.

13.
Cromwell on the Throne.

In vain (fond people) do you grutch
  and tacitly repine.
For why? my skill and strength are such —
  both poles of heaven are mine.
Your hands and purses both coher'd
  to raise us to this height:
You must protect those you have rear'd,
  or sink beneath their weight.

14.
King Charles in his Coffin.

Singing with angels, near the throne
  of the Almighty Three,
I sit, and know perdition
  (base Cromwell) waits on thee,

And on thy vile affociates :
  twelve months fhall full conclude
Your pow'r—thus fpeak the pow'rful Fates,
  then vades your interlude.

15.
The People in the Pit.

Yea, powerful Fates, hafte, hafte the time,
  the moft aufpicious day,
On which thefe monfters of our time
  to hell muft poft away.
Meanwhile, fo pare their fharpened claws,
  and fo impair their ftings,
We may no more fight for the Caufe,
  Or other *novel* things !

THE DOMINION OF THE SWORD.

A SONG MADE IN THE REBELLION.

[This admirable fong was written probably in the interval between the murder of King Charles I. and the final triumph of the Independents over the Prefbyterians and Royalifts, 1649-50.]

AY by your pleading,
Law lies a-bleeding;
Burn all your ftudies down, and throw away
your reading.

Small pow'r the word has,
And can afford us
Not half fo much privilege as the fword does.

It fofters your mafters,
It plaifters difafters,
It makes the fervants quickly greater than their mafters.

It venters, it enters,
It feeks and it centers,
It makes a 'prentice free in fpite of his indentures.

It talks of small things,
But it sets up all things;
This masters money, though money masters all things.

It is not season
To talk of reason,
Nor call it loyalty, when the sword will have it treason.

It conquers the crown, too,
The grave and the gown, too;
First it sets up a Presbyter, and then it pulls him down too.

This subtile disaster
Turns bonnet to beaver;
Down goes a bishop, sirs, and up starts a weaver.

This makes a layman
To preach and to pray, man;
And makes a lord of him that was but a drayman.

Far from the Gulpit
Of Saxby's pulpit,
This brought an Hebrew ironmonger to the pulpit.

Such pitiful things be
More happy than kings be;
They get the upper hand of Thimblebee and Slingsbee.

No gofpel can guide it,
No law can decide it,
In Church or State, till the fword has fanctified it.

Down goes your law-tricks,
Far from the matricks,
Sprung up holy Hewfon's power, and pull'd down St. Patrick's.

This fword it prevails, too,
So highly in Wales, too,
Shenkin ap Powel fwears " Cots-fplutterer nails, too."

In Scotland this fafter
Did make fuch difafter,
That they fent their money back for which they fold their mafter.

It batter'd their Gunkirk,
And fo it did their Spain-kirk,
That he is fled, and fwears the devil is in Dunkirk.

He that can tower,
Or he that is lower,
Would be judg'd a fool to put away his power.

Take books and rent 'um,
Who can invent 'um,
When that the fword replies, " *Negatur argumentum.*"

Your brave college-butlers
Muſt ſtoop to the ſutlers;
There's ne'er a library like to the cutler's.

The blood that was ſpilt, ſir,
Hath gain'd all the gilt, ſir,
Thus have you ſeen me run my ſword up to the hilt, ſir.

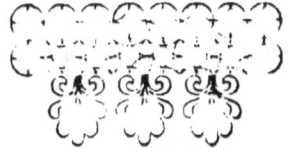

A SALT TEAR;

OR, THE WEEPING ONION,

AT THE

LAMENTABLE FUNERAL OF DR. DORISLAUS.

[Ifaac Doriflaus was a Dutchman, and doctor of civil law at Leyden, whence he came to England, and was appointed Profeffor of Hiftory at Cambridge. He next became Judge-Advocate in the King's army, but deferted Charles, and affifted in drawing up the charges againft him. Whilft agent for the Commonwealth at the Hague, he was affaffinated by twelve Scotch cavaliers, fuppofed to have been hired for that purpofe by the Marquis of Montrofe. The date of the ballad is the 18th June, 1649.]

I.

HAT though lamented—curf'd—and the high tree
Of fifty cubits was juft deftiny
(Though a deplor'd one) of that agent drew
The articles againft the holy Jew,
Good Mordecai; which by quaint, curious art
Should have contriv'd the Queen her fhare o' th' fmart.
But Providence faid, No; and Hefter taught
Proud Haman to a bloody banquet brought.
    Our upftart Hamans had a feaft: who'll bring
    Them, for digeftion's fake, to take a fwing?

2.

Doriflaus! art lamented? So was He
Who was more *Dives* than the State made thee.
If thou chance meet with him; lift up thine eyes,
And fee where Charles in Abraham's bofom lies.
O for a meffenger the Houfe to tell
And all the merry Commoners, of Hell!
How Lenthall looks! How Whitlock pales his face,
Who caught one *feal*, and loft that feal of grace!
  O how damn'd Bradfhaw quivers as he comes!
  And Fairfax groans! and Cromwell bites his
    thumbs!

3.

Egypt, no doubt, was laid in double black,
When that laft wonder, and grand land-fea wrack
Was pour'd on Pharaoh and his hoft; when waves
Reveng'd the infolence of murderous flaves,
Pharaoh muft drown, fo it doth Providence pleafe.
We have a Mofes, too, is heir o' th' feas.
  Heaven will a party in that element make:
  Your KING-SALE projects do not always take.

4.

The wife of Sifera did no doubt bewail
Sifera's fate; yet the canoniz'd nail
And hammer of ftout Jael, and the fong
Of Deborah fhow'd Heav'n fmil'd, and went along.

A Kenite did the fact. It was no lot
For perjur'd English, but a gallant Scot.
  'Tis a good omen : that as they pull'd down
  The *First*, they shall set on the *Second's* crown.
Let our deluded citizens invite,
Hug, kiss, and lick the cursed Canaanite :
What tho' their chariots be of iron ? we may
See them lie grovelling like lost Sisera.

5.

Now pray observe the pomp, the persons, state,
That did attend this alien reprobate :
Here went Lieutenant-General *Crocodile*,
And cubs, bred of the slime of our rich Nile :
Who creep before they kill, and whose false tears
Trickle from blood-shed eyes of murderers.
  Poor Island ! they have made a Nile of thee,
  We cannot find thy *head*, which fain we'd see.

6.

Next march a train of ravenous wolves, whose jaws
Yet ooze with the blood of slaughter'd King and Laws :
These are close mourners ; these the kingdoms gull :
True wolves, that never howl till they are full.
These are the beasts of prey, whose sharp fang tears
Not *cavies* now, but the harmless *levellers* ;
  By whom they rose unto this greatness. We,
  We are distasted, well as Monarchy.

7.

Clofe unto thefe, in grave deportment, march
The City changelings in *Thanksgiving* ftarch,
A fort of whelps, taught by that wolfifh kind,
Who, if one howl'd, ftraight the whole kennel whin'd.
Thefe, at the whip of cunning Oliver,
Do feaft, or elfe drop a diffembling tear.
All thefe attend their *Agent's* funeral;
This honour 's but a trap, the States' fly call
  To get another throat cut, but in vain,
  Doriflaus cries from Hell
      'TWILL BE NO GAIN!

THE STATE'S NEW COIN.

[Shortly after the abrogation of the monarchy, the Parliament iffued a new coinage. It confifted of pieces having on the obverfe a fhield with St. George's crofs, encircled by a laurel and palm branch, furrounding the fimple infcription "The Commonwealth of England." On the reverfe was the equally fimple legend "God with us," and two fhields bearing the arms of England and Ireland. The fhields being conjoined at top were at once declared to refemble the breeches of the Rump; a declaration which continued to be a ftanding joke with the Cavaliers during the times of the Commonwealth, and with others long after the reftoration of the monarchy. The other abfurdities fo ingenioufly fitted to this innocent coinage will be beft underftood by a perufal of the ballad itfelf.]

SAW you the State's money new come from
  the Mint?
 Some people do fay it is wonderous fine;
 And that you may read a great myftery in't,
Of mighty King Nol, the lord of the coin.

They have quite omitted his politic head,
 His worfhipful face, and his excellent nofe;
But the better to fhow the life he had led,
 They have fix'd upon it the print of his hofe.

For, if they had set up his picture there,
  They needs must ha' crown'd him in Charles' stead;
But 'twas cunningly done, that they did forbear,
  And rather would set up aught else than his head.

'Tis monstrous strange, and yet it is true,
  In this Reformation we should have such luck,
That crosses were always disdain'd by you,
  Who before pull'd them down, should now set them up.

On this side they have circumscrib'd *God with us,*
  And in this stamp and coin they confide;
Common-Wealth on the other, by which we may guess,
  That *God* and the *States* were not both of a side.

On this side they have cross and harp,
  And only a cross on the other set forth;
By which we may learn, it falls to our part
  Two crosses to have for one fit of mirth!

UPON THE GENERAL PARDON PASS'D
BY THE RUMP.

[After his decifive victory at Worcefter, Cromwell immediately refumed his Parliamentary duties, and, to further his ambitious views, forced from the reluctant "Rump" their affent to a refolution of amnefty fo wide, that it almoft ftruck at the root of the Commonwealth. They affented, Ludlow obferves, "the Parliament being unwilling to deny Cromwell anything for which there was the leaft colour of reafon." It was, in effect, refolved that all political offences committed before the battle of Worcefter fhould be forgiven, with the exception of a few cafes; a decifion which, though it implied a grofs injuftice to thofe who had already been mulcted heavily, relieved the royalifts from all apprehenfion of farther penalties.]

EJOICE, rejoice, ye Cavaliers,
    For here comes that difpels your fears;
    A General Pardon is now paft,
    What was long look'd for, comes at laft.

It pardons all that are undone;
The Pope ne'er granted fuch a one:
So long, fo large, fo full, fo free,
O what a glorious State have we!

Yet do not joy too much, my friends,
Firft fee how well this pardon ends;
For though it hath a glorious face,
I fear there's in't but little grace.

'Tis faid the mountains once brought forth,
And what brought they? a moufe, in troth;
Our States have done the like, I doubt,
In this their Pardon now fet out.

We'll look it o'er, then, if you pleafe,
And fee wherein it brings us eafe:
And firft, it pardons words, I find,
Againft our State — words are but wind.

Hath any pray'd for th' King of late,
And wifh'd confufion to our State?
And call'd them rebels? He may come in
And plead this Pardon for that fin.

Has any call'd King Charles that's dead
A Martyr — he that loft his head?
And villains thofe that did the fact?
That man is pardon'd by this act.

Hath any faid our Parliament
Is fuch a one as God ne'er fent?
Or hath he writ, and put in print,
That he believes the Devil's in't?

Or hath he faid there never were
Such tyrants anywhere as here?
Though this offence of his be high,
He's pardon'd for his blafphemy.

You see how large this Pardon is,
It pardons all our *Mercuries* *,
And poets too, for you know they
Are poor, and have not aught to pay.

For where there's money to be got,
I find this Pardon pardons not;
Malignants that were rich before,
Shall not be pardon'd till they're poor.

Hath any one been true to th' Crown,
And for that paid his money down,
By this new act he shall be free,
And pardon'd for his loyalty.

Who have their lands confiscate quite,
For not compounding when they might;
If that they know not how to dig,
This Pardon gives them leave to beg.

Before this act came out in print,
We thought there had been comfort in't;
We drank some healths to the higher pow'rs,
But now we've seen't they'd need drink ours.

For by this act it is thought fit
That no man shall have benefit,

---

* Alluding to the newspapers of the day, the whole of which were so named.

Unless he first engage to be
A rebel to eternity.

Thus, in this Pardon it is clear,
That nothing's here and nothing's there;
I think our States do mean to choke us
With this new act of *Hocus Pocus.*

Well, since this act's not worth a pin,
We'll pray our States to call it in,
For most men think it ought to be
Burnt by the hand of Gregory.*

Then, to conclude, here's little joy
For those that pray *Vive le Roy!*
But since they'll not forget our crimes,
We'll keep our mirth till better times.

---

* The common hangman.

THE HOUSE OUT OF DOORS.

[Mr. Carlyle, in his *Letters and Speeches of Oliver Cromwell*, gives the following graphic defcription of the laft fcene in the Long Parliament (20th April, 1653): "'You call yourfelves a Parliament,' continues my Lord General in clear blaze of conflagration; 'You are no Parliament; I fay you are no Parliament! Some of you are drunkards,' and his eye flafhes on poor Mr. Chaloner, an official man of fome value, addicted to the bottle; 'fome of you are ———,' and he glares into Harry Martin, and the poor Sir Peter, who rofe to order, lewd livers both; 'living in open contempt of God's commandments. . . . . Corrupt, unjuft perfons; fcandalous to the profeffion of the Gofpel: how can you be a Parliament for God's people? Depart, I fay, and let us have done with you. In the name of God,— go!' . . . Hiftory reports with a fhudder that my Lord General, 'ifting the facred mace itfelf, faid, 'What fhall we do with this bauble? Take it away,' and gave it to a mufketeer. And now, 'Fetch him down!' fays he to Harrifon, flafhing on the Speaker. Speaker Lenthall, more like an ancient Roman than anything elfe, declares he will not come till forced; 'Sir,' faid Harrifon, 'I will lend you a hand;' on which Speaker Lenthall came down, and gloomily vanifhed. They all vanifhed; flooding gloomily, clamouroufly out, to their ulterior bufinefs and refpective places of abode: the Long Parliament is diffolved!"]

I.

WILL you hear ftrange news ne'er heard of before,
A ballad of news without any lies?
The Parliament now is turn'd out of doors,
And fo is the Council of State likewife.

Brave Oliver came into the Houfe like a fpright,
   His fiery looks made the Speaker* dumb;
You muft be gone hence, quoth he, by this light,
   D' you mean to fit here till Doomfday come.

2.

At this the Speaker look'd pale with fear,
   And if he had been with the nightmare rid,
Infomuch that fome did think that were there
   He did e'en as much as the Alderman did;
For Oliver, though he were Doctor of Law,
   He chofe to play the Phyfician here;
His phyfic fo wrought in the Speaker's maw,
   That he gave him a *ftool* inftead of a *chair*.

3.

Brave Arthur† thought Oliver wondrous bold,
   (I mean the knight that was one of the *five*)
He was very unwilling to lofe his freehold ‡,
   But needs he muft go whom the Devil doth drive;

---

* Lenthall.

† Haslerigg, who was one of the five obnoxious members perfonally demanded by the King, January 4, 1642.

‡ A petition was prefented, 23rd Dec. 1651, to the Long Parliament by one Jofiah Prymato, leather-feller of London, who therein not only charged Sir Arthur Haflerigg with fraudulently procuring the fequeftration of the petitioner's collieries in Durham, which were worth 5000*l.* per annum, but alfo taxed four of the Compounding Commiffioners " with not daring to oppofe the will and pleafure of the faid Sir Arthur." The Houfe difmiffed the petition " as falfe,

And gone he is into the north country,
　　Hoping therein to make fome ftir—
Yet, in the meantime, take it from me,
　　Brave Arthur muft yield to brave Oliver.

4.

Harry Martin wonder'd to fee fuch a thing
　　Done by a faint of fo high a degree,
An act which he did not expect from a king,
　　Much lefs from fuch a *Dry-bone* as he.
Brave Oliver, laying his hand on his fword,
　　Upbraided him with his adultery;
Then Martin gave not fo much as a word,
　　But humbly thanked his Majefty.

5.

Much wit he had fhow'd if that he had dar'd,
　　But filent he was for fear of fome knocks,
Thought he, if I catch you within my ward,
　　I may chance fend you home with a ——.
Next Allen *, the Copperfmith, was in great fear,
　　He did us much harm fince the war began:
A broken citizen for many a year,
　　And now he's a broken Parliament man!

---

malicious, and fcandalous;" and fined the petitioner 3000*l.* to the Commonweath, 2000*l.* to Sir Arthur, and 500*l.* to each of the four Commiffioners for his impertinence!

　* The goldfmith, whom Cromwell openly taxed with "cheating the public."

6.

Brave Oliver told him what he had been,
 And him a cheating knave did call;
Which put him into a fit of the spleen,
 But now he muſt give an account for all.
It went to the heart of Sir Harry Vane
 To think what a terrible fall he ſhould have;
For he that did late in the Parliament reign,
 Was call'd (as I heard) *a diſſembling knave.*

7.

Who gave him that name you may eaſily know,
 'Twas one that had learn'd that art full well;
You may ſwear it was true if he call'd him ſo,
 For what's to diſſemble I'm ſure he can't tell.
Preſident Bradſhaw, as proud as a Pope,
 That loves upon kings and princes to trample,
Now the Houſe is diſſolv'd I cannot but hope
 To ſee ſuch a Parliament made an example.

8.

Then room for the Speaker, without his mace,
 And room for the reſt of the rabble-rout;
My maſters, methinks 'tis a pitiful caſe,
 Like the ſnuff of a candle thus to go out!
'Tis wondrous ſtrange you ſhould not agree,
 You that have been ſuch brethren in evil;
A diſſolution there needs muſt be,
 When the Devil's divided againſt the Devil!

9.

Some think that Cromwell with Charles is agreed,
   And 'twere good policy if it were so;
Left the Hollander, French, the Dane, and the Swede,
   Bring him whether we will or no.
And now I would gladly conclude my song
   With a prayer, as ballads were wont to do;
But yet I'll forbear, for I think ere long,
   We *shall* have a King and a Parliament too.

THE PARLIAMENT ROUTED;

OR, HERE'S A HOUSE TO BE LET.*

I HOPE THAT ENGLAND, AFTER MANY JARS,
SHALL BE AT PEACE, AND GIVE NO WAY TO WARS:
O LORD, PROTECT THE GENERAL, THAT HE
MAY BE THE AGENT OF OUR UNITY.

To the tune of " Lucina, or, Merrily and Cherrily."

CHEER up, kind countrymen, be not difmay'd,
    true news I can tell ye concerning the nation,
That fpirits are quench'd, the tempeft is lay'd,
    (and now we may hope for a good reformation).
The Parliament bold and the Council of State
    do wifh them beyond fea, or elfe at Virginie;
For now all their orders are quite out of date,
    twelve Parliament men fhall be fold for a penny.

---

* Vide introductory note to the preceding ballad.

Full twelve years and more thefe rooks they have fat,
   to gull and to cozen all true-hearted people;
Our gold and our filver have made them fo fat,
   that they look'd more big and mighty than Paul's fteeple:
The freedom of fubject they much did pretend,
   but fince they bare fway we never had any;
For every member promoted felf-end;
   twelve Parliament men are now fold for a penny.

Their acts and their orders, which they have contriv'd,
   was ftill in conclufion to multiply riches;
The Commonwealth fweetly by thefe men have thriv'd,
   as Lancafhire did with the jemets of witches *:
Oh! our freedom was chain'd to the Egyptian yoke,
   as it hath been felt and endured by many,
Still making religion their author and cloke;
   twelve Parliament men fhall be fold for a penny.

Both city and country are almoft undone
   by thefe caterpillars, which fwarm'd in the nation;
Their imps and their goblins did up and down run,
   Excife-men I mean, all knaves of a fafhion:
For all the great treafure that daily came in,
   the foldier wants pay, 'tis well known by a many;

---

   * The people of this county were proverbially fuperftitious.

To cheat and to cozen they held it no fin;
   twelve Parliament men fhall be fold for a penny.

The land and the livings which thefe men have had,
   'twould make one admire what ufe they've made of it;
With plate and with jewels they have been well clad;
   the foldier fared hard, whilft they got the profit:
Our gold and our filver to Holland they fent,
   but being found out, this is known by a many,
That no one would own it for fear of a fhent,
   twelve Parliament men are fold for a penny.

'Tis judged by moft people that they were the caufe
   of England and Holland their warring together*,
Both friends and dear lovers to break civil laws,
   and in cruel manner to kill one another:
What cared they how many did lofe their dear lives,
   fo they by the bargain did get people's money,
Sitting fecure, like bees in their hives?
   twelve Parliament men are now fold for a penny.

---

* An allufion to the Dutch war of 1651-52.

The Second Part.

To the same tune.

They voted, unvoted, as fancy did guide,
    to pass away time, but increasing their treasure;
(When Jack is on cock-horse he'll galloping ride,
    but falling at last he'll repent it at leisure).
The widow, the fatherless, gentry and poor,
    the tradesman and citizen, with a great many,
Have suffer'd full dearly to heap up their store;
    but twelve Parliament men shall be sold for a penny.

These burthens and grievances England hath felt,
    so long and so heavy, our hearts are e'en broken,
Our plate, gold and silver, to themselves they have dealt,
    (all this is true, in good time be it spoken).
For a man to rise high, and at last to fall low,
    it is a discredit: this lot falls to many,
But 'tis no great matter these men to serve so;
    twelve Parliament men are now sold for a penny.

The General* perceiving their lustful desire
    to covet more treasure, being puff'd with ambition,
By their acts and their orders to set all on fire,
    pretending religion to rout superstition:

---

* Cromwell.

He bravely commanded the foldiers to go,
  in the Parliament Houfe, in defiance of any;
To which they confented, and now you do know
  that twelve Parliament men may be fold for a penny.

The foldiers, undaunted, laid hold on the mace,
  and out of the chair they removed the Speaker;
The great ones were then in a pitiful cafe,
  and Taffy* cried out, All her cold muft forfake her!
Thus they were routed, pluckt out by the ears,
  the Houfe was foon empty, and rid of a many
Ufurpers, that fat there this thirteen long years;
  twelve Parliament men may be fold for a penny.

To the Tower of London away they were fent,
  as they have fent others by them captivated;
O what will become of this old Parliament,
  and all their compeers, that were royally ftated?
What they have deferv'd I wifh they may have,
  and 'tis the defire I know of a many;
For us to have freedom, O that will be brave!
  but twelve Parliament men may be fold for a penny.

Let's pray for the General and all his brave train,
  he may be an inftrument for England's blefling,

---

* It was a common practice to hold up the Welfh to derifion in the time of the Commonwealth, becaufe they failed to make fo ftout a refiftance to Cromwell and his Ironfides as was expected of them.

Appointed in heaven to free us again,
   for this is the way of our burdens redreſsing:
For England to be in glory once more,
   it would ſatisfy, I know, a great many;
But ending, I ſay, as I ſaid before,
   twelve Parliament men are now ſold for a penny.

THE SALE OF REBELLIOUS HOUSE-HOLD STUFF.

[This humorous, and at one time moſt popular ſong, alſo relates to the violent diſmiſſal of the Rump, 20th April, 1653.]

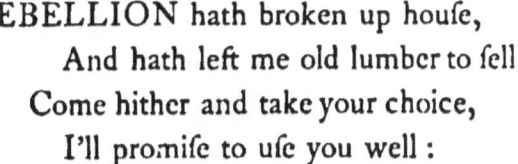EBELLION hath broken up houſe,
    And hath left me old lumber to ſell,
    Come hither and take your choice,
    I'll promiſe to uſe you well :
Will you buy the old Speaker's chair?
    Which was warm and eaſy to ſit in,
And oft has been clean'd I declare,
    Whereas it was fouler than fitting.
        Says old Simon the King,
        Says old Simon the King,
With his ale-dropt hoſe, and his malmſey noſe,
    Sing, hey ding, ding-a-ding, ding.

Will you buy any bacon flitches,
    The fatteſt that ever were ſpent?
They're the ſides of the old committees,
    Fed up in the Long Parliament.
Here's a pair of bellows and tongs,
    And for a ſmall matter I'll ſell ye 'um,

They are made of the Presbyter's lungs,
　　To blow up the coals of rebellion.
　　　　　　　Says old Simon, &c.

I had thought to have given them once
　　To some blacksmith for his forge;
But now I have considered on't,
　　They are consecrate to the Church:
So I'll give them unto some quire,
　　They will make the big organs roar,
And the little pipes to squeak higher
　　Than ever they could before.
　　　　　　　Says old Simon, &c.

Here's a couple of stools for sale,
　　One's square, and t'other is round;
Betwixt them both the tail
　　Of the Rump fell down to the ground.
Will you buy the State's Council-table,
　　Which was made of the good wain-Scot?
The frame was a tottering Babel
　　To uphold th' Independent plot.
　　　　　　　Says old Simon, &c.

Here's the besom of Reformation,
　　Which should have made clean the floor;
But it swept the wealth out of the nation,
　　And left us dirt good store.

Will you buy the State's fpinning-wheel,
 Which fpun for the roper's trade?
But better it had ftood ftill,
 For now it has fpun a fair thread.
  Says old Simon, &c.

Here's a glyfter-pipe well tried,
 Which was made of a butcher's ftump,
And has been fafely applied
 To cure the colds of the Rump.
Here's a lump of Pilgrim's-falve,
 Which once was a juftice of peace,
Who Noll and the Devil did ferve,
 But now it is come to this.
  Says old Simon, &c.

Here's a roll of the State's tobacco,
 If any good fellow will take it;
No Virginia had e'er fuch a fmack-o,
 And I'll tell you how they did make it:
'Tis th' Engagement and Covenant cook't
 Up with the Abjuration oath;
And many of them, that have took 't,
 Complain it was foul in the mouth.
  Says old Simon, &c.

Yet the afhes may happily ferve
 To cure the fcab of the nation,

Whene'er 't has an itch to swerve
  To Rebellion by innovation.
A Lanthorn here is to be bought,
  The like was scarce ever gotten,
For many plots it has found out
  Before they ever were thought on.
            Says old Simon, &c.

Will you buy the Rump's great saddle,
  With which it jockey'd the nation?
And here is the bit and the bridle,
  And curb of Dissimulation:
And here's the trunk-hose of the Rump,
  And their fair dissembling cloak;
And a Presbyterian jump,
  With an Independent smock.
            Says old Simon, &c.

Will you buy a Conscience oft turn'd,
  Which served the high-court of Justice,
And stretch'd until England it mourn'd —
  But Hell will buy that if the worst is.
Here's Joan* Cromwell's kitchen-stuff tub,
  Wherein is the fat of the Rumpers,

---

* This was a cant name given to Cromwell's wife by the Royalists, who taxed her with exchanging the kitchen-stuff for the candles used in the Protector's household. In a little work (12mo. Lond. 1664) described by Baker as " Liber rarus, et præterea nihil,"

With which old Noll's horns she did rub,
When he was got drunk with false bumpers.
          Says old Simon, &c.

Here's the purse of the public faith;
Here's the model of the Sequestration,
When the old wives upon their good troth
Lent thimbles to ruin the nation.
Here's Dick Cromwell's Protectorship,
And here are Lambert's Commissions,
And here is Hugh Peters his scrip,
Cramm'd with tumultuous Petitions.
          Says old Simon, &c.

And here are old Noll's brewing vessels,
And here are his dray and his slings;

---

and entitled *The Court and Kitchen of Elizabeth, commonly called Joan Cromwell, the wife of the late Usurper, truly described and represented*, there is a portrait of this lady, with a monkey making mouths at her, and these lines appended:—

"From feigned glory and usurped throne,
And all the greatness to me falsely shown,
And from the arts of government set free,
See how Protectress and a Drudge agree."

The most ardent Royalist could prefer no weightier charge against her than an exclusive devotion to the domestic concerns of her family.

Here are Hewſon's awl and his briſtles*;
With diverse other odd things:
And what is the price doth belong
To all these matters before ye?
I'll ſell them all for an old ſong,
And ſo I do end my ſtory.
                    Says old Simon, &c.

---

* Col. Hewſon, before the breaking out of the Rebellion, had been a cobbler.

A CHRISTMAS SONG,

WHEN THE RUMP WAS FIRST DISSOLVED.

[The diffolution of the Rump, which for so many years, by fanéti-
fied pretences, had oppreffed in turn all parties in the State, was
hailed, more particularly by the lower orders, with exuberant delight.
They saw in the downfall of their late hypocritical mafters a fpeedy
reftoration of that comparative freedom which they had enjoyed
prior to the firft meeting of the Long Parliament in 1640. In the
plenitude of their power nothing was too infignificant for the confideration or interference of that extraordinary affembly. Amongft
other acts, they not only abolifhed the feftival of Chriftmas, but
even interdicted the eating of the cuftomary pies, — fuch dainties
being regarded as " profane viands " by the fanctimonious Puritans.]

To the tune of " *I tell thee, Dick.*"

HIS Chriftmas time, 'tis fit that we
Should feaft, and fing, and merry be,
It is a time of mirth ;
For never fince the world began
More joyful news was brought to man,
Than at our Saviour's birth.

But fuch have been thefe times of late,
That holidays are out of date*,

---

* All holidays were abolifhed by the Puritans, and recreation on
the fabbath ftrictly prohibited, fo that, in fact, no time was left for
relaxation of any kind. See note, p. 54.

And holiness to boot;
For they that do despise and scorn
To keep the day that Christ was born,
Want holiness no doubt.

That Parliament that took away
The observation of that day *,
We know it was not free;
For if it had, such acts as those
Had ne'er been seen in verse or prose,
You may conclude with me.

'Twas that Assembly did maintain
'Twas law to kill their Sovereign,
Who by that law must die;
Though God's anointed ones are such,
Which subjects should not dare to touch,
Much less to crucify.

'Twas that which turn'd our Bishops out
Of house and home, both branch and root,
And gave no reason why,
And all our clergy did expel,
That would not do like that rebel —
This no man can deny.

---

* On the 3rd June, 1647, it was ordained by Lords and Commons in Parliament that the Feast of the Nativity of Christ should no longer be observed.

It was that Parliament that took
Out of our churches our *Service-book* *,
    A book without compare ;
And made God's Houfe (to all our griefs),
That Houfe of Prayer, a den of thiefs,
    Both here and everywhere.

They had no head for many years
Nor heart (I mean the House of Peers),
    And yet it did not die ;
Of thefe long fince it was bereft,
And nothing but the tail was left,
    You know as well as I.

And in this tail there was a tongue,
Lenthal † I mean, whofe fame hath rung
    In country and in city ;
Not for his worth or eloquence,
But for a rebel to his prince,
    And neither wife nor witty.

This Speaker's words muft needs be wind,
Since they proceeded from behind ;
    Befides, you may remember,

---

  * The *Book of Common Prayer*, which was fuppreffed by an ordinance of Parliament, 4th Jan. 1645.
  † William Lenthal was chofen Speaker of the Commons in 1640, and occupied the chair when Cromwell, in 1653, forcibly diffolved the Parliament.

From thence no act could be difcreet,
Nor could the fenfe o' the Houfe be fweet,
　　Where Atkins was a member.

This tale's now done, the Speaker's dumb,
Thanks to the trumpet and the drum ;
　　And now I hope to fee
A Parliament that will reftore
All things that were undone before,
　　That we may Chriftians be.

A JOLT ON MICHAELMAS DAY.

["The Protector (says Echard) having affumed the whole power of the nation to himfelf, and fent ambaffadors and agents to all foreign States, was again courted by them, and prefented with rarities and curiofities of feveral countries; among the reft the Duke of Holftein made him a prefent of a noble fet of grey Friezeland coach-horfes, with which, taking the air in Hyde Park, attended only by his fecretary, Thurloe, and his guard of Janizaries, he thought fit to mount the box and take the place of his coachman, as if he believed the three pair of horfes would prove as tame as the three nations now ridden by him; and therefore, not content with their ordinary pace, he lafhed and drove them on with his ufual fury, but they, unacquainted with fuch a rough manager, ran away at full fpeed, and never ftopt till they had violently thrown him off the box, with which fall his piftol fired in his pocket, though without any hurt to himfelf. This became the fubject of mirth and ridicule among feveral, and of fevere lampoons among others, and occafioned fome boldly to fay, 'that this ought to have inftructed him how dangerous it was to intermeddle with thofe things in which he had no experience.'"]

To the tune of
"To himfelf that hath fool'd
More than Mahomet could."

T fell on a day
When good people fay
  St. Michael beat the dragon,
My Lord the Protector
Did drive, like a Hector,
  A coach inftead of a wagon.

Becaufe he did hear
The charioteer
   Did antiently wear a crown,
Up went the horfe-heels,
Round, round went the wheels,
   Till his Highnefs came head-long down.

He rein'd them fo hard,
They look'd back and were fcar'd,
   To fee him fo red and fo grim ;
Away then they fled,
And tho' he uf'd to lead,
   This new-modell'd horfe would lead him.

But O, how they fnuff
When his piftol went off,
   For which all the Saints fufpect him :
Doth Providence attend him,
Thirty thoufand defend him,
   Yet a poor pocket-piftol protect him ?

How many a hurl
Had poor Mr. *Thurl-*
   -Lo ! he in the coach did pranck it ;
He thought he had fate
Chief Secretary of State,
   But was toft like a dog in a blanket.

Nay, had they run fafter,
He'd follow his mafter
　Through all the fcenes of this mad-fhow :
A brewer, a colonel,
A preacher, a general,
　A Protector, a King—then comes Bradfhaw.

They flander my lord,
With a bug-bear word
　That he like Phaëton did drive;
But his highnefs tried
Six horfes to guide,
　And Phaëton had but *five*.

Mad Phaëton hurl'd
Fire all o'er the world,
　Then dead in a river was found ;
But my lord had no aim
To fet all in a flame,
　And never was born to be drown'd.

'Twas Nero did ftrive
Such chariots to drive,
　And publicly fhow'd his work ;
But when my lord fticks
Up his bills to fhow tricks,
　He'll undo t'other dancing Turk.

But if you look high,
There's some reason why
   These jades did so fling and skip;
For tho' we afford
Him the " power o' the sword,"
   He had no command of the whip.

Enthron'd in his chair,
(Pray what brought him there?)
   He took such Protectory courses;
He seem'd horse and mule,
But 'tis easier to rule
   Three kingdoms than six horses.

Not a day nor an hour
But we felt his power,
   And now he would show us his art;
His first reproach
Is a fall from a coach,
   And his last will be from a cart!

A FREE PARLIAMENT LITANY.

[The following paffage from Mr. Fofter's *Life of Cromwell* affords a fair commentary upon this Ballad :—" After the gallanteft fight for liberty that had ever been fought by any nation in the world, fhe [England] found herfelf trampled under foot by a military defpot. All the vices of old kingly rule were nothing to what was now impofed upon her. Some reftraint had ftill been kept on the worft of her preceding fovereigns; now fhe found herfelf hopelefs and helplefs, her faith in all that fhe once held nobleft broken, and her fpirits unequal to any further ftruggle. * * * * The true caufe of the death of Charles I. was his refiftance to the facred principle of popular reprefentation. He laid down his head upon the block becaufe he broke violently and in fucceffion three Englifh parliaments. Oliver Cromwell had now merited far more richly that felf-fame doom; for he had committed, in circumftances of greater atrocity, the felf-fame fin. But Charles was weak, and Cromwell ftrong; and the people had undergone that worft and moft fad recoil from a virtuous and quick-fpirited enthufiafm, to the debafing fenfe of failure, depreffion, and indifference."]

To the tune of "An Old Soldier of the Queen's."

ORE Ballads!—here's a fpick and fpan new
  Supplication,
  By order of a Committee for the Reforma-
  tion
To be read in all churches and chapels of this nation,
Upon pain of flavery and fequeftration.
 From Fools and Knaves, in our Parliament free,
  Libera nos Domine.

From thofe that ha' more Religion and lefs confcience than
  their fellows ;
From a Reprefentative that's fearful and zealous ;
From a ftarting jadifh people that is troubled with the
  yellows,
And a prieft that blows the coal (a crack in his bellows).
            From Fools and Knaves, &c.

From fhepherds that lead their flocks into the briars,
And then fleece 'em — From Vow-breakers and King-
  tryers ;
— Of Church and Crown lands, from both fellers and
  buyers ;
From the children of him that's the Father of Liars.
            From Fools and Knaves, &c.

From the Doctrine and Difcipline of *Now and anon :*   Sedgwi
Preferve us and our wives from John T and Saint John,   John a
Like Mafter like Man, every way but one :   John a
The Mafter has a large confcience, and the Man has
  none.
            From Fools and Knaves, &c.

---

* William Sedgwick, a fanatical preacher, who, for having ven-
tured to foretell the day of judgment, which he furvived, was ever
afterwards called *Doomfday Sedgwick.*

From Major-Generals, Army-officers, and that phanatique crew;
From the parboil'd pimp Scot, and from Goodface, the Jew;
From old Mildmay*, that in Cheapſide miſtook his queu; [Repulſed by a citizen's wife.]
And from him that wont pledge — give the Devil his due.
   From Fools and Knaves, &c.

From long-winded ſpeeches, and not a wiſe word;
From a Goſpel miniſtry ſettled by th' ſword;
From the act of a Rump, that ſtinks when 'tis ſtirr'd;
From a Knight of the Poſt, and a cobling lord.†
   From Fools and Knaves, &c.

From all the rich people that ha' made us poor;
From a Speaker‡ that creeps to the Houſe by a back-door;
From that badger, Robinſon§ (that limps and bites ſore);
And that dog in a doublet, Arthur ‖ — that will do ſo no more.
   From Fools and Knaves, &c.

From a certain ſly Knave with a beaſtly name;
From a Parl'ment that's wild, and a people that's tame;

---

 * Sir Henry Mildmay, Bart., M.P. for Malden.
 † Col. Hewſon, one of Cromwell's lords, but originally a cobbler.
 ‡ Lenthal.
 § Luke Robinſon, who was an active member of the Houſe, and ſubſequently employed as parliamentary agent to negotiate terms with Monk.
 ‖ Sir Arthur Haslerigg.

From Skippon *, Titchbourne †, Ireton ‡,—and another
of the fame;
From a dung-hill cock, and a Hen of the game.
     From Fools and Knaves, &c.

From all thofe that fat in the High Court of Juftice;
From Ufurpers that ftyle themfelves the People's truftees;
From an old Rump, in which neither profit nor guft is;
And from the recov'ry of that which now in the duft is.
     From Fools and Knaves, &c.

From a backfliding Saint that pretends t' acquiefce;
From croffing of proverbs (let 'um hang that confefs);
From a fniveling caufe, in a pontificall drefs;
<small>Jacks both.</small> And two Lawyers, with the Devil and his dam in a
mefs.
     From Fools and Knaves, &c.

From thofe that trouble the waters, to mend the fifhing,
And fight the Lord's battles under the Devil's commiffion;

---

 * Major-General Skippon, "the pious," a Privy Councillor in 1653; and, in 1655, one of Cromwell's military fatraps appointed to command one of the eleven diftricts into which England was divided in that year.
 † Alderman Sir Robt. Titchbourne, a commiffioner for the Sale of State Lands, and a member of the Committee for Regulating the Cuftoms—offices by which he made a large fortune.
 ‡ Alderman Ireton, brother to the General of that name, and a member of the Cuftoms' Committee.

Such as eat up the Nation, whilft the Government's a-
difhing:
And from a people when it fhould be doing, ftands wifh-
ing.
     From Fools and Knaves, &c.

From an Everlafting mock-Parliament—and from *none*;
From Strafford's old friends— Harry, Jack, and John;
From our Solicitor's wolf-law deliver our King's fon;
And from the Refurrection of the Rump that is dead and
gone.
     From Fools and Knaves, &c.

From foreign invafion and commotions at home;
From our prefent diftraction, and from work to come;
From the fame hand again, Smectymnus* or the Bum,
And from taking Geneva in our way to Rome.
     From Fools and Knaves, &c.

---

* The title given to a club of five divines, the initials of whofe names formed this otherwife fenfelefs word, namely, *S*tephen *M*arfhall, *E*dmund *C*alamy, *T*homas *Y*oung, *M*atthew *N*ewcomen, and *W*illiam *S*purftow. They were authors of a once-popular book againft Epifcopacy and the Liturgy. Cleveland thus alludes to them:

> " *Smectymnus!* The Goblin makes me ftart;
> I' th' name of Rabbi Abraham, what art?
> Syriac? or Arabic? or Welfh? What fkil't?
> Ape all the bricklayers that Babel built.
> Some conjurer tranflate, and let me know it—
> Till then 'tis fit for a Weft Saxon poet.

From a hundred thoufand pound tax, to keep knaves by the fcore ;
(But it is well giv'n to thefe that turn'd thofe out of door) ;
From undoing ourfelves in plaiftering old fores ;
He that fet them a-work, let him pay their fcores.
     From Fools and Knaves, &c.

From Saints and tender Confciences in Buff;
From Mounfon in a foam, and Haflerig in a huff ;
From both Men and Women that think they never have enough ;
And from a fool's head that looks thro' a chain and a duff.
     From Fools and Knaves, &c.

From thofe that would divide the Gen'ral and the City ;
From Harry Martin's girl, that was neither fweet nor pretty ;
From a Faction that has neither brain nor pity ;
From the Mercy of a phanatique Committee.
     From Fools and Knaves, &c.

  But do the brotherhood, then, play their prizes,
  Like mummers in religion, with difguifes?
  Out-brave us with a name in rank and file—
  A name, which, if 'twere train'd would fpread a mile ?
  The faints' monopoly, the zealous clufter,
  Which like a porcupine prefents a mufter,
  And fhoots his quills at Bifhops and their Sees,
  A devout litter of young Maccabees."

Preferve us, good Heaven, from entrufting thofe
That ha' much to get, and little to lofe ;
That murther'd the Father, and the Son would depofe ;
(Sure they can't be our friends that are their Country's foes).
      From Fools and Knaves, &c.

From Bradfhaw's prefumption, and from Hoyle's* defpairs,
From rotten members, blind guides, preaching aldermen, and falfe may'rs ;
From long knives, long ears, long Parliaments, and long pray'rs ;
In mercy to this Nation — Deliver us and our heirs.
      From Fools and Knaves, &c.
      Libera nos Domine.

---

  * Alderman Hoyle, M.P., who committed fuicide.

THE PROTECTING BREWER.

[It was commonly believed that the Protector had followed the occupation of a brewer in early life, and was, therefore, frequently satirifed under that defignation; but Heath, who was one of his bittereft enemies, and loft no opportunity of reviling him for the meannefs of his origin, his irregularities in youth, and his political conduct towards the clofe of his life, pofitively afferts the contrary in his *Flagellum*. Before the commencement of the Civil Wars, Cromwell had been a farmer and malfter at St. Ives, in Huntingdonfhire; hence, probably, the vulgar opinion. *The Protecting Brewer* is an admirable epitome of his public life.]

BREWER may be a Burgefs grave,
   And carry the matter fo fine and fo brave,
   That he the better may play the knave,
      Which nobody can deny.

A Brewer may put on a Nabal face,
And march to the wars with fuch a grace,
That he may get a Captain's place,
      Which nobody, &c.

A Brewer may fpeak fo wondrous well,
That he may rife (ftrange things to tell)
And fo be made a Colonel,
      Which nobody, &c.

A Brewer may make his foes to flee,
And rife his fortunes, fo that he
Lieutenant-General may be,
    Which nobody, &c.

A Brewer may be all in all,
And raife his powers both great and fmall,
That he may be a Lord General,
    Which nobody, &c.

A Brewer may be like a fox in a Cub,
And teach a Lecture out of a Tub,
And give the wicked world a rub,
    Which nobody, &c.

A Brewer, by's Excife and Rate,
Will promife his Army he knows what,
And fet upon the College-gate,
    Which nobody, &c.

Methinks I hear one fay to me,
Pray why may not a Brewer be
Lord Chancellor o' the Univerfity ?
    Which nobody, &c.

A Brewer may be as bold as Hector,
When as he had drank his cup o' nectar;
And a Brewer may be a Lord Protector,
    Which nobody, &c.

Now here remains the ſtrangeſt thing,
How this Brewer about his liquor did bring
To be an Emperor or a King,
                Which nobody, &c.

A Brewer may do what he will,
And rob the Church and State, to ſell
His ſoul unto the Devil in Hell,
                Which nobody, &c.

A BALLAD.

By SAMUEL BUTLER.

[This farcaſtic ballad, by the author of Hudibras, was ſuggeſted by the Parliament of 1657, at the inſtigation of Alderman Sir Chriſtopher Pack, M.P. for London, tendering the crown to Oliver.]

S cloſe as a gooſe
   Sat the Parliament-houſe,
      To hatch the royal gull;
   After much fiddle-faddle,
The egg proved addle,
   And Oliver came forth *Noll*.

Yet old Queen Madge*,
Tho' things do not fadge,
   Will ſerve to be Queen of a May-pole;
Two Princes of Wales †,
For Whitſun-ales,
   And her grace, Maid Marion Clay-pole.*

---

* Cromwell's wife and daughter.
† Richard and Henry Cromwell, ſons of the Protector.

In a robe of cow-hide
Sat yeafty Pride*,
  With his dagger and his fling;
He was the pertinenft peer
Of all that were there,
  T' advife with fuch a King.

A great Philofopher †
Had a goofe for his lover,
  That follow'd him day and night:
If it be a true ftory,
Or but an allegory,
  It may be both ways right.

Strickland ‡ and his fon,
Both caft into one,
  Were meant for a fingle Baron;
But when they came to fit,
There was not wit
  Enough in them both to ferve for one!

---

* The " purging Colonel," and one of Cromwell's " Lords," who was originally a drayman.

† Butler has here confounded Amphilocus (of whom Pliny and others relate that a goofe fell in love with him) with the fon of Amphiaraus and Eriphyle.

‡ Walter Strickland, M.P. for Minehead, Cornwall, and fome time Ambaffador to the Hague. He was likewife one of the peers created by Cromwell, as well as a member of his Privy Council.

Wherefore 'twas thought good
To add Honeywood *;
But when they came to trial,
Each one prov'd a fool,
Yet three knaves in the whole,
And that made up a *pair-royal*.†

---

* Colonel Sir Thomas Honeywood, "a knight of the old ftamp," a committee-man in the time of the Long Parliament, and one of the peers created by Cromwell.

† The wit of this lies in the ambiguity of the term pair-royal, which is applicable to three knaves at the game of Brag, and, at the fame time, fignifies a *peer* or *baron* in French.

A NEW BALLAD TO AN OLD TUNE.
TOM OF BEDLAM.

[This very chara&eriftic ballad exhibits the anarchy which foi lowed the depofition of Richard Cromwell, when there appeared nc better hope for the nation than a military defpotifm even worfe than that of his father.]

MAKE room for an honeft Red-coat
  (And that you'll fay 's a wonder).
    The gun and the blade
    Are the tools,—and his trade
Is for *pay*, to *kill*, and *plunder*.
  Then away with the laws,
  And the " Good-old-Caufe." *
Ne'er talk o' the Rump, or the Charter;
  'Tis the cafh does the feat,
  All the reft's but a cheat,
Without *that* there's no Faith nor Quarter.

'Tis the mark of our coin GOD WITH US †,
  And the grace of the Lord goes along with 't:
    When the *Georges* are flown,
    Then the Caufe goes down,
  For the Lord has departed from it.
              Then away with, &c.

---

* The political cry, or by-word, of the Puritans, comprehending " religion and the laws."
† See " The State's New Coin," p. 94.

For Rome, or for Geneva,
   For the Table or the Altar,
      This spawn of a vote,
      He cares not a groat —
   For the *pence* he's your dog in a halter.
                              Then away, &c.

Tho' the name of King or Bishop
   To nostrils pure may be loathsome;
      Yet many there are,
      That agree with the May'r,
   That their lands are wondrous toothsome.
                              Then away, &c.

When our masters are poor, we leave 'em,
   'Tis the Golden Calf we bow to,
      We kill and we flay,
      Not for conscience, but pay;
   Give us *that* we'll fight for you, too.
                              Then away, &c.

'Twas *that* first turn'd the King out;
   The Lords next; then the Commons:
      'Twas that kept up Noll,
      Till the Devil fetch'd his soul;
   And then it set the *Rump* on 's.*
                              Then away, &c.

---

* The Rump was restored the 6th May, 1659, turned out again the 13th Oct., and once more restored the 26th Dec. Of these

Drunken Dick was a lame Protector,
And Fleetwood * a back-flider :
Thefe we ferv'd as the reft,
But the City's the beaft,
That will never caft her rider.
       Then away, &c.

When the Mayor holds the ftirrup,
And the Shrieves cry, God fave your honors,

---

frequent refufcitations of the Long Parliament, juft previous to the Reftoration of Charles II., Butler fays :

 " The learned rabbins of the Jews
 Write there's a bone, which they call *luez*,
 I' th' rump of man, of fuch a virtue,
 No force in nature can do hurt to ;
 And therefore, at the laft great day,
 All th' other members fhall, they fay,
 Spring out of this, as from a feed
 All forts of vegetals proceed :
 From whence the learned fons of art,
 Os facrum, juftly ftyle that part.
 Then what can better reprefent,
 Than this rump-bone, the Parliament ;
 That, after feveral rude ejections,
 And as prodigious refurrections,
 With new reverfions of nine lives,
 Starts up, and, like a cat, revives ! "
     Hudibras, part iii. c. ii. 1615-1630.

 * Fleetwood had been appointed by the officers of the army their general ; but fhortly afterwards, upon the invitation of the Parliament, he accepted a feat in the New Council of State, which was formed in oppofition to the Military Council of Twenty-three.

Then 'tis but a jump,
And up goes the Rump,
That will spur to the Devil upon us.
      Then away, &c.

And now for fling at your Thimbles,
 Your Bodkins, Rings, and Whistles * ;
  In truck for your toys,
  We'll fit you with boys
('Tis the doctrine of Hugh's† *Epistles*).
      Then away, &c.

When your Plate is gone, and your Jewels,
 You must be next entreated,
  To part with your bags,
  And to strip you to rags,
And yet not think you're cheated.
      Then away, &c.

The truth is, the Town deserves it,
 'Tis a *brainless, heartless monster;*
  At a club they may bawl,
  Or declare at their Hall,
And yet at a push not one stir.
      Then away, &c.

---

  * See note, p. 47.
  † Hugh Peters, the celebrated Puritan divine.

Sir Arthur * vow'd he'll treat 'em,
  Far worfe than the men of Chefter †;
    He's *bold* now they're cow'd,
    But he was nothing fo loud,
    When he lay in the ditch at Lefter.‡
                              Then away, &c.

The Lord has left John Lambert §,
  And the Spirit, Feak's ‖ anointed;
    But why, O Lord,
    Haft Thou fheath'd thy fword?
    Lo! thy faints are difappointed.
                              Then away, &c.

Tho' Sir Henry be departed,
  Sir John makes good the place now,
    And to help out the work
    Of the glorious Kirk,
    Our brethren march apace too. ¶
                              Then away, &c.

---

* Sir Arthur Haflerigg.

† Alluding to the garrifon of Chefter, which, when that city was befieged by the Parliamentarians, in Feb. 1645-6, was conftrained to feed on horfes, dogs, cats, &c.

‡ Alluding to the fuccefsful affault upon Leicefter by Charles I., on 30th May, 1645.

§ Alluding to the defertion of the troops under his command whilft he was ftationed at Newcaftle.

‖ Feakes was a violent anabaptift preacher at Blackfriars, who had fuffered incarceration in the Tower for his repeated attacks upon Cromwell.

¶ Alluding to Monk's progrefs towards London to fettle the difputes between the Parliament and army.

Whilſt Divines and Stateſmen wrangle,
　Let the Rump-ridden Nation bite on 't;
　　There are none but we
　　That are ſure to go free,
For the ſoldier's ſtill in the right on 't.
　　　　　　　　Then away, &c.

If our Maſters won't ſupply us
　With money, food, and clothing,
　　Let the State look to 't,
　　We'll find one that will do 't,
Let him live—we will not damn.
　　Then away with the laws,
　　And the good old Cauſe,
Ne'er talk o' the Rump, or the Charter;
　　'Tis the caſh does the feat,
　　All the reſt's but a cheat,
Without *that* there's no *faith* nor *Quarter*.

WIN AT FIRST AND LOSE AT LAST;

OR, A NEW GAME AT CARDS.

To the tune of "Ye Gallants that delight to play."

[This humorous piece, in which the events of the time are narrated in a suppofed game of cards, clofes the fatiric chronicle of the Commonwealth. It is one of the very few ballads, written againſt the Rump Parliament between the years 1639 and 1661, that is entirely free from licentioufnefs, virulence, and falfehood.]

E merry hearts that love to play
At Cards, fee who hath won the day;
You that once did fadly fing
The Knave of Clubs hath won the King;
Now more happy times we have,
    The King hath overcome the Knave,
    The King hath overcome the Knave.

Not long ago a game was play'd,
When three Crowns at the ſtakes were laid;
England had no caufe to boaſt,
Knaves won that which Kings had loſt:
Coaches gave the way to carts,
    And Clubs were better cards than Hearts,
    And Clubs were better cards than Hearts.

Old Noll was the Knave o' Clubs,
And Dad of fuch as preach in tubs,
Bradfhaw, Ireton, and Pride,
Were three other Knaves befide ;
And they play'd with half the pack,
  Throwing out all cards but Black,
  Throwing out all cards but Black.

But the juft Fates threw thefe four out,
Which made the loyal party fhout ;
The Pope would fain have had the ftock,
And with thefe cards have whipt his dock ;
But foon the Devil thefe cards fnatches,
  To dip in brimftone, and make matches,
  To dip in brimftone, and make matches.

But ftill the fport for to maintain,
Bold Lambert, Haflerigg, and Vane,
With one-eyed Hewfon, took their places,
Knaves were better cards than Aces ;
But Fleetwood he himfelf did fave,
  Becaufe he was more fool than Knave,
  Becaufe he was more fool than Knave.

Cromwell, tho' he fo much had won,
Yet he had an unlucky fon ;

He sits still, and not regards,
Whilst cunning gamesters set the Cards;
And thus, alas, poor silly Dick,
    He play'd awhile and lost his trick,
    He play'd awhile and lost his trick.

The Rumpers that had won whole Towns,
The spoils of martyrs and of Crowns,
Were not contented, but grew rough,
As though they had not won enough;
They kept the cards still in their hands,
    To play for Tithes and College lands,
    To play for Tithes and College lands.

The Presbyters began to fret,
That they were like to lose the sett;
Unto the Rump* they did appeal,
And said it was their turn to deal;
Then dealt the Presbyterians, but
    The Army swore that they would cut,
    The Army swore that they would cut.

---

* The origin of this celebrated term is thus given in the preface to *The Rump; or, Collection of Songs and Ballads made upon those who would be a Parliament, and were but the Rump of our House of Commons, five times dissolved* (12mo. Lond. 1660.):—" Now if you ask who named it Rump, know 'twas so stiled in an honest sheet of paper (call'd the Bloudy Rump) written before the Triall of our late Soveraign of Glorious Memorie: But the Word obtain'd not universal notice till it flew from the mouth of Major-General Brown at a Public Assembly in the days of Richard Cromwell."

The Foreign Lands began to wonder,
To fee what gallants we liv'd under,
That they, which Chriftians did forfwear,
Should follow gaming all the year—
Nay more, which was the ftrangeft thing,
    To play fo long without a King,
    To play fo long without a King!

The bold Phanatics prefent were,
Like butlers with their boxes there;
Not doubting but that every game
Some profit would redound to them;
Becaufe they were the gamefters' minions,
    And ev'ry day broach'd new opinions,
    And ev'ry day broach'd new opinions.

But Chefhire men (as ftories fay)
Began to fhew them gamefters' play;
Brave Booth*, and all his army, ftrives
To fave the ftakes, or lofe their lives;
But, O fad fate! they were undone,
    By playing of their Cards too foon,
    By playing of their Cards too foon.

---

* Sir George Booth, who, in the month of July, 1659, furprifed Chefter, but was fhortly afterwards defeated and captured by Lambert, who alfo recovered the city.

Thus all the while a Club was trump,
There's none could ever beat the Rump ;
Until a noble General came,
And gave the cheaters a clear flam ;
His finger did outwit their noddy,
  And fcrew'd up poor Jack Lambert's body,
  And fcrew'd up poor Jack Lambert's body.

Then Haflerig began to fcowl,
And faid the General play'd foul :
Look to him, partners, for I tell ye,
This Monk has got a King in 's belly :
Not fo, quoth Monk, but I believe,
  Sir Arthur has a Knave in 's fleeve,
  Sir Arthur has a Knave in 's fleeve.

When General Monk did underftand
The Rump were peeping into 's hand,
He wifely kept his cards from fight,
Which put the Rump into a fright ;
He faw how many were betray'd,
  That fhew'd their Cards before they play'd,
  That fhew'd their Cards before they play'd.

At length, quoth he, fome cards we lack,
I will not play with half a pack ;

What you caft out I will bring in,
And a new game we will begin :
With that the ftanders-by did fay,
    They never yet faw fairer play,
    They never yet faw fairer play.

But prefently this game was paft,
And for a fecond Knaves were caft ;
All new cards, not ftain'd with fpots,
As was the Rumpers and the Scots—
Here good gamefters play'd their parts,
    And turn'd up the King of Hearts,
    And turn'd up the King of Hearts.

After this game was done, I think,
The ftanders-by had caufe to drink,
And all loyal fubjects fing,
Farewell Knaves, and welcome King :
For, till we faw the King return'd,
    We wifh'd the Cards had all been burn'd,
    We wifh'd the Cards had all been burn'd.

CHARLES II.

THE NOBLE PROGRESS:

OR, A TRUE RELATION OF THE LORD-GENERAL MONK'S POLITICAL PROCEEDINGS WITH THE RUMP, THE CALLING IN THE SECLUDED MEMBERS, THEIR TRANSCENDANT VOTE FOR HIS SACRED MAJESTY, WITH HIS RECEPTION AT DOVOR, AND ROYAL CONDUCT THRO' THE CITY OF LONDON, TO HIS FORMER PALACE AT WHITEHALL.

[This curious street ballad, the original of which is in black letter, was discovered forming part of the lining of an old trunk. It is, probably, *unique*. The first part relates to the final dismission of the Rump, and the election, with the concurrence of Monk, of a free Parliament, or Convention, which voted the restoration of the exiled King. The second part describes the triumphal progress of Charles II. from Dovor to Whitehall, accompanied by the principal nobility and gentry of the kingdom.]

The tune is " When first the Scottish Wars began."

OOD people hearken to my call,
I'll tell you all what did befall,
  And happened of late ;
  Our noble valiant General Monk,
Came to the Rump, who lately stunk,
  With their Council of State.

Admiring what this man would do,
His secret mind there's none could know,
They div'd into him as much as they could,
George would not be won with their silver nor gold.
> The Sectarian Saints at this lookt blew,
> With all the rest of the factious crew;
> They vapor'd awhile and were in good hope;
> But now they have nothing left but the rope.*

Another invention then they sought,
Which long they wrought for to be brought
> To clasp him with they :
Quoth Vane and Scot, I'll tell you what,
We'll have a Plot, and he shall not,
> We'll carry the sway.†
Let's vote him a thousand pound a-year,
And Hampton Court for him and his heir.
Indeed, quoth George, ye're Free-Parliament men,
To cut a thong out of another man's skin.
> The Sectarian Saints, &c.

---

* At this time, the Independent leaders were so unpopular that they dared not show their faces in the street, and were scarcely safe in their own dwellings.

† Alluding to Sir Henry Vane's proposal, when he was President of the Provisional Council of State, for the future and permanent settlement of the government, namely:—"That it is destructive to the people's liberties to admit any earthly king, or single person, to the legislative or executive power over this nation."

They fent him then with all his hofts,
To break our pofts and raife our ghofts,
  Which was their intent;
To cut our gates and chains all down
Unto the ground, this trick they found,
  To make him be fhent :
This Plot the Rump did fo accord,
To caft an odium on my Lord,
But in this tafk he was hard put unto 't
'Twas enough to infect both his horfe and his foot.
    The Sectarian Saints, &c.

But when my Lord perceiv'd that night
What was their fpight, he brought to light
  Their knaveries all ;
The Parliament of *Forty-eight*,
Which long did wait, came to him ftraight,
  To give them a fall :
And fome fanatical people knew,
That George would give 'em their fatal due :
Indeed he did requite them agen,
For he pull'd the Monfter out o' the den.
    The Sectarian Saints, &c.

To the Houfe, our worthy Parliament,
With good intent they boldly went,
  To vote home the King;
And many hundred people more

Stood at the door and waited for
    Good tidings to bring :
But some in the House had their hands much in blood,
And in great opposition the traitors they stood.
But yet, I believe, it is very well known
That those that were for him were twenty to one.
    But the Sectarian Saints at this lookt blew,
    With all the rest of the factious crew ;
    They vapour'd awhile and were in good hope,
    But now they have nothing left but the Rope.

Second Part.

THEY call'd the League and Covenant in,
    To read again to every man,
      But what comes next?
    All Sequestrations null and void,
The people said none should be paid,
    For this was the text.
For as I heard all the people say,
They voted King Charles the first of May ;
Bonfires burning, bells did ring,
And our streets did echo with "God bless the King."
    At this the Sectarian Saints, &c.

Our General then to Dovor goes,
In fpite of foes, or deadly blows,
 Saying, " Vive le Roy:"
And all the Glories of the land,
At his command there they did ftand
 In triumph and joy.
Good Lord! what a fumptuous fight 'twas to fee
Our good Lord-General fall on his knee,
To welcome home his Majefty,
And own his facred fovereignty.
     But the Sectarian Saints, &c.

Then all the worthy, noble train
Came back again with *Charlemagne*,
 Our Sovereign great:
The Lord Mayor in his fcarlet gown,
In 's chain fo long, went thro' the town,
 In pomp and ftate.
The Livery-men each line the way,
Upon this great triumphant day,
Five rich maces carried before,
And my Lord himfelf the Sword he bore.
 Then *Vive le Roy* the Gentry did fing,
 For General Monk rode next to the King,
 With acclamations, fhouts, and cries,
 I thought they would have rent the fkies.

The conduits raviſhed with joy,
As I may ſay, did run all day
    Great plenty of wine;
And every gentleman of note
In 's velvet coat that could be got,
    In glory did ſhine.
There were all the Peers and Barons bold,
Richly 'tir'd in ſilver and gold,
March'd through the ſtreet ſo brave—
No greater pomp a King could have.
           At this the Sectarian Saints, &c.

And thus conducted all along,
Throughout the throng, till he did come
    Unto Whitehall;
Attended by theſe Noble-men,
Bold Hero's kin that brought him in,
    With the Generall.
Who was the man that brought him home,
And placed him on his Royal Throne?
'Twas General Monk did do this thing—
So God preſerve our gracious King!
           And now the Sectarian Saints, &c.

A BALLAD.

[In this loyal effusion, the author compares Britain to a Barbary mare, and amusingly recapitulates the various attempts by the parliamentary factions, throughout the course of the Rebellion, to bestride and manage her; ending his ballad with a flattering avowal of the superior judgment and tact exhibited on the part of her legitimate possessor—the restored King.]

LD England is now a brave Barbary made,
    And every one has an ambition to ride her;
King Charles was a horseman that long us'd the trade,
    But he rode in a snaffle, and that could not guide her.

Then the hungry Scot comes with spur and with switch,
    And would teach her to run a Geneva career;
His grooms were all Puritan, traitor, and witch,
    But she soon threw them down, with their pedlary geer.

The Long Parliament next came all to the block,
    And they this untameable palfrey would ride;
But she would not bear all that numerous flock;
    At which they were fain themselves to divide.

Jack Prefbyter firft gets the fteed by the head,
    While the reverend Bifhops had hold of the bridle :
Jack faid through the nofe, they their flocks did not feed,
    But fat ftill on the beaft, and grew aged and idle :

And then comes the Rout, with broomfticks infpir'd,
    And pull'd down their graces, their fleeves and their train,
And fets up Sir Jack, who the beaft quickly tir'd,
    With a journey to Scotland, and thence back again.

Jack rode in a doublet, with a yoke of prick-ears,
    A curfed fplay-mouth, and a Covenant-fpur ;
Rides fwitching and fpurring with jealoufies and fears,
    Till the poor famifh'd beaft was not able to ftir.

Next came th' Independent, a dev'lifh defigner,
    And got himfelf call'd by a holier name,
Makes Jack to unhorfe, for he was diviner,
    And would make her travel as far 's Amfterdam :

But Noll, a rank rider, gets firft in the faddle,
    And made her fhow tricks, and curvate and rebound ;
She quickly perceiv'd that he rode widdle-waddle,
    And, like his coach-horfes, threw his highnefs to ground.

Then Dick, being lame, rode holding by the pommel,
    Not having the wit to get hold of the rein ;

But the jade did fo fnort at the fight of a Crom'ell,
    That poor Dick and his kindred turn'd foot-men again.

Next Fleetwood and Vane, with their rafcally pack,
    Would every one put their feet in the ftirrup ;
But they pull'd the faddle quite off of her back,
    And were all got under her—before they were up.

At laft the King mounts her, and then fhe ftood ftill,
    As his Bucephalus, proud of this rider ;
She cheerfully yields to his power and fkill,
    Who is careful to feed her, and fkilful to guide her.

THE CAVALIER'S COMPLAINT.

[The Cavaliers were much difappointed at the neglect with which their claims to the royal favour were treated at the Reftoration, and expreffed great diffatiffaction at the preferments beftowed upon the Prefbyterians, whofe return to loyalty was thus conciliated and confirmed. It was commonly faid of the "Act of Oblivion and Indemnity," that the King had paffed an "act of oblivion for his friends, and of indemnity for his enemies." The famous divine, Dr. Ifaac Barrow, who may be accepted as a fair exponent of the views of the Royalifts at this juncture, conveyed, in the following diftich, his fenfe of the inattention he experienced:

"Te magis optavit rediturum, Carole, nemo,
Et nemo fenfit te rediiffe minus."

"Oh! how my breaft did ever burn
To fee my lawful King return;
Yet whilft his happy fate I blefs,
No one has felt his influence lefs."]

To the tune of "*I tell thee, Dick.*"

COME, Jack, let's drink a pot of ale,
And I fhall tell thee fuch a tale,
Will make thy ears to ring;
My coin is fpent, my time is loft,
And I this only fruit can boaft,
That once I faw my King.

But this doth moſt afflict my mind :
I went to Court in hope to find
   Some of my friends in place ;
And walking there I had a ſight
Of all the crew, but, by this light !
   I hardly knew one face.

'S' life ! of ſo many noble ſparks,
Who on their bodies bear the marks
   Of their integrity ;
And ſuffered ruin of eſtate,
It was my damned unhappy fate,
   That I not one could ſee.

Not one, upon my life, among
My old acquaintance all along
   At Truro and before ;
And I ſuppoſe the place can ſhew
As few of thoſe whom thou didſt know
   At York or Marſton Moor.

But truly there are ſwarms of thoſe
Who lately were our chiefeſt foes,
   Of pantaloons and muffs ;
Whilſt the old ruſty Cavalier
Retires, or dare not once appear,
   For want of coin and cuffs.

When none of thefe I could defcry,
Who better far deferved than I,
  Calmly I did reflect;
" Old fervices (by rule of State)
Like almanacs grow out of date,—
  What then can I expect?"

Troth! in contempt of fortune's frown,
I'll get me fairly out of town,
  And in a cloifter pray,
That fince the ftars are yet unkind
To Royalifts, the King may find
  More faithful friends than they.

AN ECHO TO THE CAVALIER'S COMPLAINT.

I MARVEL, Dick, that having been
So long abroad, and having feen
　The world as thou haft done,
　Thou fhould'ft acquaint me with a tale
As old as Neftor, and as ftale
　As that of *Prieft and Nun*.

Are we to learn what is a court?
A pageant made for Fortune's fport,
　Where merits fcarce appear;
For bafhful merit only dwells
In camps, in villages, and cells;
　Alas! it dwells not there.

Defert is nice in its addrefs,
And merit ofttimes doth opprefs,
　Beyond what guilt would do;
But they are fure of their demands
That come to Court with golden hands,
　And brazen faces too.

The King, they say, doth still profess
To give his party some redress,
   And cherish honesty;
But his good wishes prove in vain,
Whose service with his servants' gain
   Not always doth agree.

All princes (be they ne'er so wise)
Are fain to see with others' eyes,
   But seldom hear at all;
And courtiers find their interest,
In time to feather well their nest,
   Providing for their fall.

Our comfort doth on time depend,
Things when at their worst will mend;
   And let us but reflect
On our condition t' other day,
When none but tyrants bore the sway—
   What did we then expect?

Meanwhile a calm retreat is best,
But discontent (if not suppressed)
   Will breed disloyalty;
This is the constant note I sing,
I have been faithful to my King,
   And so shall ever be.

A TURN-COAT OF THE TIMES:

WHO DOTH BY EXPERIENCE PROFESS AND PROTEST THAT OF ALL PROFESSIONS, A TURN-COAT'S THE BEST.

[This, like the preceding ballad, is obviously penned by some disappointed Royalist, and exhibits the culpable partiality of the restored King in the dispensation of his favours.]

S I was walking thro'
   Hyde Park as I us'd to do,
     Some two or three months ago,
   I laid me all along,
Without any fear of wrong,
And listen'd unto a song:
It came from a powder'd thing,
As fine as a lord or a king;
   He knew not that I
   Was got so nigh,
And thus he began to sing.

   I am a Turn-coat knave,
Altho' I do bear it brave,
   And do not shew all that I have;
I can, with tongue and pen,
Court every sort of men,
   And kill 'em as fast agen:

With zealots I can pray,
With Cavaliers I can play;
　With fhop-keepers I
　Can cog and lie,
And cozen as faft as they.

When firft the wars began,
And 'prentices led the van,
　'Twas I that did fet them on;
When they cry'd Bifhops down,
In country, court, and town,
Quoth I, and have at the Crown:
The Covenant I did take,
For form and fafhion's fake,
　But when it would not
　Support my plot,
'Twas like an old Almanack.

When Independency
Had fuperiority,
　I was of the fame degree;
When Keepers did command,
I then had a holy hand
In Deans' and in Chapters' land;
But when I began to fpy
Protectorfhip drew nigh,
　And Keepers were
　Thrown o'er the bar,
Old Oliver! then cry'd I.

When Sectarifts got the day,
I uf'd my *yea* and *nay*,
   To flatter and then betray;
In Parliament I gat,
And there a Member fat,
To tumble down Church and State,
For I was a trufty trout,
In all that I went about,
   And there we did vow
   To fit till now,
But Oliver turn'd us out.

We put down the Houfe of Peers,
We kill'd the Cavaliers,
   And tippl'd the widows' tears;
We fequefter'd men's eftates,
And made 'em pay monthly rates
To trumpeters and their mates.
Rebellion we did print,
And alter'd all the Mint;
   No knavery then
   Was done by men
But I had a finger in't.

When Charles was put to flight,
Then I was at Wor'fter fight,
   And got a good booty by't;

At that moſt fatal fall
I kill'd and plunder'd all,
The weakeſt went to the wall;
Whilſt my merry mates fell on,
To pillaging I was gone,
   There is many (thought I)
   Will come by and bye,
And why ſhould not I be one.

We triumph'd like the Turk,
We crippl'd the Scottiſh Kirk,
   That ſet us firſt to work;
When Cromwell did but frown,
They yielded every town,
St. Andrew's Croſs went down;
But when old Noll did dye,
And Richard his ſon put by,
   I knew not how
   To guide my plow,
Where now ſhall I be? thought I.

I muſt confeſs the Rump
Did put me in a dump,
   I knew not what would be trump;
When Dick had loſt the day,
My gaming was at a ſtay,
I could not tell what to play;

CHARLES II.

When Monk was upon that fcore
I thought I would play no more,
   I did not think what
   He would be at,
I ne'er was fo mumpt before.

But now I am at Court,
With men of the better fort,
   And purchafe a good report;
I have the eyes and ears
Of many brave noble peers,
And flight the poor Cavaliers,
Poor knaves, they know not how
To flatter, cringe, and bow,
   For he that is wife,
   And means to rife,
He muft be a Turn-coat too.

THE OLD CLOAK.

[In the autumn of 1663, whilſt the King and his newly-married Queen were making a tour of pleaſure in the weſtern provinces, a conſpiracy was diſcovered, carried on by the old Republicans, to reſtore the Commonwealth; for which twenty perſons concerned in it were tried, convicted, and ſuffered early in the following year. The ballad ſets forth all the evils conſequent upon the former revolution, when "the old cloak," or Preſbyterian party, gained the aſcendancy; and concludes, as is uſual in the ſatires of the time, by implicating the Papiſts, who were ſuppoſed to aſſociate themſelves, in turn, with every diſaffected party in the State.]

OME buy my new Ballet,
    I have't in my wallet,
    But 'twill not, I fear, pleaſe ev'ry pallet;
    Then mark what in sooth
I ſwear by my youth,
That every line in my wallet is truth;
A Ballad of wit, a brave Ballad of worth,
'Tis newly printed, and newly come forth:
    'Twas made of a Cloak that fell out with a Gown,
    That crampt all the Kingdom, and crippl'd the Crown.

    I tell you in brief,
    A ſtory of grief,
Which happen'd when Cloak was commander-in-chief:

It tore *Common-prayers*,
  Imprifon'd Lord Mayors ;
In one day it voted down prelates and players ;
It made people perjur'd, in point of obedience,
A Covenant cut off the Oath of Allegiance.
  Then let us endeavor to pull this Cloak down,
  That crampt all the Kingdom, and crippl'd the Crown.

It was a black Cloak,
  In good time be it fpoke,
That kill'd many thoufands, but never ftruck ftroke ;
  With hatchet and rope,
  The forlorn hope,
Did join with the Devil to pull down the Pope:
It fet all the Sects in the City to work,
And rather than fail, 'twould have brought in the Turk.
  Then let us endeavor to pull the Cloak down,
  That crampt all the Kingdom, and crippl'd the Crown.

It feiz'd on the Tower-guns,
  Thofe fierce demi-gorgons ;
It brought in the Bag-pipes, and pull'd down the Organs ;
  The pulpits did fmoke,
  The churches did choke,
And all our Religion was turn'd to a Cloak :
It brought in lay-elders could not write nor read ;
It fet Public Faith up, and pull'd down the *Creed*.
  Then let us endeavor to pull the Cloak down,
  That crampt all the Kingdom, and crippl'd the Crown.

This pious Impoſter
Such fury did foſter,
It left us no penny, nor no *Pater-noſter;*
   It threw to the ground
   Ten Commandments down,
And ſet up twice twenty times ten of its own;
It routed the King and villains elected
To plunder all thoſe whom they thought diſaffected.
   Then let us endeavor to pull the Cloak down,
   That crampt all the Kingdom, and crippl'd the Crown.

   To blind people's eyes,
   This Cloak was ſo wife,
It took off Ship-money, but ſet up Exciſe *;
   Men brought in their plate,
   For reaſons of State,
And gave it to Tom Trumpeter and his mate:
In Pamphlets it writes many ſpecious epiſtles,
To cozen poor wenches of bodkins and whiſtles.
   Then let us endeavor to pull the Cloak down,
   That crampt all the Kingdom, and crippl'd the Crown.

   In pulpits it mov'd,
   And was much approv'd,
For crying out, " Fight the Lord's battles, belov'd!"

---

* The arbitrary manner in which the exciſe was levied, not only upon liquors but alſo upon proviſions, to ſupport the war againſt Charles I., difguſted people, and more particularly the poorer claſſes, more than all the other meaſures of the Long Parliament. See note to page 25.

It bob-tail'd the Gown,
Put Prelacy down,
It trod on the Mitre to reach at the Crown;
And into the field it an army did bring,
To aim at the Council, but fhot at the King.
   Then let us endeavor to pull the Cloak down,
   That crampt all the Kingdom, and crippl'd the Crown.

It raif'd up ftates,
Whofe politic pates
Do now keep their quarters on the City-gates :
   To father and mother,
   To fifter and brother,
It gave a Commiffion to kill one another;
It took up men's horfes, at very low rates,
And plunder'd our goods to fecure our eftates.
   Then let us endeavor to pull the Cloak down,
   That crampt all the Kingdom, and crippl'd the Crown.

This Cloak did proceed
To a damnable deed,
It made the beft mirror of Majefty bleed;
   Tho' Cloak did not do 't,
   He fet it on foot,
By rallying and calling his journeymen to 't [*];

---

[*] An allufion to the Scots felling Charles the Firft to the Independents, who afterwards butchered him.

For never had come such bloody disaster,
If Cloak had not first drawn a sword at his Master.
   Then let us endeavor to pull the Cloak down,
   That crampt all the Kingdom, and crippl'd the Crown.

     Let's pray that the King,
     And his Parliament,
In sacred or secular things may be content;
     So righteously firm,
     And religiously free,
That Papists and Atheists suppressed may be:
And as there's one Deity that doth over-rule us,
One Faith, and one Form, and one Church doth continue 's;
   Then Peace, Truth, and Plenty, our Kingdom will crown,
   And all Popish Plots and their Plotters shall down.

CLARENDON'S HOUSE-WARMING.

BY ANDREW MARVEL.

[Charles II., in the year 1664, granted to his Chancellor, the Earl of Clarendon, in confideration of his lordfhip's eminent fervices both at home and abroad, a valuable tract of land immediately fronting the royal palace of St. James's, whereon the earl determined to erect a fuitable manfion for himfelf and heirs. The coft of doing fo, as too frequently happens, proved three times as great as the original eftimate—amounting, in fact, to 60,000*l.* Thofe who were intriguing at court for the downfall of the Chancellor, availed themfelves of the opportunity of expofing, by all the means their fpitefulnefs and ingenuity could fuggeft and invent, his recklefs expenditure at a time when the nation was proftrated by war, peftilence, and fire; and fucceeded as well in alienating from him the good will of the King, as exciting almoft to madnefs the mind of the public againft him. "Some called it (fays Burnet) Dunkirk-houfe, intimating that it was built by his fhare of the price of Dunkirk; others called it Holland-houfe, becaufe he was believed to be no friend to the war; fo it was given out that he had money from the Dutch." The fame authority informs us, that the unfortunate earl, when driven out of England, ordered his fon to tell all his friends that if they could excufe the vanity and folly of Clarendon-houfe, he would undertake to anfwer for all the reft of his actions himfelf. In 1683, the houfe and lands furrounding it were purchafed by Sir Thomas Bond, who demolifhed the former, and erected on its fite Bond and Albemarle-ftreets.]

WHEN Clarendon had difcern'd beforehand,
  (As the *caufe* can eafily foretell the *effect*)
  At once three Deluges * threat'ning our land,
'Twas the feafon he thought to turn Architect.

As Mars, and Apollo, and Vulcan confume;
  While he the betrayer of England and Flander,
Like the king-fifher choofeth to build in the broom,
  And neftles in flames like the falamander.

But obferving that mortals run often behind,
  (So unreafonable are the rates they buy at)
His omnipotence therefore much rather defign'd
  How he might create a houfe with a *fiat*.

He had read of Rhodope, a lady of Thrace,
  Who was courted so often ere fhe did marry;
And wifh'd that his daughter had had as much grace
  To erect him a Pyramid out of a quarry.†

But then recollecting how the harper, Amphyon,
  Made Thebes dance aloft while he fiddl'd and fung,

---

  * Alluding to the plague, the great fire of London, and the difgraceful war with the Dutch.
  † A difgufting allufion to the clandeftine marriage of the earl's eldeft daughter to the Duke of York, afterwards James II.

He thought (as an inftrument he was moft free on)
  To build with the Jews-trump of his own tongue.

Yet a precedent fitter in Virgil he found,
  Of African Poultney, and Tyrian Dide,
That he begg'd for a Palace fo much of his ground
  As might carry the meafure and name of an *hyde*.*

Thus daily his gouty invention him pain'd,
  And all for to fave the expenfes of brickbat,
That engine fo fatal, which Denham had brain'd,
  And too much refembled his wife's chocalate.

But while thefe devices he all doth compare,
  None folid enough feem'd for his ftrong caftor;
He himfelf would not dwell in a caftle of air,
  Though he had built full many a one for his Mafter.

Already he had got all our money and cattle,
  To buy us for flaves, and purchafe our lands;
What Jofeph by famine, he wrought by fea-battle †,—
  Nay fcarce the prieft's portion could 'fcape from his hands.

And hence like Pharoah that Ifrael 'preft
  To make mortar and brick, yet allow'd 'em no ftraw,
He cared not though Egypt's ten plagues us diftreft,
  So he could to build but make policy law.

---

* The patronymic of the earl.
† 'Twas believed that the earl had been bribed by the Dutch to treat of a peace.

The Scotch forts and Dunkirk, but that they were fold,
 He would have demolifht to raife up his walls;
Nay, e'en from Tangier have fent back for the mould,
 But that he had nearer the ftones of St. Paul's. *

His wood would come in at an eafier rate,
 So long as the yards had a deal or a fpar:
His friend in the Navy would not be ingrate,
 To grudge him the timber who fram'd him the War.

To proceed with the model he call'd in his Allons —
 The two Allons when jovial, who ply him with gallons—
The two Allons who ferve his blind juftice for ballance—
 The two Allons who ferve his injuftice for talons.†

They approve it thus far and faid it was fine,
 Yet his Lordfhip to finifh it would be unable,
Unlefs all abroad he divulg'd the defign,
 For his houfe then would grow like a vegetable.

---

* Part of the Houfe was built with ftones defigned, before the civil war, for the repair of Old St. Paul's. The Chancellor was accufed of turning to a profane ufe what he had purchafed with a bribe.

† The two Allons, or Allens, were probably members of the Vintners' Company. Clarendon Houfe was built (fays Eachard) in the Chancellor's abfence in the Plague-year, principally at the charge of the Vintners' Company, who, defigning to monopolife his favour, made it abundantly more large and magnificent than ever he intended or defired.

His rent would no more in arrear run to Wor'ster * ;
  He should dwell more noble, and cheap too at home,
While into a fabrick the presents would muster,
  As by hook and by crook the world cluster'd of atom.

He liked th' advice, and then soon it assayed,
  And presents crowd head-long to give good example:
So the bribes overlaid her that Rome once betrayed:
  The Tribes ne'er contributed so to the Temple.†

Strait judges, priests, bishops, true sons of the seal,
  Sinners, governors, farmers, bankers, patentees,
Bring in the whole mite of a year at a meal,
  As the Cheddar clubs dairy to th' incorporate cheese.

Bulteel's, Beaken's, Morley, Wren's fingers with telling
  Were shrivell'd, and Clutterbuck, Eager's and Kips;
Since the Act of Oblivion was never such selling,
  As at this Benevolence out of the snips.‡

---

* Alluding to Worcester House, in the Strand, where the Earl resided before building Clarendon House.

† Lord Dartmouth relates, in his notes on Burnet, that Clarendon House was chiefly furnished with Cavaliers' goods, brought thither for peace-offerings.

‡ In reference to this voluntary contribution made by the people to Charles II., with which Marvel compares the "peace-offerings" of the Cavaliers to the Chancellor, Pepys writes in his *Diary* (31st August, 1661):—" The Benevolence proves so little, and an occasion of so much discontent everywhere, that it had better it had never been set up. I think to subscribe 20*l*. We are at our office quiet, only for lack of money all things go to rack. Our very bills offered to be sold upon the Exchange at 10 per cent. loss."

'Twas then that the Chimney-contractors he fmok'd ;
   Nor would take his beloved Canary in kind ;
But he fwore that the patent fhould ne'er be revok'd —
   No! would the whole Parliament falute him behind.

Like Jove under Ætna, o'erwhelming the giant,
   For foundation the Briftol funk in the earth's bowel ;
And St. John muft now for the leads be compliant,
   Or his right hand fhall elfe be cut off with a trowel.

For furveying the building 'twas Prat did the feat,
   But for th' expenfe he rely'd on Worftenholm,
Who fat heretofore at the King's receipt,
   But receiv'd now and paid the Chancellor's cuftom.

By fubfidies thus both cleric and laic,
   And with matter profane cemented with holy,
He finifht at laft his palace mofaic,
   By a model more excellent than Lefly's folly.*

And upon the *turrus*, to confummate all,
   A lanthorn, like Fawk's, furveys the burnt Town,
And fhews on the top, by the regal gilt ball,
   Where you are t' expect the *Sceptre and Crown*.†

---

   * Alluding to Dr. John Leflie, the famous linguift and bifhop of the Orkneys, whence he was tranflated to the fee of Raphoe in Ireland (1633), where he built a palace, fo ftrongly fortified, that he was the laft who furrendered to the arms of Cromwell.
   † A fimilar idea occurs in another and feverer contemporary lampoon quoted by Difraeli, in his *Curiofities of Literature* :—

Fond City ! its rubbifh and ruins that builds
  Like chymifts vain, a flow'r from its afhes returning* ;
Your metropolis-houfe is in St. James' Fields,
  And till there you remove, you fhall never leave burning.

This Temple, of War and of Peace is the fhrine,
  Where this Idol of State fits ador'd and accurft ;
And to handfel his altar and noftrils divine,
  Great Buckingham's † sacrifice muft be the firft.

> Lo! his whole ambition already divides
> The fceptre between the Stuarts and Hydes;
> Behold ! in the depth of our plague and wars,
> He built him a palace outbraves the ftars,
> Which Houfe (we Dunkirk, he Clarendon names)
> Looks down with fhame upon Saint James;
> But 'tis not his golden-globe will fave him,
> Being lefs than the Cuftom-houfe farmers gave him ;
> His chapel for confecration calls,
> Whofe facrilege plunder'd the ftones from St. Pauls.
> When Queen Dido landed, fhe bought as much ground
> As the *hide* of a lufty fat ox would furround ;
> But when the faid *hide* was cut into thongs,
> A city and kingdom to *Hyde* belongs ;
> So here in court, church, and country far and wide,
> Here's nought to be feen but *Hyde! Hyde! Hyde!*
> Of old, and where law the kingdom divides,
> 'Twas our *hides* of land, 'tis now our land of *Hydes.*

  * The refurrection, or *palingenefis*, of incinerated plants by means of fermentation, was one of thofe philofophical amufements that captivated the mind in the feventeenth century, much in the fame manner as fpirit-rapping, table-turning, &c., in our day.

  † The Chancellor, by his grave and haughty conduct, had rendered himfelf extremely obnoxious to Buckingham and the other

Now some (as all builders muſt cenſure abide)
  Throw duſt in its front, and blame ſituation;
And others as much reprehend his backſide,
  As too narrow by far for his expatiation;

But do not conſider how in proceſs of times
  That for name-ſake he may with Hyde-park it enlarge,
And with that convenience he ſoon for his crimes
  At Tyburn may land, and ſpare the Tower barge:

Or rather how wiſely his ſtall was built near,
  Left with driving too far his tallow impair;
When like the good ox, for public good cheer,
  He comes to be roaſted next St. James' fair.

---

licentious perſons about the court. "He often (ſays Eachard) took liberty to give ſuch reproofs to theſe perſons of wit and gallantry as were very unacceptable to them; and ſometimes thought it his duty to adviſe the King himſelf in ſuch a manner, as they took advantage of him, and as he paſſed the court would often ſay, "There goes your ſchoolmaſter!" The chief of thoſe was the Duke of Buckingham, who had a ſurpriſing talent of ridicule and hypocriſy; and that he might make way to his ruin, he often did act and mimic this great man in the preſence of the King, walking ſtately with a pair of bellows before him for the *purſe*, and Col. Titus carrying a fire-ſhovel on his ſhoulder for the *mace*, with which ſort of banter and farce the King was too much delighted and captivated."

ON THE LORD MAYOR AND COURT OF ALDERMEN PRESENTING THE KING AND THE DUKE OF YORK WITH A COPY OF THEIR FREEDOM.

BY ANDREW MARVEL.

[In November, 1674, on the acceffion of Sir Robert Vyner to the mayoralty, Charles the Second was magnificently entertained at the Guildhall; when he was pleafed to accept the freedom of the city, the copy and feal of which were conveyed with great pomp to his palace at Whitehall, in two boxes of maffive gold. In the *Spectator* (No. 462) is told the ftory of Sir Robert Vyner's fuccefsfully urging the King, at this entertainment, "to return and take t'other bottle." The author of this ballad was difgufted at the fycophancy of the citizens of London, who had lately been fo groffly defrauded by Charles, when he fuddenly clofed the Exchequer.]

HE Londoners Gent. to the King do prefent
   In a box the City Maggot;
'Tis a thing full of weight that requires the might
   Of the Guildhall team to drag it.

Whilft their churches unbuilt, their houfes undwelt,
   And their orphans want bread to feed 'em;
Themfelves they've bereft of the little wealth they had left,
   To make an offering of their " freedom."

O ye addled-brain'd cits! who, henceforth in their wits,
   Would entruſt their youth to your heading,—
When in diamonds and gold you have him thus enroll'd,
   You know both his friends and his breeding—?

Beyond ſea he began, where ſuch a riot he ran,
   That every one there did leave him;
And now he's come o'er ten times worſe than before,
   When none but ſuch fools would receive him!

He ne'er knew, not he, how to ſerve or be free,
   Though he has paſt through ſo many adventures;
But e'er ſince he was bound (that is, he was crown'd)
   He has every day broke his Indentures.

He ſpends all his days in running to plays,
   When he ſhould in the ſhop be ſtaying;
And he waſtes all his nights in his conſtant delights
   Of revelling, drinking, and playing.

Throughout Lombard Street, each man he did meet,
   He would run on the ſcore and borrow;
When they aſk'd for their own he was broke and gone,
   And his creditors left to ſorrow.*

---

   * The citizens of London were the principal ſufferers by the ſudden ſhutting up of the Exchequer two years previouſly. The Lord Mayor, Sir Robert Vyner, loſt upwards of 400,000*l.* by that unparalleled act of fraud.

Tho' oft bound to the peace, yet he never would ceafe
  To vex his poor neighbours with quarrels;
And when he was beat, he ftill made his retreat
  To his Clevelands, his Nells, and his Carwells.

Nay, his company lewd, were twice grown fo rude,
  That had not fear taught him fobriety;
And the Houfe being well barr'd, with guard upon guard,
  They'd robb'd us of all our propriety.

Such a plot was laid, had not Afhley betray'd,
  As had cancell'd all former difafters,
And your wives had been ftrumpets to his Highnefs'
    trumpets,
  And foot-boys had all been your mafters.

So many are the debts, for his numerous brats,
  Which muft all be defray'd by London;
That notwithftanding the care of Sir Thomas Player*,
  The chamber muft needs be undone.

His words, nor his oath, can bind him to troth,
  And he values not credit or hiftory;
And tho' he has ferv'd thro' two 'prenticefhips now,
  He knows not his trade or myftery.

---

* The Chamberlain of the City.

Then London rejoice in thy fortunate choice
  To have made him free of thy fpices ;
And do not miftruft he may once grow more juft,
  When he 'as worn off his folly and vices.

And what little thing is that which you bring
  To the Duke, the kingdom's darling—?
Ye hug it and draw, like ants at a ftraw,
  Tho' too fmall for the griftle of Sterling.

Is it a box of pills to cure the Duke's ills
  (He is too far gone to begin it !)
Or, does your fine fhow in proceffioning go
  With the pix and the hoft within it—?

The very firft head of the oath you him read,
  Show you all how fit he 's to govern ;
When in heart (you all knew) he ne'er was, nor will be true
  To his country, or to his fovereign.

And who could fwear, that he would forbear
  To cull out the good of an alien,
Who ftill doth advance the government of France,
  With a wife and religion Italian—?

And now, worshipful firs, go fold up your furs,
  And Vyners turn again, turn again,
I see who e'er's freed, you for slaves are decreed,
  Until you *burn again, burn again.**

---

  * Alluding to the great fire of London in 1666.

THE HISTORY OF INSIPIDS.
BY JOHN WILMOT, EARL OF ROCHESTER.

[Bifhop Burnet relates, in his *Life of Rochefter*, that the Earl once, being drunk, intended to prefent King Charles the Second with a libel that he had written on fome ladies connected with the Court; but by a miftake he handed him one written on himfelf. It this is the libel in queftion, the merry monarch muft have been very much of Andrew Marvel's opinion, that the profligate earl "was a man who had the true vein of fatire in him." Probably no feverer lampoon than this was ever penned; certainly no one more richly merited it than the object of it; and, unhappily, no one was lefs affected by fuch expofures than the regal penfioner of France. Rochefter was not the only one who expofed to his face the unpatriotic and fenfual conduct of the King. Pepys records Tom Killigrew having told Charles, in the prefence of Cowley the poet, that matters were in a very ill ftate, but yet there was one way to help all. "There is (faid he) a good, honeft, able man, that I could name, that if your Majefty would employ and command to fee all things well executed, all things would foon be mended; and this is one Charles Stuart, who now fpends his time employing his lips about the Court, and hath no other employment; he were the fitteft man in the world to perform it." To this Pepys adds: "This is moft true, but the King do not profit by any of this, but lays all afide, and remembers nothing, but to his pleafures again; which is a forrowful confideration." *Diary*, 8 Dec. 1666.]

I.

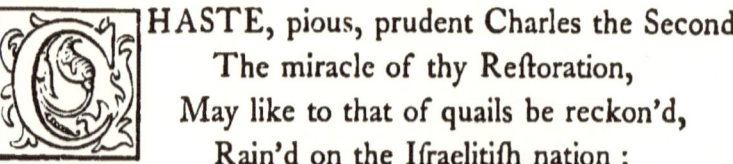CHASTE, pious, prudent Charles the Second,
The miracle of thy Reftoration,
May like to that of quails be reckon'd,
Rain'd on the Ifraelitifh nation:

The wish'd-for blessing from Heav'n sent,
Became their curse and punishment.

2.

The virtues in thee, Charles, inherent,
   Albeit thy face is somewhat odd,
Proves thee as proper a vicegerent
   As e'er was Harry ordain'd by God;
For chastity and pious deeds
His grandsire Harry, Charles exceeds.

3.

Our Romish bondage-breaker, Harry,
   Espoused half a dozen wives;
Charles only one resolv'd to marry;
   With other men's he never lives;—
Yet hath he sons and daughters more
Than e'er had Harry by three score.

4.

Never was such a faith's defender,
   He like a politic prince, and pious,
Gives liberty to conscience tender,
   And doth to no religion tie us:
Jews, Turks, Christians, Papists, he'll please us
With Moses, Mahomet, or Jesus.

5.

In all affairs of Church or State,
  He very zealous is, and able;
Devout at pray'rs, and fits up late,
  At the Cabal and Council-table;
His very dog at Council-board
Sits grave and wife as any lord.

6.

Let Charles his policy no man flout,
  The wifeſt kings have all ſome folly;
Nor let his piety any doubt;
  Charles, like a ſovereign wife and holy,
Makes young men judges of the bench,
And biſhops thoſe that love a wench.

7.

His father's foes he doth reward,
  Preſerving thoſe that cut off 's head;
Old Cavaliers, the Crown's beſt guard,
  He lets them ſtarve for want of bread:
Never was any king indued
With ſo much grace and gratitude.

8.

Blood*, that wears treaſon in his face,
  Villain complete, in parſon's gown,—

---

* The noted deſperado, Colonel Thomas Blood, who, notwithſtanding his atrocious attempt to murder the Duke of Ormond, and,

How much is he at Court in grace
For ſtealing Ormond and the crown!
Since loyalty does no man good,
Let's ſteal the King and out-do Blood.

9.

A Parliament of knaves and ſots,
Members by name you muſt not mention,
He keeps in pay, and buys their votes,
Here with a place, there with a penſion:
When to give money he can't cologue 'em,
He doth with ſcorn prorogue, prorogue 'em.*

---

in the ſame year (1670), difguiſed as a prieſt, to ſteal the regalia from the Tower, was not only freely pardoned, but liberally penſioned by Charles!

* Marvel has alſo expoſed this common expedient of the King in the following ſtinging epigram:

> " There's a Houſe to be let,
>   For Charles Bawd ſwore,
> By infamous Portſmouth,
>   He wou'd ſhut up the door.
> Inquire at the lodgings,
>   Next door to the Pope,
> At Duke Lauderdale's head,
>   With a cravat of rope.
> And there you will hear
>   How next he will let it;
> If you pay the old price
>   You will certainly get it.
> He holds it in tail
>   From his father, who faſt
> Did keep it long ſhut,
>   But paid for't at laſt."

10.

But they long fince by too much giving,
    Undid, betray'd, and fold the nation;
Making their memberfhips a living,
    Better than e'er was fequeftration:
God give thee, Charles, a refolution
To damn the knaves by diffolution.

11.

Fame is not grounded on fuccefs,
    Though victories were Cæfar's glory;
Loft battles make not Pompey lefs,
    But left them ftiled great in ftory:
Malicious fate doth oft devife
To beat the brave, and fool the wife.

12.

Charles in the firft Dutch war ftood fair
    To have been fovereign of the deep;
When Opdam blew up in the air*,
    Had not his Highnefs† gone to fleep:
Our fleet flack'd fails, fearing his waking,
The Dutch elfe had been in fad taking.

---

* Alluding to the memorable defeat of the Dutch, off Harwich, 3rd June, 1665, when the fhip of Opdam, their admiral, blew up, and himfelf, with 500 of his men, perifhed in the explofion. Rochefter bore a part in that great fea fight.

† The Duke of York. The charge of his having retired to reft in order to avoid a continuance of the battle, was inveftigated by Parliament, which exonerated the Duke.

13.

The Bergen* bufinefs was well laid,
  Though we paid dear for that defign;
Had we not three days parling ftaid,
  The Dutch fleet there, Charles, had been thine:
Though the falfe Dane agreed to fell 'um,
He cheated us, and faved Skellum.

14.

Had not Charles fweetly chouf'd the States,
  By Bergen-baffle grown more wife,
And made them pay him higher rates,
  By their rich Smyrna fleet's furprife:
Had haughty Holms † but call'd in Spragg ‡,
Horns had been put into a bag.

15.

Mifts, ftorms, fhort victuals, adverfe winds,
  And once the natives' wife divifion,

---

* The fort of Bergen, in Norway, in the harbour of which town the Dutch Eaft India fleet had taken refuge, where, with the connivance of the King of Denmark (the port being a neutral one), a defperate attempt was made by the Englifh to capture the merchantmen, which alone were valued at 25,000,000 livres. The failure of this enterprife, in which Rochefter alfo bore a part, created much unpleafant fpeculation at the time.

† Vice-Admiral Sir Robert Holms, known in his day as "the curfed beginner of the two Dutch wars."

‡ Admiral Sir Edward Spragg, who was fubfequently drowned (1673).

Defeated Charles his beſt deſigns,
  Till he became his foes deriſion :
But he had ſwing'd the Dutch at Chatham,
Had he had ſhips but to come at 'em.*

16.

Our Blackheath hoſt, without diſpute,
  Raiſ'd (put on board, why no man knows)
Muſt Charles have render'd abſolute,
  Over his ſubjects or his foes :
Has not the French King made us fools,
By taking Maeſtricht with our tools?

17.

But Charles, what could thy object be
  To run ſo many ſad diſaſters ;
To join thy fleet with falſe D'Eſtrées†,
  To make the French of Holland maſters?

---

* Alluding to the national diſgrace, when the Dutch ſailed up the Medway (11th June, 1667), captured Sheerneſs, burnt the magazines and ſeveral men of war, and blew up the fortifications.

† The French Admiral, Count D'Eſtrées, who was aſſociated with, but rendered little aſſiſtance to, the Duke of York and Lord Sandwich, when they were oppoſed to the Dutch in Solebay (28th May, 1672). Rocheſter, of courſe, was ignorant of the diſgraceful arrangements which had been privately entered into between Charles and Louis.

Was 't Carwell*, Brother James, or Teague,
That made thee break the Triple-league ?

18.

Could Robin Viner† have forefeen
The glorious triumphs of his mafter,

---

* Louife de Quéroualle (which the Englifh pronounced "Carwell"), Duchefs of Portfmouth, and one of the King's miftreffes. She was alfo the reputed fpy of Louis XIV. Her portrait is thus defcribed in 1682, when fhe had paffed the meridian of life :

"Who can on this picture look,
And not ftraight be wonder-ftruck,
That fuch a fneaking dowdy thing
Shou'd make a beggar of a king ;
Three happy nations turn to tears,
And all their former love to fears ;
Ruin the great and raife the fmall,
Yet will by turns betray them all.
Lowly born and meanly bred,
Yet of this nation fhe is head :
For half Whitehall makes her their court,
Tho' t'other half makes her their fport.
Monmouth's tamer, Jeffrey's advance,
Foe to England, fpy to France ;
Falfe and foolifh, proud and bold,
Ugly, as you fee, and old."

† Sir Robert Vyner, Lord Mayor of London in 1675. He converted an equeftrian ftatue of John Sobiefki, King of Poland, into the reprefentation of Charles II., and fet it up at the north end of St. Mary Woolnoth Church, Lombard Street. This ftatue excited the wit of the contemporary fatirifts, as much as the circumftances

The Wool-church ſtatue gold had been,
  Which now is made of alabaſter:
But wiſe men think, had it been wood,
  'Twere for a bankrupt King too good.

19.

Thoſe that the fabric well conſider,
  Do of it diverſely diſcourſe;
Some paſs their cenſure on the rider,
  Others their judgment on the horſe;
Moſt ſay the ſteed's a goodly thing,
But all agree 'tis a lewd King.

---

under which it was placed there. It is thus deſcribed in another lampoon of the day:

> " By all it appears, from the firſt to the laſt,
> To be as revenge and malice forecaſt,
> Upon the King's birthday to ſet up a thing
> That ſhows him a monkey more like than a king.
> When each one that paſſes finds fault with the horſe,
> Yet all do aſſure that the King is much worſe:
> And ſome by the likeneſs Sir Robert ſuſpect
> That he did for the King his own ſtatue erect.
> To ſee him ſo diſguiſed the herb-women chide,
> Who upon panniers more decently ride;
> And ſo looſe are his feet that all men agree,
> Sir William Peak ſits much faſter than he.
> But a market, they ſay, doth fit the King well,
> Who oft Parliaments buys and revenues ſell;
> And others, to make the ſimilitude hold,
> Say his Majeſty himſelf is oft bought and ſold."

20.

By the Lord Mayor and his grave coxcombs,
　Freeman of London Charles is made ;
Then to Whitehall a rich gold box comes,
　Which was beſtow'd on the French jade :
But wonder not it ſhould be ſo, ſirs,
　When monarchs rank themſelves with grocers.*

21.

Cringe, ſcrape no more, ye City fops,
　Leave off your feaſting and fine ſpeeches ;
Beat up your drums, ſhut up your ſhops,
　The Courtiers then will kiſs your breeches :
Arm'd, tell the Popiſh Duke † that rules,
You're free-born ſubjects, not French mules.

22.

New upſtarts, pimps, baſtards, wh—s,
　That locuſt-like devour the land,
By ſhutting up the Exchequer doors ‡,
　When thither our money was trepann'd ;

---

* Vide p. 185.
† James, Duke of York.
‡ Alluding to the King's flagitious conduct on the 2nd Jan. 1672, when, during the prorogation of Parliament, he ſuddenly cloſed the Exchequer, — an act which amounted to an avowal of national bankruptcy, and which had the immediate effect of ſpreading ruin far and wide, and of entirely uprooting credit. By this iniquitous proceeding Charles pocketed 1,300,000*l*.

Have rendered Charles his Reſtoration
But a ſmall bleſſing to the nation.

23.

Then, Charles, beware thy brother York,
   Who to thy government gives law;
If once we fall to the old ſport,
   You muſt again both to Breda:
Where ſpite of all that would reſtore you,
Grown wiſe by wrongs, we ſhall abhor you.

24.

If all Chriſtian blood the guilt
   Cries loud for vengeance unto heaven—
That ſea by treacherous Louis ſpilt,
   Can never be by God forgiven;
Worſe ſcourge unto his ſubjects, Lord!
Than peſtilence, famine, fire, or ſword.

25.

That falſe, rapacious Wolf of France*,
   The ſcourge of Europe and its curſe;
Who at his ſubjects' cry does dance,
   And ſtudies how to make 'em worſe:
To ſay ſuch kings, Lord, rule by thee,
Were moſt prodigious blaſphemy!

---

* Louis XIV.

26.

Such know no laws but their own luft ;
　Their fubjects' fubftance and their blood,
They count it tribute true and juft,
　Still fpent and fpilt for fubjects' good :
If fuch kings are by God appointed,
The Devil may be the Lord's anointed.

27.

Such kings (curft be the power and name !)
　Let all the world henceforth abhor 'em ;
Monfters which knaves facred proclaim,
　And then like flaves fall down before 'em :
What can there be in Kings divine —
The moft are wolves, goats, fheep, or fwine !

28.

Then farewell facred majefty,
　Let's pull all brutifh tyrants down ;
Where men are born and ftill live free,
　Here ev'ry head does wear a crown :
Mankind, like the unhappy frogs,
Prove wretched, king'd by Storks and Logs.

THE GENEVA BALLAD.

[The gradual development of Charles' defpotic character and aims, and more particularly his fufpected attachment to popery, not only gave offence and alarm to all moderate and well-meaning men in the country, but called into activity once more the Republican or Prefbyterian faction, which could now, with fome fhow of reafon, juftify their former oppofition to his father and himfelf. This is one of the many fervile ballads fent abroad by the Court party, in which the author retorts upon the fufpicious Prefbyterian the charges that the latter ufually preferred againft the Papifts, namely, that they fought to override both Church and State.]

To the tune of 48.

F all the factions in the Town,
 Mov'd by French fprings or Flemifh wheels,
  None treads Religion upfide down,
  Or tears pretences out at heels,
Like *Splay-mouth** with his brace of caps,
Whofe confcience might be fcann'd perhaps
By the dimenfions of his chaps.

 He whom the Sifters fo adore,
  Counting his actions all divine,
   Who, when the Spirit hints, can roar,
   And if occafion ferves can whine:

---

* The nick-name commonly applied to the Prefbyterian body both during the Rebellion and after the Reftoration.

Nay, he can bellow, bray, and bark.
Was ever fuch a Beuk-learn'd Clerk,
That fpeaks all linguas of the Ark?

To draw in profelytes like bees,
With pleafing twang he tones his profe,
   He gives his handkerchief a fqueeze,
And draws John Calvin through his nofe.
   Motive on motive he obtrudes,
   With flip-ftockin fimilitudes,
   Eight ufes more—and fo concludes.

When Monarchy began to bleed,
And Treafon had a fine new name;
When Thames was balderdafh'd with Tweed,
And pulpits did with beacons flame;
   When Jeroboam's calves were rear'd,
   And Laud was neither lov'd nor fear'd,
   This Gofpel-comet firft appear'd.

Soon his unhallow'd fingers ftripp'd
His Sov'reign Liege of power and land,
And, having fmote his Mafter, flipp'd
His fword into his fellow's hand.
   But he that wears his eyes may note,
   Ofttimes the butcher binds a goat,
   And leaves his boy to cut her throat.

Poor England felt his fury then
Outweigh'd Queen Mary's many grains;
 His very preaching flew more men,
Than Bonner's faggots, ftakes, and chains.
  With dog-ftar zeal and lungs like Boreas,
  He fought and taught; and what's notorious,
  Deftroy'd his Lord to make him glorious!

 Yet drew for King and Parliament,
As if the wind could ftand North-South;
 Broke Mofes' Law with bleft intent,
Murther'd and then he wip'd his mouth:
  Oblivion alters not his cafe,
  Nor clemency, nor acts of grace,
  Can blanch an Ethiopian's face.

 Ripe for Rebellion he begins
To rally upon the Saints in fwarms,
 He bawls aloud, *Sirs, leave your fins;*
But whifpers, *Boys, ftand to your arms.*
  Thus he's grown infolently rude,
  Thinking his gods can't be fubdu'd—
  Money, I mean, and *Multitude*.

 Magiftrates he regards no more
Than St. George or the Kings of Colen;
 Vowing he'll not conform before
The old wives wind their dead in wollen.

He calls the bifhop Grey-beard Goff,
And makes his power a mere fcoff,
As Dagon, when his hands were off.

Hark! how he opens with full cry!
Halloo, my hearts, beware of ROME!
　　Cowards that are afraid to die
Thus make domeftic broils at home.
　　How quietly great Charles might reign,
　　Would all thefe Hotfpurs crofs the main,
　　And preach down Popery in Spain!

　　The ftarry rule of Heaven is fixt,
There's no diffenfion in the fky:
　　And can there be a mean betwixt
Confufion and Conformity?
　　A place divided never thrives:
　　'Tis bad where hornets dwell in hives,
　　But worfe where children play with knives.

　　I would as foon turn back to mafs,
Or change my phrafe to *Thee* and *Thou;*
　　Let the Pope ride me like an afs,
And his priefts milk me like a cow:
　　As buckle to Smectymnuan laws,
　　The bad effects o' th' *Good Old Caufe*,
　　That have dove's plumes, but vulture's claws.

For 'twas the Haly Kirk that nurf'd
The Brownift's and the Ranter's crew;
Foul Error's motly vefture firft
Was oaded * in a Northern blue.
And what's th' enthufiaftic breed,
Or men of Knipperdoling's creed,
But Cov'nanters run up to feed?

Yet they all cry, *They love the King*,
And make boaft of their innocence:
There cannot be fo vile a thing,
But may be color'd with pretence.
Yet when all's faid, one thing I'll fwear,
No fubject like th' *old Cavalier*,
No traitor like *Jack Prefbyter*.

* Dyed.

TITUS TELLTROTH.

[The unparalleled fictions of Titus Oates (the subject of this and innumerable ballads), no doubt, would have speedily configned their wretched author to Tyburn instead of to Whitehall, but for the unfortunate and mysterious death of Sir Edmundbury Godfrey, (who had taken his evidence,) happening about the same time, an event which confirmed the delusions of the people, and rendered their prejudices absolutely incurable. "Thenceforward," remarks Hume, "to deny the reality of the [Popish] plot was to be an accomplice ; to hesitate was criminal." This ballad issued from the prolific press of Nat Thompson, the Romanist, and was penned by one Banks, as appears from a stanza in *Thompson-Tell-Lies*, a contemporary broadside :

" Titus the light of the Town,
    They call thee (and well they may) ;
  But Banks that Papistical clown
    Calls thee so in a jeering way.
  He calls thee the scorn of the Court,
    O ! pity it should be so ;
  What cattle do hither resort
    By abusing of thee we know."]

To the tune of " *Hail to the Myrtle shades.*"

AIL to the Knight of the Post,
To Titus the chief of the town ;
Titus, who vainly did boast
Of the Salamanca gown* ;

---

* Oates passed the greater part of the year 1677 in Valladolid, where he joined the Society of the Jesuits, with the sole purpose, as he afterwards acknowledged, "of betraying them."

Titus, who faw the world o'er,
　From the tower of Valladolid,
Yet ftood in the White-Horfe door*,
　And fwore to it like a creed.

Titus at Wotton in May,
　To Titus at Iflington ;
And Titus the felf-fame day,
　Both here and there again.
Titus, who never fwore truth,
　His politic plots to maintain,
And never yet baulked an oath,
　When call'd to the teft again.

Then Titus was meekeft of all,
　When never a penny in 's purfe,
And oft did on Pickering† call,
　His charity to imburfe.
But when he fwore damnable oaths,
　And lying efteem'd no fin,
Then Titus was one of thofe
　Whom the Devil had enter'd in.

---

* Alluding to the White Horfe tavern, in the Strand, where Oates fwore the Jefuits concerted their " plot."

† Thomas Pickering, a Roman Catholic prieft, and one of the earlieft victims of Oates' perjury, notwithftanding the fact of his having oftentimes befriended him in his poverty.

Then Titus the frown of heaven,
  And Titus, a plague upon earth;
Titus, who'll ne'er be forgiven,
  Curs'd from his fatal birth;
Titus, the curse and the doom
  Of the rich and the poor man too—
O Titus, thou *shred of a loom**,
  What a plague dost thou mean to do?

Titus an orthodox beast,
  And Titus a Presbyter tall;
Titus a Popish priest,
  And Titus the shame of them all †;
Titus, who ne'er had the skill,
  The wise with his plots to deceive;
But Titus whose *tongue* ‡ can kill,
  Whom nature has made a slave.

Titus, the light of the town,
  Where zealots and Whigs co-resort;

---

* Alluding to the mean origin of Oates, whose father was originally a ribbon-weaver, but afterwards an Anabaptist preacher.

† Oates had ministered successively in the churches of England and Rome, and amongst the Baptists, with whom he finally remained.

‡ A punning allusion to Dr. Ezrael Tonge, who had the credit of having instructed and qualified Oates for his desperate undertaking. The doctor, however, was the first to reveal the "plot" to the government.

Titus, the fhame of the gown,
   And Titus the fcorn of the Court* ;
Titus who fpew'd out the truth,
   To fwallow the Covenant,
But never yet blufh'd at an oath,
   Whom lying has made a faint.

Yet Titus believ'd could be
   Againft any popifh lord,
While ftill againft Shaftefbury
   The witnefs and truth's abhorr'd :
So Titus got credit and gold †
   For lying, and thought it no fin ;

---

* The King had from the beginning looked upon the Popifh plot difcoverers as little better than impoftors.

† Parliament fettled a penfion of 500*l. per ann.* upon Oates, which was fubfequently increafed to 1200*l.* as well as provided him with apartments in the palace of Whitehall. His fuccefs in the reign of Charles is humoroufly contrafted with his too tardy punifhment in that of James, in the following ftanzas from a contemporary Scotch ballad :

"Sic a trade as Titus drave,
   As Titus drave, as Titus drave,
When thefe three nations he did fave,
   He'll never drive again, jo.

"Ten pounds a-week he did receive,
   And muckle mair the *godly* gave,
And there was nought but afk and have,
   The like was never feen, jo.

"But to Tyburn Titus trigs,
   In company o' th' godly Whigs,
To dance and fing Geneva jigs,
   And there's an end o' him, jo."

But againſt Diſſenters bold
   The truth is not worth a pin.

Thus Titus ſwore on a-pace
   'Gainſt thoſe whom he never did ſee;
Yet Titus with brazen face,
   Would our *preſerver* be:
But Titus, the foreman in truſt,
   Diſcover'd this myſtery,
May Titus ſo be the firſt
   That leads to the triple-tree.

INFORMATION.

[This ballad likewife refers to the Popifh-plot mania, and was fuggefted, no doubt, by the over-zealous "addrefs of the Lords fpiritual and temporal," to the King, in which they prayed his Majefty to iffue a proclamation to the effect " that if any perfon or perfons fhall, before the 25th day of December next [1678], make any further difcovery of the late horrid defigns againft his. Majefty's facred perfon and government, . . . fhall not only receive *for every fuch difcovery* the reward of 200*l*.," but, whether principal or not in the faid defign, " fhall have his Majefty's gracious pardon." The very day on which this extraordinary proclamation was iffued, Oates and his co-jurors proceeded fo far as to accufe the Queen herfelf before the Privy Council !]

To the tune of " Conventicles are grown fo brief."

NFORMING of late is a notable trade :
    For he that his neighbor intends to invade,
    May pack him to Tyburn, no more's to be faid ;
  Such power hath information.
Be good and be juft, and fight for your King,
  Or ftand for your country's honor,
And you're fure by precife information to fwing,
  Such fpells fhe hath got upon her.

To fix hundred and fixty from forty-one,
She left not a bifhop or clergyman,
But compell'd both Church and State to run
    By the ftrength of the Nonconformift.
The dean and chapter, the fceptre and crown,
    (The lords and commons fnarling)
By bleft information came tumbling down;
    Fair fruits of an over-long parling.

'Twas this that fummon'd the bodkins all,
The thimbles and fpoons to the City-hall,
When St. Hugh* to the babes of grace did call,
    To prop up the *Caufe* that was finking:
This made the cobler take the fword,
    The pedlar, and the weaver;
By the pow'r of the fpirit, and not by the word,
    Made the tinker wear cloak and beaver.

'Tis information from Valladolid †
Makes jefuits, monks, and friars bleed;
Decapitates lords, and what not, indeed,
    Doth fuch damnable information?
It cities burnt, and ftuck not to boaft,
    Without any finning or fcruple,
Of forty thoufand black bills by the poft
    Brought in by the devil's pupil.

---

* Hugh Peters, the celebrated preacher in the days of the Commonwealth.
† Vide the preceding ballad.

This imp, with her jealoufies and fears,
Sets all men together by the ears,
Strikes at religion, and kingdoms tears,
  By voting againft the brother*:
This makes abhorrers, makes lords proteft,
  They know not why nor wherefore ;
This ftrikes at fucceffion, but aims at the reft ;
  Pray look about you therefore.

This raifeth armies in the air,
Imagining more than you need have to fear,
Keeps horfe under ground, and armies to tear
  The cities and towns in funder.
'Twas this made the knight to Newark run,
  With his *fidus Achates* behind him ;
Who brought for the father one more like the fon,
  The devil and zeal did fo blind him.

It ftrips, it whips, it hangs, it draws,
It pillories alfo without any caufe,
By falfely informing the judges and laws,
  By a trick from Salamanca :
This hurly-burlies all the town,
  Makes Smith and Harris prattle,
Who fpare neither caffock, cloak, nor gown,
  In their paltry tittle-tattle.

---

* Alluding to the daily increafing oppofition to the fucceffion of the Duke of York.

'Tis information affrights us all,
By information we stand or fall,
Without information there's no plot at all,
    And all is but information.
That Pickering stood in the Park with a gun,
    And Godfrey by Berry was strangled;
'Twas by information such stories began,
    Which the nation so much have entangled.

ON THE LORD CHANCELLOR'S SPEECH TO PARLIAMENT.

[This ballad was fuggefted by the fpeech of the Earl of Shaftfbury, when he made his memorable motion in the Lords for a committee of the whole Houfe " to confider the ftate of the nation," 25th March, 1679, a period charaƈterifed above all others for alleged plots and confpiracies, which kept the public mind in an unparalleled ftate of ferment. The fpeech (of which, it is said, 30,000 copies were printed and circulated a few days after it was delivered) was aimed againft the romanizing tendencies of the Court, and led to the adoption of Sir William Temple's ftrange plan of government by a permanent council of thirty.]

OULD you fend Kate * to Portugal,
   Great James † to be a Cardinal,
   And make Prince Rupert Admiral,
                   This is the time.

Would you turn Danby ‡ out of doors,
   Banifh rebels and French wh——,
   The worfer fort of common fhores ;
                   This is the time.

---

  * Katharine, Infanta of Portugal, and Queen of Charles II.
  † James, Duke of York, brother to the King.
  ‡ The Earl of Danby was at this time extremely obnoxious to Shaftfbury and the anti-court party, and, defpite the King's efforts to fhield him, was compelled to fly his country to efcape the vengeance of his political opponents.

Would you exalt the mighty name
Of Shaftſbury and Buckingham *,
And not forget Judge Scroggs † his fame,
      This is the time.

Would you our Sovereign difabuſe,
And make his Parliament of uſe,
Not to be changed like dirty ſhoes,
      This is the time.

Would you extirpate pimps and panders,
Diſband the reſt of our Commanders,
Send Mulgrave after Teague to Flanders,
      This is the time.

Would you remove our miniſters,
The curſed cauſe of all our fears,
Without forgetting turn-coat Meres ‡,
      This is the time.

---

* Both theſe noblemen not only fought for and obtained the freedom of the city of London, but alſo aſpired to the higheſt offices in it. Shaftſbury was pleaſed to be addreſſed by his *ſobriquet* of "the alderman."

† Sir William Scroggs, the infamous Lord Chief Juſtice of the King's Bench.

‡ Henry Booth, ſon of the firſt Lord de la Mere, created, in 1690, Earl of Warrington.

Would you once more bleſs this nation,
By changing of Portſmouth's * vocation,
And find one fit for procreation,
                    This is the time.

Would you let Portſmouth try her chance,
Believe Oats, Bedloe, Dugdale, Prance †,
And ſend Barillon ‡ into France,
                    This is the time.

Would you turn Papiſts from the Queen,
Cloiſter up fulſome Mazarine §,
Once more make Charles great again,
                    This is the time.

---

* Louiſe de Quéroualle, Ducheſs of Portſmouth, the miſtreſs of the King, and the reputed ſpy of Louis XIV.

† Bedloe and Dugdale were joint witneſſes with Oates to the alleged Popiſh plot of 1678-9, and Prance was ſuſpected of having murdered Sir Edmondbury Godfrey, 12th Oct. 1678.

‡ Barillon was the French ambaſſador to the Court of England.

§ The Ducheſs of Mazarine, who came to England in 1675, and was thought to have been ſent hither to ſupplant the Ducheſs of Portſmouth in the confidence and affections of the King.

A NEW SATIRICAL BALLAD OF THE LICENTIOUSNESS OF THE TIMES.

[This ballad, manifeftly written by a partizan of the Court, gives but a very inadequate picture of the period to which it refers. " The moft loyal Parliament that ever met in England" (as it has been characterifed by the greateft of modern hiftorians), and which had been in exiftence ever fince the reftoration of Charles, was juft diffolved; and new appeals were about to be made to the country, maddened beyond meafure by the mifgovernment of the King, and the abominable fictions of Titus Oates and his coadjutors and rivals. The religious apoftacy of the higheft perfonages in the realm, the growing influence of the Roundhead party, and the prevailing fear of Popery, were fufficient to create that "licentioufnefs" of fpeech which the author of this ballad fo much deprecates.]

To the tune of "The Blind Beggar of Bednall Green."

HE Devil has left his puritanical drefs,
And now like a hawker attends on the Prefs,
That he might thro' the town fedition difperfe,
In pamphlets and ballads, in profe and in verfe.

'Tis furely fo, for if the Devil wasn't in 't,
There would not be fo many ftrange things in print;
Now each man writes what feems good in his eyes,
And tells in bald rhymes his inventions and lies.

Some relate to the world their own cauſeleſs fears,
Endeavoring to ſet us together by the ears,
They ſtrive to make factions for two great commanders,
Tho' one be in Holland, the other in Flanders.*

They baul and they yaul aloud thro' the whole town,
The rights to ſucceſſion and claims to the Crown,
And ſnarling and grumbling like fools at each other,
Raiſe conteſts and factions betwixt ſon and brother.†

Here one doth on this ſide his verſes oppoſe,
Up ſtarts another and jouſts with him in proſe,
On Rumour a jade, they get up, and mount her,
And ſo like Don Quixote with wind-mills encounter.

Our ſun is not ſetting, it does not grow dark yet,
The King is in health ſtill, and gone to New-Market,
Let then idle coxcombs leave off their debating,
What either ſide ſays is uncommonly prating.

Another tho' he be but a ſenseleſs widgion,
Will, like an archbiſhop, determine religion:
Whate'er his opinion is that muſt be beſt,
And ſtrait he confutes, and confounds all the reſt.

---

* The Dukes of Monmouth and York; the firſt of whom, upon his diſmiſſal from the poſt of Captain-General, retired to Holland; and the ſecond, by deſire of the King, departed with his family to Bruſſels (March, 1678-9).

† Monmouth and York.

I' the coffee-houfe here one with a grave face,
When after falute, he hath taken his place,
His pipe being lighted begins for to prate,
And wifely difcourfes the affairs of the State.

Another in fury the board ftrait does thump,
And highly extols the bleft times of the Rump;
The Pope and all monarchs he fends to the devil,
And up in their places he fets Harry Nevil.*

Another who would be diftinguifh'd from cit,
And fwearing G—d d—n me, to fhew him a wit,
(Who for all his huffing one grain hath not got)
Scoffs at all religion, and the Popifh Plot.

One with an uncivil fatirical jeft,
To be thought a wit, has a fling at the prieft,
He jeers at his betters, and all men of note,
From th' Alderman to the canonical coat.

A politick citizen in his blew gown,
As gravely in fhop he walks up and down,
Inftead of attending the wares on his ftall,
Is all day relating th' intrigues of Whitehall.

---

* A confpicuous member of the Council of State appointed by the Parliament in 1659, who was oppofed to the reftoration of Charles.

And though to speak truth he be but a noddy,
He'd have you to think that he is fomebody,
With politic fhrug, e'vn as bad as a curfe,
He cries out, O ! the times, no mortal faw worfe.

Then comes a wife knight as the whole city's factor,
Speaks prologue in profe, too grave for an actor,
And being fore frighted, in a learned fpeech,
To ftand to their arms all the cits does befeech.

The cobler in ftall, did you but hear him prate,
You'd think that he fat at the helm of the State,
His awl lay'd afide, and in right hand a pot,
He roundly rips up the *foul* of the Plot.

But it is not enough to fee what is paft,
For thefe very men become prophets at laft,
And with the fame eyes can fee what is meant,
To be acted and done in the next Parliament.

His worfhip so wife, who a kingdom can rule,
Is now by dear wife at home made a fool ;
For tho' he doth fee thro' dark mifts of the State,
He can't fee the horns that fhe plants on his pate.

The women, too, prate of the Pope and the Turk,
Who fhould ceafe to play falfe, and 'tend to their work ;
But two noble virtues they 've attain'd to, I think,
To handle State matters, and to take off their drink.

Petition the players to come on the ftage,
There to reprefent the vice of the age,
That people may fee in ftage looking-glaffes
Fools of all forts, and their politic affes.

And thus I have fhewn you the vice of the nation,
Which wants of thefe things a through reformation ;
But when that will be I cannot determine,
For plenty breeds vice, as foul bodies breed vermine.

Men may prate and may write, but 'tis not their rhimes,
That can any way change, or alter the times ;
It is now grown an epidemical difeafe,
For people to talk and to write what they pleafe.

God blefs our good King who our little world rules,
And is not difturb'd at the action of fools ;
It very much helps a wife man's melancholy
To fee and obferve, and to laugh at their folly.

GENEVA AND ROME; OR, THE ZEAL OF BOTH BOILING OVER:

In an earneſt diſpute for pre-eminence
carried on at a private conference
between *Jack-a-Preſbyter* and *Believe-all-Papiſt*.

Now printed for public ſatisfaction.

[Oates' and Bedloe's aſtounding revelations of Popiſh plots in the ſouth, increaſing with the growth of the popular credulity, and the doubtful iſſue of the war which was being proſecuted againſt the Covenanters in the north, kept the public mind in a perpetual ſtate of agitation and alarm during the whole of the year 1679. King Charles was compelled to baniſh his Popiſh brother, James Duke of York, from the Court, in order to reaſſure his panic-ſtricken people, whom he had good reaſon to fear might again throw off their allegiance to him, and involve the country in civil ſtrife. The author of the following loyal ballad, whilſt affecting to contemn both Papiſts and Preſbyterians, expoſes in turn their reſpective malpractices in the two former reigns, and inſinuates that they are equally ready to repeat them in the event of once more gaining the aſcendancy in England.]

ACK Preſbyter and the ſons of the Pope
Had a late diſpute of the right of the Rope
Who'd merit hanging without any trope;
    Which nobody can deny.

First Jack held forth, and bid him remember,
The horrible plot on the *Fifth of November*,
The very month preceding December;
    Which nobody, &c.

The thirtieth of January, th' other reply'd,
We heard of 't at Rome, which can't be deny'd,
Had Jack been loyal, then Charles had not dy'd;
    Which nobody, &c.

Then John cry'd out, D——d Jesuit, thou ly'st,
I only appear'd for the Lord Jesus Christ,
Which thou, as a merit-monger, deny'st;
    Which nobody, &c.

The Powder treason, oh! horrible plot—
Why, prithee Jack Presbyter, be not so hot,
For Charles was kill'd, and Jemmy was not;
    Which nobody, &c.

Then Presbyter John his zeal was inflam'd,
And now I find it I'll make thee asham'd.
If so, prithee Jack, let the Cov'nant be nam'd;
    Which nobody, &c.

Why the Covenant named? 'tis found on record
To be an Old and New Testament word,
As I prov'd to Charles by text and by sword;
    Which nobody, &c.

Thou prove it to Charles? impertinent Afs,
What thou defign'dft old Noll brought to pafs,
And then, like a beaft, he turn'd thee to grafs;
     Which nobody, &c.

A truce! a truce! quoth Prefbyter Jack,
We both love treafon as Loyalifts fack,
And if either prevails the King goes to wrack;
     Which nobody, &c.

The Bifhops tell Charles we both have long nails,
And Charles fhall find it if either prevails,
For, like Sampfon's foxes, we're ty'd by the tails;
     Which nobody, &c.

The Jefuits, and the brats of John Knox,
Both vifited Europe with the French —,
By the means of Loyola and Calvin the fox;
     Which nobody, &c.

THE LOYAL TORIES DELIGHT;

OR,

A PILL FOR FANATICS.

[This Court effusion was suggested by the persevering and unscrupulous endeavours on the part of the Lord Chancellor Shaftesbury to change the succession to the Crown, in favour of the Duke of Monmouth, to the exclusion of the Duke of York.]

GREAT York has been debar'd of late*,
From Court by some accursed fate;
But ere long we do not fear,
We shall have him,
We shall have him, have him here.

The makers of the Plot we see,
By d—d old Tony's † treachery,
How they would have brought it about,
To have given great York the rout;
     To have given, &c.

---

* The Duke, by desire of the King, had withdrawn from the country (3rd March, 1678-9); and a few months after his return (24th Feb. 1680) was sent to Scotland.

† Anthony Ashley Cooper, Earl of Shaftesbury, who prosecuted the Duke as a Popish recusant (16th June, 1680), and supported the Exclusion Bill, which was rejected by the Lords after its passage through the Commons.

God preferve our gracious King,
And fafe tidings to us bring,
Defend us from the *ſham black box* *,
And all d—d *fanatic plots*,
        And all, &c.

Here's Charles' health I drink to thee,
And wiſh him all profperity;
God grant that he long time may reign,
To bring us home great York again;
       To bring us home, &c.

That he in fpite of all his foes,
Who loyalty and laws oppofe,
May long remain in health and peace,
Whilſt plots and plotters all ſhall ceaſe;
       Whilſt plots, &c.

Let Whigs † go down to Erebus,
And not ſtay here to trouble us,

---

* Shaftefbury, to fupport the regal pretenfions of his friend the Duke of Monmouth, propagated rumours that the King only denied his marriage with the Duke's mother (Lucy Walters) from pride; that the witneffes to the ceremony were ſtill in exiſtence, and that the contract itfelf, "enclofed in a black box," had been entruſted by the late Biſhop of Durham to the cuſtody of his fon-in-law, who had it ready to produce whenever Parliament required him to do fo.

† The Whigs had uniformly, up to this period, refifted the claims of the Romaniſts, and let ſlip no opportunity of perfecuting them; the Tories, on the other hand, had always befriended them.

With noify cant and needlefs fear,
Of ills to come they know not where,
Of ills to come, &c.

When our chief trouble they create,
For plain we fee what they be at ;
Could they but push great York once down,
They'd next attempt to fnatch the Crown;
They'd next attempt, &c.

But Heaven preferve our gracious King,
May all good fubjects loudly fing ;
And Royal James preferve likewife,
From fuch as do againft him rife,
From fuch as do, &c.

Then come again, fill round our glafs,
And loyal Tories let it pafs ;
Fill up, fill up, unto the brim,
And let each bowl with nectar fwim,
And let each bowl, &c.

Though Cloakmen that feem much precife,
'Gainft wine exclaim, with turn'd up eyes,
Yet in a corner they'll be drunk,
With drinking healths unto the RUMP;
With drinking healths, &c.

In hopes that once more they shall tear
Both Church and State, which is their pray'r;
But Heaven does still protect the Throne,
Whilst Tyburn for such slaves does groan,
  Whilst Tyburn, &c.

For now 'tis plain most men abhor
What some so strongly voted for:
Great York in favour does remain,
In spite of all the Whiggish train,
  In spite of all, &c.

And now the *Old Cause* goes to wrack,
Sedition maugre Cloak in black,
Do greatly dread the triple-tree,
Whilst we rejoice in loyalty,
  Whilst we rejoice, &c.

Then come let's take another round,
And still in loyalty abound,
And wish our King he long may reign,
To bring us home great York again;
  To bring us home great York again

THE KING'S VOWS.

BY ANDREW MARVEL.

[The precife date of this cauftic fatire is unknown, but it would appear, from certain allufions in it, to have been penned not later than the year 1679. It is characteriftic alike of the bafeft of Englifh fovereigns, and the moft patriotic of Englifh ftatefmen. In vain Charles affailed the integrity and patriotifm of Marvel :

" In awful poverty his honeft mufe
  Walks forth vindictive thro' a venal land;
  In vain Corruption fheds her golden dews,
  In vain Oppreffion lifts her iron hand :
  He fcorns them both, and arm'd with Truth alone,
  Bids Luft and Folly tremble on his throne."

Probably Lord Macaulay had in his mind *The King's Vows*, when he gave, in his hiftorical fragment, a fummary of Charles's character. " He came forth (fays he) from the fchool of adverfity with focial habits, with polite and engaging manners, and with fome talents for lively converfation, addicted beyond meafure to fenfual indulgence, fond of fauntering and frivolous amufements, incapable of felf-denial and exertion, without faith in human virtue or in human attachment, without defire of renown, and without fenfibility of reproach." Marvel, who knew Charles II. perfonally, was lefs tolerant in his judgment of him than the modern hiftorian.]

HEN plate was at pawn, and fob at an ebb,
And fpider might weave in bowels its web,
And ftomach as empty as brain ;
   Then Charles without acre,
Did fwear by his Maker,
   If e'er I fee England again :—

I'll have a religion all of my own,
Whether popish or protestant shall not be known;
And, if it prove troublesome — I will have none.

I'll have a long Parliament always to friend,
And furnish my treasure as fast as I spend,
And, if they will not—they shall have an end.

I'll have as fine bishops as were e'er made with hands,
With consciences flexible to my commands,
And, if they displease me— I'll have all their lands.

I'll have a fine navy to conquer the seas,
And the Dutch shall give caution for their Provinces,
And, if they should beat me—I'll do what they please.*

I'll have a fine Court, with ne'er an old face,
And always who beards me shall have the next grace,
And, I either will vacate,— or, buy him a place.

I'll have a privy purse without a control,
I'll wink all the while my revenue is stole,
And, if any is question'd — I'll answer the whole.

---

* This is a sarcastic allusion to the great national disgrace of 1667, when the Dutch were suffered with impunity to sail up the Medway, and destroy the fortifications of Chatham.

If this pleafe not — I'll reign then on any condition,
Mifs and I will both learn to live on exhibition,
And I'll firft put the Church — then the Crown in com-
   miffion.

I'll have a fine tunic, a flafh and a veft :
Tho' not rule like a Turk — yet I will be fo dreft,—
And who knows but the fafhion may bring in the reft ?

I'll have a Council fhall fit always ftill,
And give me a licence to do what I will ;
And two Secretaries fhall flourifh a quill.

My infolent brother * fhall bear all the fway ;
If Parliaments murmur I'll fend him away,
And call him again as foon as I may.

I'll have a rare fon †, in marrying tho' marr'd,
Shall govern (if not my kingdom) my guard,
And fhall be fucceffor to me or Gerrard. ‡

---

* James, Duke of York, whofe bigoted attachment to Roman Catholicifm began about this time to excite popular indignation againft him.

† James, Duke of Monmouth, the King's natural fon by Lucy Walters.

‡ Commonly called "Generous Gerrard," an enthufiaftic royalift, who was executed (10th July, 1654) for plotting the deftruction of Cromwell.

I'll have a new London inftead of the old *,
With wide ftreets and uniform to my own mould;
But, if they build too faft, I'll bid 'em hold.

The ancient nobility I will lay by,
And new ones create their rooms to fupply,
And they fhall raife fortunes for my own fry.

Some one † I'll advance from a common defcent,
So high that he fhall hector the Parliament,
And all wholefome laws for the public prevent.

And I will affert him to fuch a degree,
That all his foul treafons, tho' daring and high,
Under my hand and feal fhall have indemnity.

And, whate'er it coft me, I'll have a French w—,
As bold as Alice Pierce, and as fair as Jane Shore;
And when I am weary of her, I'll have more.

Which if any bold Commoner dare to oppofe,
I'll order my bravos to cut off his nofe ‡,
Tho' for't a branch of prerogative lofe.

---

    * Alluding to the deftruction of the city by fire, 1666.
    † Thomas Ofborne, Earl of Danby, who was accufed by the Commons of great mifdemeanours, April, 1675; difmiffed as Treafurer 1678; and, to fave him from the effects of an impeachment, pardoned by the King 1678-9. The Commons, however, on the 5th May 1679, voted his pardon unconftitutional and void.
    ‡ Alluding to the barbarity practifed on Sir John Coventry, who, for reflecting on the King's amours, in his place in Parliament, was

My pimp shall be my minister premier,
My bawds call ambassadors far and near,
And my wench shall dispose of *congé d'Elire*.

I'll wholly abandon all public affairs,
And pass all my time with buffoons and players,
And saunter to Nelly * when I should be at prayers.

I'll have a fine pond with a pretty decoy,
Where many strange fowl shall feed and enjoy,
And still in their language quack *Vive le roy!* †

---

waylaid by Sands and Obrian, creatures of the Court, and had his nose slit to the bone.

* Nell Gwynn, the celebrated actress, whose wit no less than her beauty captivated the King:

"When he was dumpish, she would still be jocund,
And chuck the royal chin of Charles the Second."

So reports Sir George Etherege, the licentious dramatist, with more truth than refinement.

† It was the custom of Charles to saunter almost daily into St. James' Park, where he took a great interest in the water-fowl with which it was stocked, and which it was his practice to feed with his own hand.

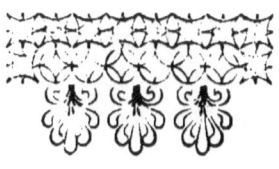

THE LOYAL SHERIFFS OF LONDON AND MIDDLESEX: UPON THEIR ELECTION.

[This, as well as the following fervile ballad, was written by a Court partizan on the occafion of the memorable election of Sheriffs for London and Middlefex in 1683, when Charles II. fo groffly invaded the rights and liberties of the citizens.

The fcheme was to prevent the regular election of Sheriffs, and to force upon the City the two Court nominees, Dudley North and Ralph Box, who had only a fmall minority of electors in their favour. In fpite of violence ufed in their behalf, the poll was going in favour of the liberal candidates, Papillion and Dubois, when the Lord Mayor, Sir John Moore, a tool of the Government, attempted to adjourn the election to another day. The Sheriffs *pro tempore*, Shute and Pilkington, who were the proper officers to prefide, continued the poll defpite Moore's oppofition, and ultimately declared the liberal candidates duly elected. Neverthelefs the Court candidates were fworn in as Sheriffs, and thofe who infifted on continuing the election after the pretended adjournment by the Mayor were profecuted for an alleged riot, and being convicted by a packed jury were heavily fined.

A pamphleteer, writing in 1703, fays: " The defpicable fcum of Sonnateers and Rhyming Scribblers were never more encouraged than at that time; the foregoing fongs are but part of 180 printed by Nat Thompfon, the popifh printer; and will Pofterity believe that an infamous fongfter has had 10 or 20 guineas at a time given him for finging one of thefe Ballads at Court?"]

TUNE, " Now at laft the Riddle," &c.

NOW at laft the matter is decided,
    Which fo long the nation has divided;
        Mifguided
By intereft and blind zeal,
Which fo well in *Forty-four* they acted.
    Now with greater heat
They again act o'er, like men diftracted,
To give to Monarchy a new defeat.

Famous North, of noble birth and breeding,
And in loyal principles exceeding,
        Is pleading
    To ftand his country's friend;
To do juftice to the King and nation
    Some fo much oppofe;
To renew the work of Reformation,
And carry on again the *Good old Caufe*.

Next, renowned Box, as high commended,
And of loyal parentage defcended,
        Intended
    To do the City right:

With true courage, and firm refolution,
  He the Hall adorns;
But the heads were all in a confufion,
Such din there was and rattling with their horns.

Prick up ears, and pufh one for another,
  Let not Box, an old malignant brother,
      Nor t'other
    Our properties command,
He's a King's-man, North is nothing better,
  They walk hand-in-hand:
He, you know, is the Lord Mayor's creature;
Therefore it is not fit that they fhould ftand.

Where are now our liberties and freedom?
Where fhall we find fuch friends, when we shou'd,
      To bleed 'em
    And pull the Tories down?
To pufh far our int'reft, who can blame us?
    Sheriffs rule in the Town,
When we lofe our darling Ignoramus :.
We lofe the combat, and the day's their own.

Then let every man ftand by his brother,
Poll o'er ten times, poll one for another.
      What a pother
    You fee the Tories make,

Now or never, now to fave your Charter,
　　Or your hearts will ache;
If it goes for them expect no quarter:
If Law and Juftice rule, our heels will fhake!

Rout, a rout! Join Prentice, boor, and peafant,
Let the White-hall party call it treafon,
　　　　'Tis treafon —
We fhould our necks defend!
Routs and riots, tumults and fedition,
　　　Poll 'em o'er again;
Thefe do beft agree with our condition —
If Monarchy prevail, we're all loft men.

The Lord Mayor is loyal in his ftation —
'Las, what will become o' th' Reformation
　　　　O' th' nation
　　If the Sheriffs be loyal too?
Wrangle, bangle, huff and keep a clatter —
　　If we lofe the field,
Poll 'em o'er again, it makes no matter,
For tho' we lofe the day, we fcorn to yield!

Ten for Box, and twenty for Papillion,
North a thoufand, Dubois a million —
　　　　What villain
　　　Our intereft dare oppofe?

With thofe noble patriots thus they fided,
   To uphold the Caufe;
But the good Lord Mayor the cafe decided,
And once again two loyal worthies chofe.

Noble North and famous Box * promoted,
By due courfe and legal choice allotted,
      They voted
   To be the City Shrieves,
And may they both to London's commendation
   Her ancient rights reftore,
To do that juftice to the King and Nation
Which former factions have deny'd before.

---

* Ralph Box had the decency to decline ferving the office to which he had been fo unfairly elected, and paid the ufual fine of 500*l.* for his exemption.

LONDON'S LAMENTATION FOR THE LOSS OF THEIR CHARTER.

[The infamous judgment in the great London *Quo Warranto* Cafe, delivered in Michaelmas term 1683, fully explains both the hiftory and object of this ballad: —
"Several times (faid Mr. Juftice Jones, the Senior Puifne judge of the King's Bench) have we met, and had conference about this matter, and we have waited on my Lord [Chief Juftice] Saunders during his ficknefs often; and upon deliberation, we are unanimoufly of opinion that a Corporation aggregate, fuch as the City of London, may be forfeited and feifed into the King's hands, on a breach of a truft repofed in it for the good government of the King's fubjects; — that to affume the power of making bye-laws to levy money is a juft caufe of forfeiture; — and that the Petition [*i.e.* of the Mayor and Citizens of London to the King, befeeching him not to diffolve his Parliament] in the pleadings mentioned is fo fcandalous to the King and his government, that it is a juft caufe of forfeiture. Therefore, the Court doth award that the liberties and franchifes of the City of London be feifed into the King's hands."]

To the tune of "Packington's Pound."

OU Freemen and Mafters, and Prentices, mourn,
For now you are left with your Charter forlorn;

Since London was London, I dare boldly say,
For your riots you never so dearly did pay;
   In Westminster Hall
   Your Dagon did fall,
That caus'd you to riot and mutiny all:
Oh! London, oh! London, thou had'st better had none,
Than thus with thy Charter to vie with the Throne.

Oh! London, oh! London, how could'st thou pretend,
Against thy Defender thy crimes to defend?
Thy freedom and rights from kind princes did spring,
And yet in contempt thou withstandest thy King:
   With bold brazen face
   They pleaded thy case,
In hopes to the Charter the King would give place.
Oh! London, thou'dst better no Charter at all,
Than thus for Rebellion thy Charter should fall.

Since Britons to London came over to dwell,
You had an old Charter to buy and to sell;
And whilst in allegiance each honest man lives,
Then you had a Charter for Lord Mayor and Shrieves:
   But when with your pride
   You began to backslide,
And London by factions did run with the tide;
Then London, oh! London, 'tis time to withdraw,
Lest the flood of your factions the land overflow.

When faction and fury of Rebels prevail'd,
When Coblers were Kings, and monarchs were jail'd,
When Masters in tumults their prentices led,
And the tail did begin to make war with the Head,
    When Thomas and Kate
    Did bring in their plate,
T'uphold the *Old cause* of the Rump of the State;
Then tell me, oh! London, I prithee now tell,
Haft thou e'er a Charter to fight and rebell?

When zealous sham-sheriffs the City oppose,
In spite of the Charter, the King, and the Laws,
And make such a riot and rout in the Town,
That never before such a racket was known,
    When rioters dare
    Arrest the Lord May'r *,
And force the King's substitute out of the Chair;
Oh! London, whose Charter is now on the lees,
Did your Charter e'er warrant such actions as these?

Alas, for the Brethren! † What now must they do
For choosing Whig-sheriffs and Burgesses too?

---

* The Mayor having committed the two presiding sheriffs for alleged contempt, the friends of the latter, in order to obtain their release, retaliated by arresting the Mayor for a debt said to have been incurred in the course of the election.
 † Alluding to the Court of Aldermen, who incriminated each other in defaming James, Duke of York, the King's brother.

The Charter with Patience * is gone to the pot,
And the Doctor † is loſt in the depth of the plot:
   Saint Stephen his flayl
   No man will prevail,
  Nor Sir Robert's ‡ dagger the Charter to bail:
Oh! London, thou'dſt better have lain in the fire,
Than thus thy old Charter ſhould ſtick in the mire.

But ſince with your folly, your faction and pride,
You ſink with the Charter, who ſtrove with the tide,
Let all the loſt rivers return to the Main;
From whence they deſcended they'll ſpring out again:
   Submit to the King
   In everything,
  Then of a new Charter new Sonnets we'll ſing;
As London — the Phœnix of England — ne'er dies,
So out of the flames a new Charter will riſe!

---

   * Alderman Sir Patience Ward, Moor's predeceſſor in the Mayoralty, who was moſt unjuſtly indicted for perjury, becauſe he refuſed to depoſe againſt his brother alderman, Pilkington, accuſed of ſcandaliſing the Duke of York.
   † Oates.
   ‡ Sir Robt. Clayton, Lord Mayor in 1680, who contended in vain for his own and fellow-citizens' rights.

VIENNA'S TRIUMPH;

WITH THE WHIGS' LAMENTATION FOR
THE OVERTHROW OF THE TURKS.

[In the fummer of 1683 the Ottomans, after fweeping over Hungary, invefted Vienna, from which the Emperor Leopold and his family had fled. All Europe was in confternation. Sobiefki, the King of Poland, was bound by no treaty to the Houfe of Auftria; but, as a Chriftian Prince, he determined to defend the eaftern bulwark of Chriftian Europe againft the univerfally dreaded foe. Having, therefore, united his own forces with thofe of Germany, he attacked the Turks in their entrenchments, and gained a decifive victory over them. On the news of the deliverance of Vienna every State in Europe refounded with acclamations—France excepted, whofe "moft Chriftian King," Louis XIV., wifhed to humble the houfe of Hapfburg to the duft. The Whigs, notwithftanding the fact that they had confiftently oppofed the foreign policy of England, and alfo condemned that of France, are here affociated with the common foe of Europe, becaufe at this time they were as unpopular in the country as hateful to Charles.]

OW, now 's the fiege raif'd,
And the numerous train
Of the Turks, Jove be praif'd,
Are defeated again :
Their Mahomet's aid
They in vain did implore,
And they fwear they'll not truft
The dull God any more :

The sham of the *Loadstone* *
At last they have found,
And their God is condemn'd
To be laid under ground.

Let the English give praise,
  Let all Christendom join,
In singing of lays
  To the Powers Divine :
Vienna once more
  Hath the victory won,
And the Turks, tho' so mighty,
  Are put to the run :
The giant Goliah
  By David was slain ;
Thus, who fight against Heav'n
  Do fight but in vain.

The Grand Vizier's fled,
  In vain he did boast ;
And 'twill cost him his head,
  Since the battle he lost :
His many of thousands
  He invincible thought,

---

* Alluding to the famous black stone in the Kaaba at Mecca, which the Mahomedans believe was brought to that place by the archangel Gabriel, and which is supposed to have become black from the kisses of the innumerable pilgrims annually attracted by it.

Yet they by few hundreds
    To confusion were brought :
To the great King of Poland
    Let the honor redound,
Whose actions with credit
    And fame do abound.

To the Duke of Lorrain
    Great praises are due,
Who had fought but in vain,
    If proud words had prov'd true:
At the Emperor's threats
    He laughs in his sleeve,
And all his great proffers
    He scorn'd to believe :
But great as he was
    He withstood all their charms,
Choosing rather to die
    In his countrymen's arms.

His loyalty true
    All the world doth admire,
But the Whigs, who look blue,
    And commotions desire :
Ruin and strife are
    Whigs' elements still,
They 're an obstinate people,
    If crost in their will :

And what their will is,
    Is as hard to be known,
As it is to find out
    The philofopher's ftone.

No devotion but their's,
    All others, they fay,
Of the Devil are fnares
    For to lead us aftray:
The Pope to avoid
    They'll do what they can,
And inftead of an image
    They'll worfhip a man:
To the Turks they no martyrs,
    But converts, would be;
But in time we may fee
    Them all die by the Tree.

DAGON'S FALL.

[When the plan of deſtroying all the free inſtitutions of England, and of eſtabliſhing arbitrary rule, was openly avowed by the ſervile ſupporters of the Court, Lord Shafteſbury, knowing that he was marked out for the royal vengeance, ſeriouſly contemplated raiſing an inſurrection in the City of London, with a view to ſet aſide the popiſh Duke of York, as ſucceſſor to the Crown, as well as to get rid of the King's evil Councillors. Learning, however, that there was an intention once more to arreſt him, he made his eſcape to Holland (18th November, 1682), where he was received with great reſpect, and admitted into the magiſtracy. He died at Amſterdam, after a very brief illneſs, on the 21ſt January, 1683. The ballad was publiſhed before the news of his deceaſe had reached this country.]

H! cruel bloody fate,
    What canſt thou now do more?
    Alas, 'tis now too late
    Poor Tony to reſtore!
Why ſhould the flatt'ring fates perſuade
    That Tony ſtill ſhould live
In England here, or in Holland there,
    Yet all our hopes deceive?

A noble peer he was,
    And of notorious fame;
But now he's gone, alas!
    A pilgrim o'er the main.

The prop and pillar of our hope,
    The patron of our cauſe,
The ſcorn and hate of Church and State,
    The urchin of the laws.

Of matchleſs policy
    Was this renowned peer;
The bane of monarchy,
    The people's hope and fear;
The joy of all true proteſtants,
    The Tories' ſcorn and dread:
But now he's gone who curſ'd the throne;
    Alas, poor Tony's dead!

For Commonwealth he ſtood,
    Pretending liberty;
And, for the public good,
    Would pull down Monarchy.
The Church and State he would divorce,
    The holy cauſe to wed,
And in time did hope to confound the Pope,
    And be himſelf the head.

A tap in 's ſide did bore,
    To broach all ſorts of ill,
For which ſeditious ſtore
    The crowd ador'd him ſtill:

He spit his venom thro' the town,
  With which the saints possest
Would preach and prate 'gainst Church and State,
  While he perform'd the rest.

When any change of State,
  Or mischief was at hand,
He had a working pate
  And devil at command:
He forg'd a plot*, for which the heads
  Of faction gave their votes:
But now the plot has gone to pot —
  What will become of Oates?

Under the fair pretence
  Of right, religion, law,
Excluding the true prince,
  The Church he'd overthrow:
With such religious shams he brought
  The rabble to his side;
And for his sport, the town and court,
  In parties he'd divide.

---

* Lord Shaftesbury early had the credit of being the contriver of the popish plot, which he framed (according to Dalrymple) "in order to bring the Duke [of York], and, perhaps, the King, under the weight of the national fear and hatred of popery."

Now what's become of all
    His fquinting policy,
Which wrought your Dagon's fall,
    From juftice forc'd to flee?
Old and decrepid, full of pains,
    As he of guilt was full,
He fell to fate, and now too late
    He leaves us to condole.

Now learn, ye Whigs, in time,
    By his deferved fall,
To expiate his crime,
    Ere fate revenge you all:
For rights, religion, liberty,
    Are but the fham pretence
To anarchy—but loyalty
    Obeys the lawful Prince.

JAMES II.

A SHORT LITANY.

No prince had been so generally unpopular and so severely satirised as James the Second before his accession to the throne. After that event, the ballad-writers appear to have been restrained in a great measure by their fear of him. When, however, his tyranny became quite insupportable, and there was a prospect of the country being ridded of his presence, their courage revived, and they renewed their daily attacks upon him with increased virulence. The coarsest ballads and squibs, as well as the most unfeeling lampoons, pursued the bigoted monarch in his flight to France.

As this and the following ballads refer to the closing months of his brief reign, it will not be necessary to give a separate introduction to each; the foot-notes will elucidate, where necessary, the text of them.

The entire rule of James is well expressed in the subjoined lampoon :—

> "Unhappy Age! and we in it,
>   When Truth doth go for Treason;
> Every blockhead's will for law,
>   And coxcomb's sense for reason.
> Religion's made a band of State,
>   To serve the pimps and panders,
> Our Liberty a prison gate,
>   And Irishmen commanders.
>
> "Oh! wretched is our fate—
>   What dangers do we run!
> We must be wicked to be great,
>   And to be just, undone.
> 'Tis thus our Sovereign keeps his word,
>   And makes the nation great;
> To Irishmen he trusts the sword,
>   To Jesuits the State."

To the tune of " Cock-laurel."

ROM an old Inquifition*, and new Declaration †,
From freedom of Confcience, and Whig Toleration,
'Gainft Confcience impofing upon the whole Nation,
For ever, good Heaven, deliver me!

From Knaves would fet up a Difpenfative power,
To pull down the Teft unto which we have fwore,
By impofing a greater than any before,
      For ever, &c.

From the Court's Triumvirate's Council in vain,
The father-confeffor ‡, that cheater of men,
The hypocrite Lobb ‡, and that Jefuit Pen ‡,
      For ever, &c.

---

 * An allufion to the extraordinary conduct of the King in extorting a promife from every clafs of public officials "to live in friendfhip with people of all religious perfuafions."

 † The memorable Declaration of Indulgence (publifhed on the 4th April, 1687), which fufpended and difpenfed with the penal laws and tefts on admiffion into offices civil and military.

 ‡ Father Edward Petre, vice-provincial of the Jefuits, who was fworn a member of the Privy Council, 11th November, 1687; Stephen Lobb, a member of the Jefuitical Cabal, employed to gain over the Independents to the Court; and William Penn, the quaker, who publicly preached in favour of James and his Declaration of Indulgence. All were members of the "Jefuitical Cabal."

From lofing the Set in a paffion and flame,
By taking feven men up, and hoping the fame
To recover by playing an after-back game,
        For ever, &c.

From a fchifmatic State, and a Catholic Court,
From packing a jury in hopes to be for 't,
From fhopping the bifhops*, the Church to fupport,
        For ever, &c.

From Puritans' malice, and Jefuits' fpite,
From fhowing our teeth, without pow'r to bite,
Againft our own Confcience from doing of right,
        For ever, &c.

From making a pannel the prelates to blaft,
In hopes with St. Peter their lordfhips to caft,
And finding it all *Ignoramus* at laft,
        For ever, &c.

---

* Alluding to the incarceration and trial of the Seven Bifhops for protefting againft the King's famous Declaration.

THE ADVICE.

OULD you be famous and renown'd in ſtory,
And after having run a ſtage of glory,
Go ſtraight to Heaven, and not to Pur-
gatory;
This is the time.

Would you ſurrender your Diſpenſing power,
And ſend the Weſtern Hangman* to the Tower,
From whence he'll find it difficult to ſcour;
This is the time.

Would you ſend Father Pen, and Father Lob,
Aſſiſted by the poet-laureate Squab†,
To teach obedience paſſive to the mob;
This is the time.

Would you let Reverend Father Peters know
What thanks the Church of England to him owe
For favors paſt, he did on them beſtow;
This is the time.

---

* The infamous Chief Juſtice Jeffreys.
† Dryden.

Would you with expedition fend away
Thofe four dim lights made bifhops t'other day,
To convert Indians in America;
      This is the time.

Would you the reft of that bald-pated train
No longer flatter with thin hopes of gain,
But fend 'em to St. Om'r's back again;
      This is the time.

Would you (inftead of holding birchen-tool)
Send Pulton* to be lafh'd at Bufby's fchool,
That he in print no longer play the fool;
      This is the time.

Would you that Jack of all religions fcare,
Bid him for hanging fpeedily prepare,
That Harry H   s may vifit Harry Care†;
      This is the time.

Would you let Ireland no more fear McDonnel,
And all the rabble under Phelim O'Neel,
And Clarendon‡ again fucceed Tyrconnel;
      This is the time.

---

 * Andrew Pulton, a jefuit and controverfialift, whofe ignorance of Englifh compofition made him the laughing-ftock of his contemporaries.

 † A nonconformift, who had bitterly affailed the King when Duke of York, but now was as loud in his adulation of him.

 ‡ Clarendon had been appointed Lord Deputy of Ireland in 1685, and was recalled in the following year, to make place for Tyrconnel, who was dreaded alike by Proteftants and Romanifts.

Would you Court ear-wigs banifh from your ears,
Thofe carpet-knights and interefted peers,
And rid the Kingdoms from impending fears;
This is the time.

Would you at once make all the *Hogans Mogans** yield,
And be at once their terror, and our fhield,
And not appear by proxy in the field;
This is the time.

Would you no more a woman's counfel take,
But love your Kingdoms for your Kingdoms' fake,
Make fubjects love, and enemies to quake;
This is the time.

---

* Cant expreffions for the Dutch.

THE CATHOLIC BALLAD:

OR,
AN INVITATION TO POPERY, UPON CONSIDERABLE GROUNDS AND REASONS.

BY WALTER POPE, A.M.

INCE Popery of late is so much in debate,
   And great strivings have been to restore it,
I cannot forbear, openly to declare,
   That the ballad-makers are for it.

We'll dispute no more then, these heretical men
   Have exposed our books unto laughter,
So that many do say, 'twill be the best way,
   To sing for the cause hereafter.

O the Catholic Cause! now assistance, my muse,
   Now earnestly do I desire thee;
Neither will I pray to St. Bridget to-day,
   But only to thee to inspire me!

Whence should purity come, but from Catholic Rome?
   I wonder much at your folly—

For St. Peter was there, and left an old chair,
　　Enough to make all the world holy.

For this facred old wood is fo excellent good,
　　If our doctors may be believed,
That whoever fits there needs never more fear
　　The danger of being deceived.

If the Devil himfelf fhould (God blefs us!) get up,
　　Though his nature we know to be evil,
Yet whilft he fat there, as divers will fwear,
　　He would be an infallible Devil.

Now who fits in the feat, but our father the Pope?
　　Which is a plain demonftration,
As clear as noon-day, we are in a right way,
　　And all others are doom'd to damnation.

If this will not fuffice yet to open your eyes,
　　Which are blinded with bad education;
We have arguments plenty, and miracles twenty,
　　Enough to convince a whole nation.

If you give but good heed, you fhall fee the hoft bleed,
　　And if anything can perfuade ye,
An image fhall fpeak, or at leaft it fhall fqueak,
　　In the honor of our Lady.

You shall see, without doubt, the devil cast out,
　　As of old by *Erra Pater*;
He shall skip about and tear, like a dancing bear,
　　When he feels the holy water.

If yet doubtful you are we have relics most rare,
　　We can shew you the sacred manger;
Several loads of the Cross, as good as e'er was,
　　To preserve your souls from danger.

Should I tell you of all, it would move a stone wall,
　　But I spare you a little for pity,
That each one may prepare, and rub up his ear,
　　For the second part of my ditty.

The Second Part.

NOW listen again to those things that remain,
　　They are matters of weight, I assure you,
And the first thing I say, throw your bibles away,
　　'Tis impossible else for to cure you.

O that pestilent book! never on it more look,
　　I wish I could sing it out louder:

It has done men more harm, I dare boldly affirm,
    Than th' invention of guns and powder.

As for matters of faith, believe what the Church faith,
    But for Scripture leave that to the learned;
For thefe are edge-tools, your laymen are fools,
    If you touch them you're fure to be harmed.

Be the Church's good fon, and your work is half done,
    After that you may do your own pleafure;
If your beads you can tell, and fay *Ave Mary* well,
    Never doubt of the heavenly treafure.

For the Pope keeps the Keys, and can do what he pleafe,
    And without all peradventure,
If you cannot at the fore, yet at the back-door
    Of Indulgence you may enter.

But firft by the way, you muft make a fhort ftay
    At a place call'd Purgatory,
Which the learned us tell, in the buildings of hell,
    Is about the middlemoft ftory.

'Tis a monftrous hot place, and a mark of difgrace,
    In the torment on't long to endure,
None are kept there but fools, and poor pitiful fouls
    Who can no ready money procure.

For a handsome round sum, you may quickly begone,
    So the Church has wisely ordained;
And they who build crosses, and pay well for masses,
    Would not there be too long detained.

And that 'tis a plain case, as the nose on one's face,
    They are in the surest condition,
Since none but poor fools, and some niggardly awls,
    That can fall into utter perdition.

And it faileth you then, O ye great and rich men,
    For that you will not hearken to reason;
And as long as you've pence, y'need scruple no offence,
    For murder, advoutery, treason.

And ye sweet-natured women, who hold all things common,
    My addresses to you are most hearty,
And to give you your due, you are to us most true,
    And we hope we shall gain the whole party.

If you happen to fall, your penance is small,
    And although you cannot forego it,
We have for you a cure, if of this you be sure,
    To confess before you go to it.

There is one reason yet, which I cannot omit,
   To those who affect the French nation,
Hereby we advance the religion of France,
   The religion that's only in fashion.

If these reasons prevail (as how can they fail?),
   To have Popery entertained,
You cannot conceive, and will hardly believe,
   What benefits hence may be gained.

For the Pope shall us bless (that's no small happiness),
   And again we shall see restored
The Italian trade, which formerly made
   This land to be so much adored.

O the pictures and rings, the beads and fine things,
   The good words as sweet as honey,
All this, and much more, shall be brought to our door,
   For a little dull English money.

Then shall Justice and Love, and whatever can move,
   Be restored again to our Britain;
And Learning so common, that ev'ry old woman
   Shall say her prayers in Latin.

Then the Church shall bear sway, and the State shall
   obey,
   Which is now lookt upon as a wonder,

And the proudeſt of Kings, with all temporal things,
  Shall ſubmit and truckle under.

And the Parliament too, who have tak'n us to do,
  And have handled us with ſo much terror,
May chance on that ſcore ('tis no time to ſay more),
  They may chance t'acknowledge their error.

If any man yet ſhall have ſo little wit
  As ſtill to be refractory,
I ſwear by the Maſs, he is a mere aſs,
  And ſo there's end of the ſtory.

THE TRUE PROTESTANT LITANY.

ROM such as the honest intentions oppose
   Of our true-hearted friends, and are led by
      the nose,
   By the specious pretences and wiles of our
      foes :
Libera nos, Domine.

From such as the Protestant cause would betray,
And give up their lives to the Pope for a prey;
If they will not sell Heaven as freely as they :
Libera nos.

From Judges opprest with such dimness of sight,
That they cannot discern what is *wrong*, or what's *right*;
If a spider's *gold*-web do but hang in their light :
Libera nos.

From those, who to finish their treasons begun,
When they fear'd that their work would be left but half
    done,
Did consult by the stars how to darken our *Sun* :
Libera nos.

From perſons, who under a handſome diſguiſe,
Would perſuade us the only way to be wiſe,
Is to forfeit our reaſon and put out our eyes:
Libera nos.

From thoſe who would learnedly make it appear,
That it is factious either to ſhun or to fear
The moſt imminent dangers, though never ſo near:
Libera nos.

From infallible fops, who would make us believe
We muſt pin our faith to their Catholic ſleeve,
Till we ſuffer a bondage beyond a reprieve:
Libera nos.

From the factors of *Rome*, who hither are ſent,
To raiſe cauſeleſs diſlikes of the King's government;
And to ſeparate him and his Parliament:
Libera nos.

From ſuch as will whiſper the *traitor's* defence,
And do own they believe their avouch'd innocence,
Thereby to diſparage the King's evidence:
Libera nos.

From Powis * and Peters, and all the whole crew,
And from all that would have them come fhort of their due;
From friars, and priefts, and Jefuits too:
> *Libera nos.*

And, laftly, from all that wifh ill to the King,
Or Popery into this Nation would bring;
Who merit no lefs than a Paddington fwing:
> *Libera nos.*

---

* Wm. Herbert, Earl of Powis, a Catholic Peer, who had been recently admitted into the Privy Council.

PRIVATE OCCURRENCES;

OR,

THE TRANSACTIONS OF THE FOUR LAST YEARS,

WRITTEN IN IMITATION OF THE OLD BALLAD OF

" *Hey, brave Oliver, Ho, brave Oliver.*"

PROTESTANT Mufe, yet a lover of
Kings,
On th' Age, grown a little fatirical, fings
Of Papifts, their counfels, and other fine
things.
Sing hey brave Popery, ho rare Popery,
Oh! fine Popery, O dainty Popery, ho!

She hopes fhe offends no Englifhman's patience,
Tho' Satire's forbid on all fuch occafions,
She's too good a fubject to read Declarations,
      Sing hey, &c.

If the faying be good of *Let him laugh that wins,*
Sure a lofer may fmile without any offence,
My Mufe, then, is gamefome, and thus fhe begins,
      Sing hey, &c.

When Charles deceaf'd, to his kingdom's difmay,
By an apoplex, or elfe fome other way *,
Our Brother with fhouts was proclaimed the fame day,
        Sing hey, &c.

His firft Royal promife was never to touch
Our Rights, nor Religion, nor Privilege grutch,
But Peters fwore, D—n him! he granted too much.
        Sing hey, &c.

Then Monmouth came in with an army of fools,
Betray'd by his cuckold † and other dull tools,
That painted the turf of green Sedgemoor with *Gules*,
        Sing hey, &c.

That Victory gotten (fome think to our wrong),
The priefts bray'd out joy in a thankfgiving fong,
And Teague with the bald-pates were at it ding dong.
        Sing hey, &c.

---

 * In reference to the death of Charles II. (relates Macaulay) "Wild ftories without number were repeated and believed by the common people. His Majefty's tongue had fwelled to the fize of a neat's tongue. A cake of deleterious powder had been found in his brain. There were blue fpots on his breaft. There were black fpots on his fhoulder. Something had been put into his fnuff-box. Something had been put into his broth. Something had been put into his favourite difh of eggs and ambergreafe. The Duchefs of Portfmouth had poifoned him in a cup of chocolate. The Queen had poifoned him in a jar of dried pears. Such tales ought to be preferved; for they furnifh us with a meafure of the intelligence and virtue of the generation which eagerly devoured them."

 † Lord Grey.

Then straight a strong army was levied in haste,
To hinder Rebellion — a very good jest —
But some folks will swear 'twas to murder the Test,
      Sing hey, &c.

A politique law which recusants did doom
That into our Senate they never might come,
But Equivalent since was proposed in its room.
      Sing hey, &c.

As if a true friend should in kindness demand
A tooth in my head, which firmly doth stand,
To give for't another he had in his hand.
      Sing hey, &c.

Then Term after Term this matter was weigh'd,
Old Judges turn'd out and new blockheads made,
That Coke or wise Littleton never did read.
      Sing hey, &c.

The good Church of England with speed was run down,
Whose loyalty ever stood fast to the Crown,
And Presbyter John was made Mayor of the Town.
      Sing hey, &c.

The bishop's disgrace made the clergy to sob,
A prey to old Petre and President Bob*,
And hurried to prison as if they did rob.
      Sing hey, &c.

---

* The versatile Robert Spencer, Earl of Sunderland, in whom, remarks Macaulay, " the political immorality of his age was personified in the most lively manner."

Then into the world a dear Prince of Wales flipt,
'Twas plain, for we hear a great minifter peept,
The Bricklayer for prating had lik'd t'a been whipt*.
       Sing hey, &c.

Thus England's diftreffes more fierce than the plague,
That during three years of no quiet could brag,
The Prince van Auraignia has brought from the Hague.
       Sing hey, &c.

A ftrong fleet and army t' invade us are bent,
We know not the caufe, tho' there's fomething in 't,
But we doubt not ere long we fhall fee it in print.
       Sing hey, &c.

Ah! England, that never could'ft value thy peace,
Had matters been now as in Elizabeth's days,
The Dutch had ne'er ventur'd to fifh in our feas!
       Sing hey, &c.

---

* Alluding to one of the indecent reports refpecting the legitimacy of James Frederic Edward, Prince of Wales (afterwards known as the Chevalier de St. George). Burnet has reprefented him as the fruit of *fix* different impoftures! Dryden, however, in his *Britannia Rediviva*, thus difpofes of thefe grofs calumnies:—

  " Born in broad daylight, that the ungrateful rout
  May find no room for a remaining doubt;
  Truth, which is light itfelf, doth darknefs fhun,
  And the true caglet fafely dares the fun."

LILLI BURLERO.*

BY THOMAS, MARQUIS OF WHARTON.

[This famous doggrel ballad, written on the occasion of General Dick Talbot being created Earl of Tyrconnel, and nominated by James II. to the lieutenancy of Ireland in 1686—1688, is attributed to Lord Wharton in a small pamphlet, entitled "A true relation of the several facts and circumstances of the intended riot and tumult on Queen Elizabeth's birth-day," &c., London, 1712, wherein it is said "A late Vice-roy [of Ireland] who has so often boasted himself upon his talent for mischief, invention, lying, and for making a certain *Lilli Burlero* song ; with which, if you will believe himself, he sung a deluded Prince out of Three Kingdoms."]

HO! broder Teague†, dost hear de decree?
Lilli Burlero, bullen a-la.*
Dat we shall have a new deputie,
Lilli Burlero, bullen a-la.
Lero lero, lilli Burlero, lero lero, bullen a-la.
Lero, lero, lilli burlero, lero lero, bullen a la.

Ho! by Shaint Tyburn, it is de Talbote,
Lilli, &c.
And he will cut de Englishman's troate,
Lilli, &c.

---

* *Lilli Burlero* and *Bullen-a-la* are said to have been the words of distinction used among the Irish Papists in their massacre of the Protestants in 1641.

† A cant name, in this age, for an Irishman.

Dough by my fhoul de Englifh do praat,
  Lilli, &c.
De law's on dare fide, and Creifh knows what,
  Lilli, &c.

But if difpence do come from de Pope,
  Lilli, &c.
We'll hang Magna Charta and dem in a rope
  Lilli, &c.

For de good Talbot is made a lord,
  Lilli, &c.
And with brave lads is coming abroad,
  Lilli, &c.

Who all in France have taken a fware,
  Lilli, &c.
Dat dey will have no Proteftant heir,
  Lilli, &c.

Ara! but why does he ftay behind?
  Lilli, &c.
Ho! by my fhoul 'tis a proteftant wind.
  Lilli, &c.

But fee de Tyrconnel is now come afhore,
  Lilli, &c.
And we fhall have commiffions gillore,
  Lilli, &c.

And he dat will not go to de mafs,
   Lilli, &c.
Shall be turn out, and look like an afs,
   Lilli, &c.

Now, now de heretics all go down,
   Lilli, &c.
By Chris and Shaint Patric, de nation's our own,
   Lilli, &c.

Dare was an old prophecy found in a bog,
   Lilli, &c.
" Ireland fhall be rul'd by an afs and a dog,"
   Lilli, &c.

And now dis prophecy is come to pafs,
   Lilli, &c.
For Talbot's de dog, and James is de afs.
   Lilli, &c.

A NEW SONG OF AN ORANGE.

To that excellent old tune, " Of a Pudding," &c.

GOOD people come buy
  The fruit that I cry,
That now is in feafon, tho' Winter is nigh,
  'Twill do you all good,
  And fweeten your blood,
I'm fure it will pleafe you when once underftood.
        'Tis an Orange.

  Its cordial juice
  Does much vigor produce,
I may well recommend it to every man's ufe;
  Tho' fome it quite chills,
  And with fear almoft kills,
Yet certain each honeft man benefit feels
        by an Orange.

  To make claret go down,
  Sometimes there is found
A jolly good health to pafs pleafantly round;
  But yet I'll proteft,
  Without any jeft,
No flavor is better than that of the tafte
        of an Orange.

Perhaps you may think
At Whitehall they ftink,
Becaufe that our neighbors come over the fea;
But fure 'tis prefum'd
That may be perfum'd
By the fcent of a clove when once it is ftuck
        in an Orange.

If they'd cure the ails
Of the Prince of Wales,
When the *Milk of Milch Tyler* does not well agree;
Though he's fubject to caft,
They may better the tafte,
Yet let 'em take heed left it curdle at laft
        with an Orange.

Old Stories rehearfe,
In profe and in verfe,
How a Welfh child was found by loving of cheefe;
So this will be known
If it be the Queen's own;
For the tafte it utterly then will difown
        of an Orange.

Though the mobile bawl,
Like the Devil and all,
For Religion, Property, Juftice, and Laws;

Yet, in very good footh,
I'll tell you the truth,
There nothing is better to ftop a man's mouth
      than an Orange.

We are certainly told
That by Adam of old,
Himfelf and his bearns for an Apple was fold;
 And who knows but his fon,
 By ferpents undone,
And his juggling *Eve* may chance lofe her own
      for an Orange?

TO THE FIRST VOLUME.

Allen, 102.
Allons, 180.
Armstrong, the Jester, 15.
Ashley, 187.
Atkins, Alderman Sir John, 44, 120.

Barillon, 218.
Baxter, Colonel, 65.
Beaken, 181.
Bedloe, 218, 224.
Berry, 215.
Blood, Colonel Thomas, 192.
Bob, President (see Sunderland, Earl of.)
Booker, the Astrologer, 10.
Booth, Sir George, 147.
Booth, Henry (Lord Delamere), 217.
Box, Ralph, 236, 238, 239, 240.
Bradshaw, John, 91, 103, 123, 131, 145.
Brandon, the Hangman, 6.
Buckingham, Duke of, 183, 217.
Bulteel, 181.
Burges, Dr. Cornelius, 36.
Burley, Captain, 50.
Butler, Samuel, the Poet, 28, 135.

Care, Henry, 259.

Carwell, 187 (see also Quérouaille, Louise de, and Portsmouth, Duchess of.)
Chaloner, 45, 50.
Clarendon, First Earl of, 178.
Clarendon, Second Earl of, 259.
Claypole, Lady, 135.
Clayton, Alderman Sir Robert, 244.
Cleveland, John, the Poet, 28.
Cleveland, Lady, 187.
Clotworthy, Sir John, 42.
Clutterbuck, 181.
Coventry, Sir John, 234.
Crocodile, Lieutenant-General, 92 (see Cromwell, Oliver.)
Cromwell, Henry, 135.
Cromwell, Joan, 114.
Cromwell, Oliver, 49, 67, 91, 104, 145, 161, 168, 169, 170 (see also Crocodile, General, the, Noll.
Cromwell, Richard, 115, 135, 138, 140, 146, 160, 170.

Dade, the Astrologer, 10.
Dagon (see Shaftesbury, Earl of.)
Danby, Earl of, 216, 234.
Deering, Sir Edward, 4.
Denham, 179.

INDEX OF NAMES

Derrick, the Hangman, 6, 58.
D'Eſtrées, Count, 196.
Doriſlaus, Dr. Iſaac, 90.
Dove, the Aſtrologer, 10.
Dryden, John, the Poet, 258 (ſee *Squab.*)
Dubois, 236, 239.
Duck, Dr. Arthur, 5, 18.
Dugdale, 218.

Eager, 181.
Elizabeth, the Princeſs, 61.
Eſſex, Earl of, 47.

Fairfax, Sir Thomas, 41, 47, 49, 56, 58, 61, 67, 91.
Feakes, 142.
Finch, Lord Keeper, 17, 18.
Fleetwood, General, 140, 145, 161.
Forbes, Lord, 24.

General, The, 108 (*ſee* Cromwell, Oliver).
Gerrard, the "Generous," 233.
Glynn, Serjeant John, 40, 41.
Godfrey, Sir Edmundbury, 207, 215.
Gregory, the Hangman, 99.
Gwynne, Eleanor, 235 (*ſee* Nell.)

Hampden, John, 42.
Hangman, Weſtern (*ſee* Jeffreys, Lord Chief Juſtice).
Harlow (i.e. Harley) Colonel Edward, 41.
Harriſon, Major-General, 113.
Haſlerigg, Sir Arthur, 101, 127, 130, 142, 145, 148.
Herbert, Admiral William, 271 (*ſee* Powis, Earl of.)
Hewſon, Colonel, 66, 88, 116, 127, 145.
Holms, Sir Robert, 195.

Honeywood, Sir Thomas, 137.
Hollis, Denzil, 40.
Hotham, Sir John, 56.
Hoyle, Alderman, 131.
Hyde, 183 (*ſee* Clarendon, Earl of.)

Ingleby, Lady Anne, 25.
Ireton, Alderman, 128.
Ireton, Colonel, 145.

Jeffreys, Lord Chief Juſtice, 258 (ſee *Hangman, Weſtern.*)
Jenkins, Judge David, 50.
Jones, Mr. Juſtice, 241.

Katharine, Queen of Charles II., 216.
Kent, Counteſs of, 46.
Killigrew, Thomas, 190.
Kipps, 181.

Lamb, Dr. 5, 18.
Lambert, Colonel John, 67, 142, 145, 147, 148.
Laud, Archbiſhop, 3, 13, 21.
Lauderdale, Duke of, 193.
Lenthall, William, 91, 101, 119, 127.
Leopold, Emperor of Auſtria, 245.
Leſlie, Biſhop, 182.
Lewis, Sir William, 41.
Lobb, Stephen, 256, 258.
Long, Walter, 42.
Lorrain, Duke of, 247.
Louis XIV., 200, 245.

Macdonnel, 259.
Madge, Queen, 135 (*ſee* Cromwell, Joan).
Mancheſter, Earl of, 47.
Martin, Henry, 45, 49, 50, 69, 102, 130.
Marvel, Andrew, 177, 181, 190, 193, 231.

Maynard, Sir John, 41.
Mildmay, Sir Henry, 45, 127.
Monk, General, 142, 148, 153, 154, 157, 158, 171.
Monmouth, Duke of, 220, 227, 233, 272.
Moore, Alderman Sir John, 236.
Morley, 181.
Mounſon, Sir William, 130.
Mulgrave, Earl of, 217.

Needham, Marchmont, 19, 24, 26, 73.
Nell, 187 (ſee Gwynne, Eleanor).
Nevill, Henry, 221.
Nichols, Anthony, 42.
Nol, King, 94, 115, 135, 139, 145, 160, 170 (ſee Cromwell, Oliver).
North, Dudley, 236, 237, 240.
Northumberland, Duke of, 61.

Oates, Titus, 207, 208, 212, 218, 224, 244, 251 (ſee *Telltroth, Titus*).
Okey, Colonel, 66.
Oliver, 93, 101, 102 (ſee Cromwell, Oliver).
O'Neil, Phelim, 259.
Opdam, Admiral, 194.
Ormonde, Duke of, 193.

Pack, Alderman Sir Chriſtopher, 135.
Papillon, 236, 239.
Parker, Martin, the Ballad writer, 10.
Penn, William, 256, 258.
Pepys, Samuel, 181, 190.
Peters, Hugh, 115, 141, 213.
Petre, Father Edward, 256, 258.
Pickering, Thomas, 208, 215.
Player, Sir Thomas, 187.
Pond, the Aſtrologer, 10.
Pope, Walter, 261.
Portſmouth, Ducheſs of, 218 (ſee Carwell and Quérouallé).

Powis, Earl of, 270 (ſee Herbert, William).
Prance, 218.
Pride, Colonel, 66, 136, 145.
Prymato, Joſiah, 101.
Prynne, William, 34.
Pulton, Andrew, 259.
Pym, John, 22, 26, 42, 63, 72.

Quéroualle, Louiſe de, 197 (ſee Carwell, and Portſmouth, Ducheſs of).

Rich, Colonel, 65.
Rivers, the Aſtrologer, 10.
Robinſon, Luke, 127.
Rocheſter, John Wilmot, Earl of, 190, 194.
Rupert, Prince, 216.

Say and Sele, Lord, 34.
Sandwich, Earl of, 196.
Saunders, Lord Chief Juſtice, 241.
Saxby, 87.
Scroggs, Lord Chief Juſtice, 217.
Sedgwick, William, 126.
Selden, John, 46.
Shafteſbury, Earl of, 217, 228, (ſee Dagon and Tony).
Skippon, Major General, 128.
Smectymnus, 129.
Sobieſki, John, King of Poland, 245, 247.
Spragg, Sir Edward, 195
Squab, Poet-Laureate (ſee Dryden).
Staines, 67.
Stapleton, Sir Philip, 40.
Strafford, Earl of, 8, 129.
Strickland, Walter, 136.
Stroud, 42.
Sunderland, Robert Spencer, Earl of, 273.
Swallow, the Aſtrologer, 10.

Telltroth, Titus, 207 (fee Oates, Titus).
Thomond, Earl of, 24.
Thurloe, 122.
Tichbourne, Sir Robert, 128.
Titus, Colonel, 184.
Tonge, Dr. Ezrael, 209.
Tony, 227, 249 (fee Shaftefbury, Earl of).
Tyler, Milch, 279 (fee Wales, Prince of).
Tyrconnel, Richard Talbot, Earl of, 259, 275.

Vane, Sir Harry, 45, 50, 103, 145, 154, 161.
Vyner, Sir Robert, 185, 186, 189, 197.

Ufher, Archbifhop, 71.

Wales, Prince of, 274 (fee Tyler, Milch).
Walter, Sir William, 41.
Ward, Sir Patience, 244.
Watfon, 67.
Wharton, Marquis of, 275, 279.
Whitelock, Bulftrode, 91.
Williams, Dr., Archbifhop of York, 8.
Windebanke, Sir Francis, 17.
Worftenholm, 182.
Wortley, Sir Francis, 40.
Wray, Sir John, 45.
Wren, 181.
Wren, Dr. Matthew, Bifhop of Ely, 4, 17, 18,

York, Archbifhop of (fee Williams).
York, James, Duke of, 178, 194, 196, 199, 220, 227, 228, 233, 243, 251.

END OF THE FIRST VOLUME.

LONDON
PRINTED BY SPOTTISWOODE AND CO.
NEW-STREET SQUARE

A CATALOGUE
OF
NEW WORKS IN GENERAL LITERATURE
PUBLISHED BY
LONGMAN, GREEN, LONGMAN, AND ROBERTS
39 PATERNOSTER ROW, LONDON.

CLASSIFIED INDEX

Agriculture and Rural Affairs.

Bayldon on Valuing Rents, &c.	5
Cecil's Stud Farm	8
Hoskyns's Talpa	11
Loudon's Agriculture	14
Morton on Landed Estates	17
" (J. C.) Handbook of Dairy Husbandry	17

Arts, Manufactures, and Architecture.

Brande's Dictionary of Science, &c.	6
" Organic Chemistry	6
Cresy's Civil Engineering	8
Fairbairn's Information for Engineers	9
" on Mills and Millwork	9
Falkener's Dædalus	9
" Museum of Classical Antiquities	9
Goodeve's Elements of Mechanism	9
Gwilt's Encyclopædia of Architecture	10
Harford's Plates from M. Angelo	10
Humphreys's Parables Illuminated	12
Jameson's Sacred and Legendary Art	12
" Commonplace-Book	12
König's Pictorial Life of Luther	10
Loudon's Rural Architecture	14
Love's Art of Dyeing	14
Lowndes's Engineers' Handbook	14
MacDougall's Campaigns of Hannibal	15
" Theory of War	14
Moseley's Engineering	17
Piesse's Art of Perfumery	18
" Laboratory of Chemical Wonders	18
Richardson's Art of Horsemanship	19
Scoffern on Projectiles, &c.	20
Steam Engine, by the Artisan Club	6
Ure's Dictionary of Arts, &c.	23

Biography.

Arago's Lives of Scientific Men	5
Baillie's Memoir of Bate	5
Brialmont's Wellington	6
Bunsen's Hippolytus	7
Bunting's (Dr.) Life	7
Crosse's (Andrew) Memorials	8
Green's Princesses of England	10
Harford's Life of Michael Angelo	10
Lardner's Cabinet Cyclopædia	13
Marshman's Life of Carey, Marshman, and Ward	15
" Life of Havelock	15

Maunder's Biographical Treasury	15
Mountain's (Col.) Memoirs	17
Palleske's Life of Schiller	18
Parry's (Admiral) Memoirs	18
Peel's Sketch of Sir R. Peel's Life and Character	18
Piozzi's Autobiography and Letters	19
Russell's Memoirs of Moore	16
" (Dr.) Life of Mezzofanti	20
SchimmelPenninck's (Mrs.) Life	20
Shee's Life of Sir M. A. Shee	21
Southey's Life of Wesley	21
Stephen's Ecclesiastical Biography	22
Strickland's Queens of England	22
Sydney Smith's Memoirs	21
Waterton's Autobiography and Essays	24

Books of General Utility.

Acton's Cookery-Book	5
Black's Treatise on Brewing	6
Cabinet Gazetteer	7
" Lawyer	7
Cust's Invalid's Own Book	8
Hensman's Handbook of the Constitution	11
Hints on Etiquette	11
Hudson's Executor's Guide	12
" on Making Wills	12
Hunter's Art of Writing Précis	12
Kesteven's Domestic Medicine	13
Lardner's Cabinet Cyclopædia	13
Loudon's Lady's Country Companion	14
Maunder's Treasury of Knowledge	15
" Biographical Treasury	15
" Geographical Treasury	16
" Scientific Treasury	15
" Treasury of History	16
" Natural History	15
Piesse's Art of Perfumery	18
Pitt's How to Brew Good Beer	18
Pocket and the Stud	10
Pycroft's English Reading	19
Richardson's Art of Horsemanship	19
Riddle's Latin Dictionaries	19
Roget's English Thesaurus	19
Rowton's Debater	20
Short Whist	21
Simpson's Handbook of Dining	21
Sleigh's Personal Wrongs and Legal Remedies	21
Thomson's Interest Tables	22
Walford's Handybook of the Civil Service	23
Webster's Domestic Economy	23
West's How to Nurse Sick Children	21
Willich's Popular Tables	21
Wilmot's Blackstone	24

A

Botany and Gardening.

Hassall's British Freshwater Algæ	10
Hooker's British Flora	11
" Guide to Kew Gardens	11
Lindley's Introduction to Botany	13
" Synopsis of the British Flora	13
" Theory of Horticulture	13
Loudon's Hortus Britannicus	14
" Amateur Gardener	14
" Trees and Shrubs	13
" Gardening	13
" Plants	14
Pereira's Materia Medica	18
Rivers's Rose-Amateur's Guide	10
Wilson's British Mosses	24

Chronology.

Brewer's Historical Atlas	6
Bunsen's Ancient Egypt	7
Haydn's Beatson's Index	10
Jaquemet's Abridged Chronology	12

Commerce and Mercantile Affairs.

Gilbart's Logic of Banking	9
Lorimer's Young Master Mariner	13
M'Culloch's Commerce and Navigation	15
Thomson's Interest Tables	22
Tooke's History of Prices	23

Criticism, History, and Memoirs.

Brewer's Historical Atlas	6
Bunsen's Ancient Egypt	7
" Hippolytus	7
Burke's Vicissitudes of Families	7
Chapman's Gustavus Adolphus	8
Clough's Greek History from Plutarch	8
Conolly's Sappers and Miners	8
Conybeare and Howson's St. Paul	8
Crowe's History of France	8
Frazer's Letters during the Peninsular and Waterloo Campaigns	9
Gurney's Historical Sketches	10
Hayward's Essays	11
Hensman's Handbook of the Constitution	11
Herschel's Essays and Addresses	11
Jeffrey's (Lord) Contributions	12
Kemble's Anglo-Saxons	13
Lardner's Cabinet Cyclopædia	13
Latham's Works on the English Language	13
Lowe's Campaigns in Central India	14
Macaulay's Critical and Hist. Essays	14
" History of England	14
" Miscellaneous Writings	14
" Speeches	14
Mackintosh's Miscellaneous Works	15
" History of England	15
M'Culloch's Geographical Dictionary	15
Maunder's Treasury of History	16
Merivale's History of Rome	16
" Roman Republic	16
Moore's (Thomas) Memoirs, &c.	16
Mure's Greek Literature	17
Palleske's Life and Works of Schiller	18
Piozzi's Autobiography and Letters	18
Porter's Knights of Malta	19
Raikes's Journal	19
Rich's Roman and Greek Antiquities	19
Riddle's Latin Dictionaries	19
Rogers's Essays from Edinb. Review	19
" (Sam.) Recollections	19
Roget's English Thesaurus	19

Schimmelpenninck's Memoirs of Port-Royal	20
" Principles of Beauty	20
Schmitz's History of Greece	20
Southey's Doctor	21
Stephen's Ecclesiastical Biography	22
" Lectures on French History	22
Sydney Smith's Works	21
" Lectures	21
" Memoirs	21
Thirlwall's History of Greece	22
Turner's Anglo-Saxons	23
White and Riddle's Latin Dictionary	24
Whiteside's Italy	24
Wilkins's Political Ballads	24
Wilmot's Brougham's Law Reforms	24

Geography and Atlases.

Brewer's Historical Atlas	6
Butler's Geography and Atlases	7
Cabinet Gazetteer	7
Johnston's General Gazetteer	13
M'Culloch's Geographical Dictionary	15
Maunder's Treasury of Geography	16
Murray's Encyclopædia of Geography	17
Sharp's British Gazetteer	20

Juvenile Books.

Amy Herbert	20
Cleve Hall	20
Earl's Daughter (The)	20
Experience of Life	20
Gertrude	20
Howitt's Boy's Country Book	12
" (Mary) Children's Year	11
Ivors	20
Katharine Ashton	20
Laneton Parsonage	20
Margaret Percival	20
Piesse's Chymical, Natural, and Physical Magic	18
" Laboratory of Chymical Wonders	18
Pycroft's Collegian's Guide	19

Medicine, Surgery, &c.

Brodie's Psychological Inquiries	6
Bull's Hints to Mothers	6
" Management of Children	6
Copland's Dictionary of Medicine	8
Cust's Invalid's Own Book	8
Holland's Mental Physiology	11
" Medical Notes and Reflections	11
Kesteven's Domestic Medicine	13
Pereira's Materia Medica	18
Spencer's Principles of Psychology	21
Todd's Cyclopædia of Anatomy and Physiology	22
West on Children's Diseases	24
" Nursing Sick Children	24

Miscellaneous Literature.

Bacon's (Lord) Works	5
Boase's Philosophy of Nature	6
Bray on Education of the Feelings	6
Defence of *Eclipse of Faith*	9
Eclipse of Faith	9
Greyson's Select Correspondence	10
Gurney's Evening Recreations	10
Hassall's Adulterations Detected, &c.	10
Haydn's Book of Dignities	10
Holland's Mental Physiology	11

CLASSIFIED INDEX TO CATALOGUE. 3

Hooker's New Guide	11
Howard's Gymnastic Exercises	11
Howitt's Rural Life of England	13
" Visits to Remarkable Places	12
Jameson's Commonplace-Book	12
Jeffrey's (Lord) Essays	12
Macaulay's Critical and Hist. Essays	14
" Speeches	14
Mackintosh's Miscellaneous Works	15
Martineau's Miscellanies	15
Newman on University Education	17
" Office & Work of Universities	17
" 's Lectures and Essays	17
Pycroft's English Reading	19
Rich's Dictionary of Antiquities	19
Riddle's Latin Dictionaries	19
Rowton's Debater	20
Sir Roger De Coverley	21
Smith's (Rev. Sydney) Works	21
Southey's Doctor, &c.	21
Spencer's Essays	21
Stephen's Essays	22
Stow's Training System	22
Thomson's Laws of Thought	22
Trevelyan on the Native Languages of India	22
White & Riddle's Latin Dictionary	24
Wit and Wisdom of Sydney Smith	21
Yonge's English-Greek Lexicon	24
" Latin Gradus	24
Zumpt's Latin Grammar	24

Natural History in general.

Agassiz on Classification	5
Catlow's Popular Conchology	8
Ephemera's Book of the Salmon	9
Garratt's Marvels of Instinct	9
Gosse's Natural History of Jamaica	10
Hartwig's Sea and its Living Wonders	10
Kirby and Spence's Entomology	13
Lee's Elements of Natural History	13
Maunder's Natural History	15
Quatrefages' Rambles of a Naturalist	19
Stonehenge on the Dog	22
Turton's Shells of the British Islands	23
Waterton's Essays on Natural History	23
Youatt's The Dog	24
" The Horse	24

One-Volume Encyclopædias and Dictionaries.

Blaine's Rural Sports	6
Brande's Science, Literature, and Art	6
Copland's Dictionary of Medicine	8
Cresy's Civil Engineering	8
Gwilt's Architecture	10
Johnston's Geographical Dictionary	13
Loudon's Agriculture	14
" Rural Architecture	14
" Gardening	13
" Plants	14
" Trees and Shrubs	13
M'Culloch's Geographical Dictionary	15
" Dictionary of Commerce	15
Murray's Encyclopædia of Geography	17
Sharp's British Gazetteer	20
Ure's Dictionary of Arts, &c.	23
Webster's Domestic Economy	23

Religious and Moral Works.

Afternoon of Life	5
Amy Herbert	20
Bloomfield's Greek Testament	6
Bloomfield's Supplementary Annotations on the Greek Testament	6
Bray on Education of the Feelings	6
Bunyan's Pilgrim's Progress	7
Calvert's Wife's Manual	7
Catz and Farlie's Moral Emblems	8
Cleve Hall	20
Conybeare and Howson's St. Paul	8
Cotton's Instructions in Christianity	8
Dale's Domestic Liturgy	9
Defence of Eclipse of Faith	9
Earl's Daughter (The)	20
Eclipse of Faith	9
Experience (The) of Life	20
Gertrude	20
Hoare on the Veracity of Genesis	11
Horne's Introduction to Scriptures	11
" Abridgment of ditto	11
Humphreys's *Parables* Illuminated	12
Ivors, by the Author of *Amy Herbert*	20
Jameson's Saints and Martyrs	12
" Monastic Legends	12
" Legends of the Madonna	12
" on Female Employment	12
Jeremy Taylor's Works	13
Katharine Ashton	20
König's Pictorial Life of Luther	10
Laneton Parsonage	20
Lyra Germanica	7
Maguire's Rome	15
Margaret Percival	20
Marshman's Serampore Mission	15
Martineau's Christian Life	15
" Hymns	15
" Studies of Christianity	15
Merivale's Christian Records	16
Moore on the Use of the Body	17
" Soul and Body	17
" 's Man and his Motives	17
Morning Clouds	17
Moseley's Astro-Theology	17
Neale's Closing Scene	17
Powell's Christianity without Judaism	18
" Order of Nature	19
Readings for Lent	20
" Confirmation	20
Riddle's Household Prayers	19
Robinson's Lexicon to the Greek Testament	19
Schimmel Penninck's Sacred Musings	20
Self-Examination for Confirmation	20
Sewell's History of the Early Church	20
" Passing Thoughts on Religion	20
Smith's (Sydney) Moral Philosophy	21
" (G.) Wesleyan Methodism	21
" (J.) Shipwreck of St. Paul	21
Southey's Life of Wesley	21
Spitta's Lyra Domestica	22
Stephen's Ecclesiastical Biography	22
Theologia Germanica	7
Thumb Bible (The)	22

Poetry and the Drama.

Aikin's (Dr.) British Poets	5
Arnold's Merope	5
" Poems	5
Calvert's Wife's Manual	7
Goldsmith's Poems, illustrated	9
L. E. L.'s Poetical Works	13
Linwood's Anthologia Oxoniensis	13
Lyra Germanica	7
Macaulay's Lays of Ancient Rome	14
MacDonald's Within and Without	4
" Poems	14
Montgomery's Poetical Works	17

CLASSIFIED INDEX TO CATALOGUE.

Moore's Poetical Works 16
" Selections (illustrated) . . 16
" Lalla Rookh 16
" Irish Melodies 16
" National Melodies . . . 16
" Sacred Songs (*with Music*) . 16
" Songs and Ballads . . . 16
Power's Virginia's Hand . . . 19
Shakspeare, by Bowdler 20
Southey's Poetical Works . . . 21
Spitta's Lyra Domestica . . . 22
Thomson's Seasons, illustrated . . 22
Warburton's Hunting Songs . . 23
Wilkins's Political Ballads . . . 24

The Sciences in general and Mathematics.

Arago's Meteorological Essays . . 5
" Popular Astronomy . . 5
Bosse's Philosophy of Nature . . 6
Bourne on the Steam Engine . . 6
" 's Catechism of Steam-Engine . 6
Boyd's Naval Cadet's Manual . . 6
Brande's Dictionary of Science, &c. . 6
" Lectures on Organic Chemistry 6
Conington's Chemical Analysis . . 8
Cresy's Civil Engineering . . . 8
De la Rive's Electricity 9
Grove's Correlation of Physical Forces . 10
Herschel's Outlines of Astronomy . . 11
Holland's Mental Physiology . . 11
Humboldt's Aspects of Nature . . 12
" Cosmos . . . 12
Hunt on Light 12
Lardner's Cabinet Cyclopædia . . 13
Marcet's (Mrs.) Conversations . . 15
Morell's Elements of Psychology . . 17
Moseley's Astro-Theology . . . 17
" Engineering and Architecture 17
Ogilvie's Master-Builder's Plan . . 17
Owen's Lectures on Comp. Anatomy 17 & 18
Pereira on Polarised Light . . . 18
Peschel's Elements of Physics . . 18
Phillips's Mineralogy 18
" Guide to Geology . . 18
Piesse's Laboratory of Chymical Wonders 18
Powell's Unity of Worlds . . . 18
" Christianity without Judaism 18
" Order of Nature . . . 19
Ramsay's Glaciers of North Wales and
   Switzerland 19
Smee's Electro-Metallurgy . . . 21
Steam-Engine, by the Artisan Club . 6
Tate on Strength of Materials . . 22
Twisden's Examples in Mechanics . 23
Webb's Celestial Objects for Common
   Telescopes 23

Rural Sports.

Baker's Rifle and Hound in Ceylon . 5
Blaine's Dictionary of Sports . . . 6
Cecil's Stable Practice 8
" Stud Farm 8
Dead Shot (The) 9
Ephemera on Angling 9
" Book of the Salmon . . 9
Freeman and Salvin's Falconry . . 9
Hamilton's Reminiscences of an Old
   Sportsman 10
Hawker's Young Sportsman . . . 10
Howard's Athletic Exercises . . . 11
The Hunting-Field 10
Idle's Hints on Shooting 12
Pocket and the Stud 10

Practical Horsemanship 10
Pycroft's Cricket-Field 19
Richardson's Horsemanship . . . 19
Ronalds's Fly-Fisher's Entomology . 19
Salmon Fishing in Canada . . . 5
Stable Talk and Table Talk . . . 10
Stonehenge on the Dog 22
" " Greyhound . . 22
The Stud, for Practical Purposes . . 10

Veterinary Medicine, &c.

Cecil's Stable Practice 8
" Stud Farm 8
Hunting-Field (The) 10
Miles's Horse-Shoeing 16
" on the Horse's Foot . . 16
Pocket and the Stud 10
Practical Horsemanship 10
Richardson's Horsemanship . . . 19
Stable Talk and Table Talk . . . 10
Stonehenge on the Dog 22
Stud (The) 10
Youatt's The Dog 24
" The Horse 24

Voyages and Travels.

Baker's Wanderings in Ceylon . . 5
Barth's African Travels 5
Burton's East Africa 7
" Lake Regions of Central Africa 7
" Medina and Mecca . . 7
Domenech's Deserts of North America 9
" Texas and Mexico . . 9
Forester's Sardinia and Corsica . . 9
Hill's Peru and Mexico 11
Hinchliff's Travels in the Alps . . 11
Hind's North American Exploring Expeditions 11
Howitt's Victoria 11
Huc's Chinese Empire 12
Hudson and Kennedy's Mont Blanc . 12
Humboldt's Aspects of Nature . . 12
Hutchinson's Western Africa . . . 12
Kane's Wanderings of an Artist . . 13
Lady's Tour round Monte Rosa . . 13
Lowe's Central India in 1857 and 1858 14
M'Clure's North-West Passage . . 17
Minturn's New York to Delhi . . 16
Möllhausen's Journey to the Pacific . 17
Peaks, Passes, and Glaciers . . . 18
Ramsay's Glaciers of North Wales and
   Switzerland 19
Senior's Journal in Turkey and Greece 20
Snow's Tierra del Fuego 21
Tennent's Ceylon 22
Weld's Vacations in Ireland . . . 24
" Two Months in the Highlands 24
" Pyrenees, West and East . 24
" United States and Canada . 24
Whiteside's Italy 24
Wills's "Eagle's Nest" 24

Works of Fiction.

Cruikshank's Falstaff 8
Howitt's Tallangetta 11
Moore's Epicurean 16
Sewell's Ursula 20
Simpkinson's Washingtons . . . 21
Sir Roger de Coverley 21
Sketches (The), Three Tales . . . 21
Southey's Doctor, &c. 21
Trollope's Barchester Towers . . . 22
" Warden 22

ALPHABETICAL CATALOGUE
of
NEW WORKS and NEW EDITIONS
PUBLISHED BY
LONGMAN, GREEN, LONGMAN, AND ROBERTS,
PATERNOSTER ROW, LONDON.

Miss Acton's Modern Cookery for Private Families, reduced to a System of Easy Practice in a Series of carefully-tested Receipts, in which the Principles of Baron Liebig and other eminent writers have been as much as possible applied and explained. Newly-revised and enlarged Edition; with 8 Plates, comprising 27 Figures, and 150 Woodcuts. Fcp. 8vo. 7s. 6d.

The Afternoon of Life. By the Author of *Morning Clouds*. New and cheaper Edition. Fcp. 8vo. 5s.

Agassiz. — An Essay on Classification [the Mutual Relation of Organised Beings]. By LOUIS AGASSIZ. 8vo. 12s.

Aikin's Select Works of the British Poets from Ben Jonson to Beattie; with Biographical and Critical Prefaces. New Edition, comprising Selections from more recent Poets. 8vo. 18s.

Alexander.—Salmon-Fishing in Canada. By a RESIDENT. Edited by Colonel Sir JAMES EDWARD ALEXANDER, K.C.L.S. Map and Woodcuts. Post 8vo. 10s. 6d.

Arago (F.)—Biographies of Distinguished Scientific Men. Translated by Admiral W. H. SMYTH, D.C.L., F.R.S., &c.; the Rev. BADEN POWELL, M.A.; and ROBERT GRANT, M.A., F.R.A.S. 8vo. 18s.

Arago's Meteorological Essays. With an Introduction by BARON HUMBOLDT. Translated under the superintendence of Lieut.-Col. E. SABINE, R.A., Treasurer and V.P.R.S. 8vo. 18s.

Arago's Popular Astronomy. Translated and edited by Admiral W. H. SMYTH, D.C.L., F.R.S.; and ROBERT GRANT, M.A., F.R.A.S. With 25 Plates and 358 Woodcuts. 2 vols. 8vo. price £2. 5s.

Arnold. — Merope, a Tragedy. By MATTHEW ARNOLD. With a Preface and an Historical Introduction. Fcp. 8vo. 5s.

Arnold.—Poems. By Matthew ARNOLD. FIRST SERIES. Third Edition. Fcp. 8vo. 5s. 6d. SECOND SERIES, price 5s.

Lord Bacon's Works. A New Edition, collected and edited by R. L. ELLIS, M.A., JAMES SPEDDING, M.A., and D. D. HEATH, Esq., Barrister-at-Law. VOLS. I. to V. comprising the Division of *Philosophical Works*; with a copious INDEX. 5 vols. 8vo. price £4. 6s. VOLS. VI. and VII. comprising the Division of *Literary and Professional Works*, with a full INDEX. 2 vols. 8vo. price £1. 16s.

Baker.—The Rifle and the Hound in Ceylon. By S. W. BAKER, Esq. New Edition, with 13 Illustrations engraved on Wood. Fcp. 8vo. 4s. 6d.

Baker. — Eight Years' Wanderings in Ceylon. By S. W. BAKER, Esq. With 6 coloured Plates. 8vo. 15s.

Barth.—Travels and Discoveries in North and Central Africa: Being the Journal of an Expedition undertaken under the auspices of Her Britannic Majesty's Government in the Years 1849—1855. By HENRY BARTH, Ph.D., D.C.L. With numerous Maps and Illustrations. 5 vols. 8vo. £5. 5s. cloth.

Bate. — Memoir of Captain W. Thornton Bate, R.N. By the Rev. JOHN BAILLIE. *New Edition*; with Portrait and 4 Illustrations. Fcp. 8vo. 5s.

Bayldon's Art of Valuing Rents and Tillages, and Claims of Tenants upon Quitting Farms, at both Michaelmas and Lady-day; as revised by Mr. DONALDSON. *Seventh Edition*, enlarged and adapted to the Present Time. By ROBERT BAKER, Land-Agent and Valuer. 8vo. price 10s. 6d.

Black's Practical Treatise on Brewing, based on Chemical and Economical Principles: With Formulæ for Public Brewers, and Instructions for Private Families. 8vo. 10s. 6d.

Blaine's Encyclopædia of Rural Sports; or, a complete Account, Historical, Practical, and Descriptive, of Hunting, Shooting, Fishing, Racing, &c. *New Edition*, revised and corrected; with above 600 Woodcut Illustrations, including 20 Subjects from Designs by JOHN LEECH. 8vo. price 42s.

Bloomfield.—The Greek Testament: with copious English Notes, Critical, Philological, and Explanatory. Especially adapted to the use of Theological Students and Ministers. By the Rev. S. T. BLOOMFIELD, D.D., F.S.A. Ninth Edition, revised. 2 vols. 8vo. with Map, £2. 8s.

Dr. Bloomfield's Critical Annotations on the New Testament, being a Supplemental Volume to the Ninth Edition. 8vo. 11s.

Dr. Bloomfield's College & School Edition of the Greek Testament: With brief English Notes, chiefly Philological and Explanatory. Seventh Edition; with Map and Index. Fcp. 8vo. 7s. 6d.

Dr. Bloomfield's College & School Lexicon to the Greek Testament. New Edition, revised. Fcp. 8vo. price 7s. 6d.

Boase.—The Philosophy of Nature: A Systematic Treatise on the Causes and Laws of Natural Phenomena. By HENRY S. BOASE, M.D., F.R.S., and G.S. 8vo. 12s.

Boyd.—A Manual for Naval Cadets. Published with the sanction and approval of the Lords Commissioners of the Admiralty. By JOHN M'NEILL BOYD, Captain, R.N. Second Edition; with 253 Illustrations (13 coloured). Fcp. 8vo. 12s. 6d.

Bourne.—A Treatise on the Steam Engine, in its Application to Mines, Mills, Steam Navigation, and Railways. By the Artisan Club. Edited by JOHN BOURNE, C.E. New and greatly improved Edition; with many Plates and Wood Engravings. 4to. [*Nearly ready.*

Bourne's Catechism of the Steam Engine in its various Applications to Mines, Mills, Steam Navigation, Railways, and Agriculture: With Practical Instructions for the Manufacture and Management of Engines of every class. With 89 Woodcuts. Fcp. 8vo. 6s.

Brande's Dictionary of Science, Literature, and Art; comprising the History, Description, and Scientific Principles of every Branch of Human Knowledge; with the Derivation and Definition of all the Terms in general use. Third Edition, revised and corrected; with numerous Woodcuts. 8vo. 60s.

Professor Brande's Lectures on Organic Chemistry, as applied to Manufactures, including Dyeing, Bleaching, Calico Printing, Sugar Manufacture, the Preservation of Wood, Tanning, &c. Edited by J. SCOFFERN, M.B. Fcp. Woodcuts, 7s. 6d.

Bray.—The Education of the Feelings. By CHARLES BRAY. Third Edition. 8vo. 5s.

Brewer.—An Atlas of History and Geography, from the Commencement of the Christian Era to the Present Time: Comprising a Series of Sixteen Coloured Maps, arranged in Chronological Order, with Illustrative Memoirs. By the Rev. J. S. BREWER, M.A. *Second Edition*, revised and corrected. Royal 8vo. 12s. 6d. half-bound.

Brialmont and Gleig's Life of Wellington.—History of the Life of Arthur Duke of Wellington: The Military Memoirs from the French of Captain BRIALMONT, with Additions and Emendations; the Political and Social Life by the Rev. G. R. GLEIG, M.A. With Maps, Plans of Battles, and Portraits. 4 vols. 8vo. £2. 14s.

Brodie.—Psychological Inquiries, in a Series of Essays intended to illustrate the Influence of the Physical Organisation on the Mental Faculties. By Sir BENJAMIN C. BRODIE, Bart. Third Edition. Fcp. 8vo. 5s.

Dr. Bull on the Maternal Management of Children in Health and Disease. New Edition. Fcp. 8vo. 5s.

Dr. Bull's Hints to Mothers on the Management of their Health during the Period of Pregnancy and in the Lying-in Room: With an Exposure of Popular Errors in connexion with those subjects, &c.; and Hints upon Nursing. New Edition. Fcp. 8vo. 5s.

Bunsen.—Christianity and Mankind, their Beginnings and Prospects. By Baron C. C. J. BUNSEN, D.D., D.C.L., D.Ph. Being a New Edition, corrected, re-modelled, and extended, of *Hippolytus and his Age*. 7 vols. 8vo. £5. 5s.—Or,

1. Hippolytus and his Age; or, the Beginnings and Prospects of Christianity. 2 vols. 8vo. £1. 10s.
2. Outline of the Philosophy of Universal History applied to Language and Religion; containing an Account of the Alphabetical Conferences. 2 vols. 33s.
3. Analecta Ante-Nicæna. 3 vols. 8vo. £2. 2s.

Bunsen. — Lyra Germanica. Translated from the German by CATHERINE WINKWORTH. FIRST SERIES, Hymns for the Sundays and Festivals of the Christian Year. SECOND SERIES, the Christian Life. Fcp. 8vo. 5s. each Series.

An Edition of the FIRST SERIES of *Lyra Germanica*, with Illustrations from Original Designs by JOHN LEIGHTON, F.S.A., engraved on Wood under his superintendence. Fcp. 4to. price 21s.

HYMNS from *Lyra Germanica*, 18mo. 1s.

. These selections of German Hymns have been made from collections published in Germany by Baron BUNSEN; and form companion volumes to

Theologia Germanica. Translated by SUSANNA WINKWORTH. With a Preface by the Rev. CHARLES KINGSLEY; and a Letter by Baron BUNSEN. Fcp. 8vo. 5s.

Bunsen.—Egypt's Place in Universal History: An Historical Investigation, in Five Books. By Baron C. C. J. BUNSEN, D.C.L., D.Ph. Translated from the German by C. H. COTTRELL, Esq., M.A. With many Illustrations. 4 vols. 8vo. £5. 8s.

Bunting. — The Life of Jabez Bunting, D.D.: With Notices of contemporary Persons and Events. By his Son, THOMAS PERCIVAL BUNTING. VOL. I. with 2 Portraits and Vignette. *Third Thousand*, post 8vo. 7s. 6d.; or (*large paper and Proof Engravings*) square crown 8vo. 10s. 6d.

Bunyan's Pilgrim's Progress: With 126 Illustrations engraved on Steel and on Wood from Original Designs by CHARLES BENNETT; and a Preface by the Rev. CHARLES KINGSLEY, Rector of Eversley. Fcp. 4to. price 21s. cloth.

Burke.—Vicissitudes of Families. By Sir BERNARD BURKE, Ulster King of Arms. FIRST and SECOND SERIES, crown 8vo. 12s. 6d. each.

Burton.—The Lake Regions of Central Africa: A Picture of Exploration. By RICHARD F. BURTON, Captain H.M. Indian Army; Fellow and Gold Medallist of the Royal Geographical Society. With Map and numerous Illustrations. 2 vols. 8vo. 31s. 6d.

Captain Burton's First Footsteps in East Africa; or, an Exploration of Harar. With Maps and coloured Plates. 8vo. 18s.

Captain Burton's Personal Narrative of a Pilgrimage to El Medinah and Meccah. *Second Edition*, revised; with coloured Plates and Woodcuts. 2 vols. crown 8vo. 24s.

Bishop Butler's Sketch of Modern and Ancient Geography. New Edition, thoroughly revised, with such Alterations introduced as continually progressive Discoveries and the latest Information have rendered necessary. Post 8vo. 7s. 6d.

Bishop Butler's General Atlas of Modern and Ancient Geography; comprising Fifty-four full-coloured Maps; with complete Indices. New Edition, enlarged, and greatly improved. Edited by the Author's Son. Royal 4to. 24s.

The Cabinet Lawyer: A Popular Digest of the Laws of England, Civil and Criminal; with a Dictionary of Law Terms, Maxims, Statutes, and Judicial Antiquities; Correct Tables of Assessed Taxes, Stamp Duties, Excise Licenses, and Post-Horse Duties; Post-Office Regulations; and Prison Discipline. 18th Edition, comprising the Public Acts of the Session 1860. Fcp. 8vo. 10s. 6d.

The Cabinet Gazetteer: A Popular Exposition of All the Countries of the World. By the Author of *The Cabinet Lawyer*. Fcp. 8vo. 10s. 6d.

Calvert. — The Wife's Manual; or, Prayers, Thoughts, and Songs on Several Occasions of a Matron's Life. By the Rev. W. CALVERT, M.A. Ornamented from Designs by the Author in the style of *Queen Elizabeth's Prayer-Book*. Crown 8vo. 10s. 6d.

Catlow's Popular Conchology; or, the Shell Cabinet arranged according to the Modern System: With a detailed Account of the Animals, and a complete Descriptive List of the Families and Genera of Recent and Fossil Shells. With 405 Woodcuts. Post 8vo. 14s.

Catz and Farlie's Book of Emblems.—Moral Emblems, with Aphorisms, Adages, and Proverbs of all Nations, from J. CATZ and R. FARLIE: comprising 60 circular Vignettes, 60 Tail-Pieces, and a Frontispiece composed from their works by J. LEIGHTON, F.S.A., and engraved on Wood. The Text translated, &c., by R. PIGOT. Imperial 8vo. 31s. 6d. cloth; or 52s. 6d. bound in morocco.

Cecil.—The Stud Farm; or, Hints on Breeding Horses for the Turf, the Chase, and the Road. Addressed to Breeders of Race-Horses and Hunters, Landed Proprietors, and Tenant Farmers. By CECIL. Fcp. 8vo. 5s.

Cecil's Stable Practice; or, Hints on Training for the Turf, the Chase, and the Road; with Observations on Racing and Hunting, Wasting, Race-Riding, and Handicapping: Addressed to all who are concerned in Racing, Steeple-Chasing, and Fox-Hunting. Second Edition. Fcp. 8vo. with Plate, 5s.

Chapman.—History of Gustavus Adolphus, and of the Thirty Years' War up to the King's Death: With some Account of its Conclusion by the Peace of Westphalia, in 1648. By B. CHAPMAN, M.A. 8vo. Plans, 12s. 6d.

Clough.—Greek History from Themistocles to Alexander, in a Series of Lives from Plutarch. Revised and arranged by A. H. CLOUGH, sometime Fellow of Oriel College, Oxford. Fcp. 8vo. with 44 Woodcuts, 6s.

Conington.—Handbook of Chemical Analysis, adapted to the Unitary System of Notation. By F. T. CONINGTON, M.A., F.C.S. Post 8vo. 7s. 6d. Also, *Tables of Qualitative Analysis*, designed as a Companion. Price 2s. 6d.

Connolly's History of the Royal Sappers and Miners: Including the Services of the Corps in the Crimea and at the Siege of Sebastopol. *Second Edition;* with 17 coloured Plates. 2 vols. 8vo. 30s.

Conybeare and Howson's Life and Epistles of Saint Paul: Comprising a complete Biography of the Apostle, and a Translation of his Epistles inserted in Chronological Order. *Third Edition,* revised and corrected; with several Maps and Woodcuts, and 4 Plates. 2 vols. square crown 8vo. 31s. 6d.

. The Original Edition, with more numerous Illustrations, in 2 vols. 4to. price 48s. may also be had.

Dr. Copland's Dictionary of Practical Medicine: Comprising General Pathology, the Nature and Treatment of Diseases, Morbid Structures, and the Disorders especially incidental to Climates, to Sex, and to the different Epochs of Life; with numerous approved Formulæ of the Medicines recommended. Now complete in 3 vols. 8vo. price £5. 11s. cloth.

Bishop Cotton's Instructions in the Doctrine and Practice of Christianity. Intended as an Introduction to Confirmation. 4th Edition. 18mo. 2s. 6d.

Cresy's Encyclopædia of Civil Engineering, Historical, Theoretical, and Practical. Illustrated by upwards of 3,000 Woodcuts. *Second Edition,* revised and extended. 8vo. 63s.

Crosse.—Memorials, Scientific and Literary, of Andrew Crosse, the Electrician. Edited by Mrs. CROSSE. Post 8vo. 9s. 6d.

Crowe.—The History of France. By EYRE EVANS CROWE. In Five Volumes. VOL.I. 8vo. 14s.; VOL.II. 15s.

Cruikshank.—The Life of Sir John Falstaff, illustrated in a Series of Twenty-four original Etchings by George Cruikshank. Accompanied by an imaginary Biography, by ROBERT B. BROUGH. Royal 8vo. 12s. 6d. cloth.

Lady Cust's Invalid's Own Book: A Collection of Recipes from various Books and various Countries. Fcp. 8vo. 2s. 6d.

The Rev. Canon Dale's Domestic Liturgy and Family Chaplain, in Two Parts: PART I. Church Services adapted for Domestic Use, with Prayers for Every Day of the Week, selected from the Book of Common Prayer; PART II. an appropriate Sermon for Every Sunday in the Year. Post 4to. 21s. cloth; 31s. 6d. calf; or 50s. morocco.

Separately { THE FAMILY CHAPLAIN, 12s.
THE DOMESTIC LITURGY, 10s. 6d.

PUBLISHED BY LONGMAN, GREEN, AND CO.

The Dead Shot; or, Sportsman's Complete Guide; being a Treatise on the Use of the Gun, with Rudimentary and Finishing Lessons in the Art of Shooting Game of all kinds; Dog-breaking, Pigeon-shooting, &c. By MARKSMAN. Fcp. 8vo. with 6 Illustrations, 5s.

De la Rive's Treatise on Electricity in Theory and Practice. Translated for the Author by C. V. WALKER, F.R.S. 3 vols. 8vo. Woodcuts, £3, 13s.

Domenech.—Seven Years' Residence in the Great Deserts of North America. By the ABBÉ DOMENECH. With a Map, and about Sixty Illustrations. 2 vols. 8vo. £1, 16s.

Abbé Domenech's Missionary Adventures in Texas and Mexico: A Personal Narrative of Six Years' Sojourn in those Regions. 8vo. 10s. 6d.

The Eclipse of Faith; or, a Visit to a Religious Sceptic. 10th Edition. Fcp. 8vo. 5s.

Defence of The Eclipse of Faith, by its Author. 3d Edition, revised. Fcp. 8vo. 3s. 6d.

Ephemera's Handbook of Angling; teaching Fly-fishing, Trolling, Bottom-Fishing, Salmon-Fishing: With the Natural History of River-Fish, and the best Modes of Catching them. With Woodcuts. Fcp. 8vo. 5s.

Ephemera's Book of the Salmon: The Theory, Principles, and Practice of Fly-Fishing for Salmon; Lists of good Salmon Flies for every good River in the Empire; the Natural History of the Salmon, its Habits described, and the best way of artificially Breeding it. Fcp. 8vo. with coloured Plates, 14s.

Fairbairn.—A Treatise on Mills and Millwork. By WILLIAM FAIRBAIRN, F.R.S., F.G.S. With numerous Illustrations. 2 vols. 8vo. [In the press.

Fairbairn.—Useful Information for Engineers: A First Series of Lectures delivered to the Working Engineers of Yorkshire and Lancashire. By WILLIAM FAIRBAIRN, F.R.S., F.G.S. Third Edition; with Plates and Woodcuts. Crown 8vo. 10s. 6d.

SECOND SERIES of FAIRBAIRN'S Useful Information for Engineers, uniform with the above, nearly ready.

Falkener. — Dædalus; or, the Causes and Principles of the Excellence of Greek Sculpture. By EDWARD FALKENER, Member of the Archæological Institutes of Rome and Berlin. With numerous Illustrations and 2 Medallions from the Antique. Royal 8vo. 12s.

Falkener.—Museum of Classical Antiquities: A Series of Thirty-five Essays on Ancient Art, by various Writers, edited by EDWARD FALKENER. With 25 Plates and many Woodcuts. Imperial 8vo. 42s.

Forester's Rambles in the Islands of Corsica and Sardinia: With Notices of their History, Antiquities, and present Condition. With coloured Map; and numerous Illustrations from Drawings by Lieut.-Col. M. A. Biddulph, R.A. Imperial 8vo. 28s.

Letters of Sir A. S. Frazer, K.C.B. Commanding the Royal Horse Artillery under the Duke of Wellington: Written during the Peninsular and Waterloo Campaigns. Edited by MAJOR-GENERAL SABINE, R.A. With Portrait, 2 Maps, and Plans. 8vo. 18s.

Freeman and Salvin.—Falconry: Its Claims, History, and Practice. By the Rev. G. E. FREEMAN, M.A. ("Peregrine" of the *Field*); and Captain F. H. SALVIN. Post 8vo. with Woodcut Illustrations from Drawings by Wolf, price 10s. 6d. cloth.

Garratt.—Marvels and Mysteries of Instinct; or, Curiosities of Animal Life. By GEORGE GARRATT. Second Edition, improved. Fcp. 8vo. 4s. 6d.

Gilbart's Logic of Banking: A Familiar Exposition of the Principles of Reasoning, and their Application to the Art and the Science of Banking. 12mo. with Portrait, 12s. 6d.

The Poetical Works of Oliver Goldsmith. Edited by BOLTON CORNEY, Esq. Illustrated by Wood Engravings, from Designs by Members of the Etching Club. Square crown 8vo. cloth, 21s.; morocco, £1. 16s.

Goodeve. — The Elements of Mechanism, designed for Students of Applied Mechanics. By T. M. GOODEVE, M.A., Professor of Natural Philosophy in King's College. Post 8vo. with 206 Figures, 6s. 6d.

A 2

Gosse.—A Naturalist's Sojourn in Jamaica. By P. H. GOSSE, Esq. With Plates. Post 8vo. 14s.

Green.—Lives of the Princesses of England. By Mrs. MARY ANNE EVERETT GREEN, Editor of the *Letters of Royal and Illustrious Ladies*. With numerous Portraits. Complete in 6 vols. post 8vo. 10s. 6d. each.

Greyson.—Selections from the Correspondence of R. E. GREYSON, Esq. Edited by the Author of *The Eclipse of Faith*. New Edition. Crown 8vo. 7s. 6d.

Grove.—The Correlation of Physical Forces. By W. R. GROVE, Q.C., M.A. *Third Edition*. 8vo. 7s.

Gurney.—St. Louis and Henri IV.: Being a Second Series of Historical Sketches. By the Rev. JOHN H. GURNEY, M.A. Fcp. 8vo. 6s.

Evening Recreations; or, Samples from the Lecture-Room. Edited by Rev. J. H. GURNEY. Crown 8vo. 5s.

Gwilt's Encyclopædia of Architecture, Historical, Theoretical, and Practical. By JOSEPH GWILT. With more than 1,000 Wood Engravings, from Designs by J. S. GWILT. 8vo. 42s.

Hamilton.—Reminiscences of an Old Sportsman. By Colonel J. M. HAMILTON, K.H., Author of *Travels in the Interior of Columbia*. 2 vols. post 8vo. with 6 Illustrations, 18s.

Hare (Archdeacon).—The Life of Luther, in Forty-eight Historical Engravings. By GUSTAV KÖNIG. With Explanations by Archdeacon HARE and SUSANNAH WINKWORTH. Fcp. 4to. 28s.

Harford.—Life of Michael Angelo Buonarroti: With Translations of many of his Poems and Letters; also Memoirs of Savonarola, Raphael, and Vittoria Colonna. By JOHN S. HARFORD, Esq., D.C.L., F.R.S. Second Edition, revised; with 20 Plates. 2 vols. 8vo. 25s.

Illustrations, Architectural and Pictorial, of the Genius of Michael Angelo Buonarroti. With Descriptions of the Plates, by the Commendatore CANINA; C. R. COCKERELL, Esq., R.A.; and J. S. HARFORD, Esq., D.C.L., F.R.S. Folio, 73s. 6d. half-bound.

Harry Hieover's Stable Talk and Table Talk; or, Spectacles for Young Sportsmen. New Edition, 2 vols. 8vo. Portrait, 24s.

Harry Hieover.—The Hunting-Field. By HARRY HIEOVER. 2d Edition; with 2 Plates. Fcp. 8vo. 5s.

Harry Hieover. — Practical Horsemanship. Second Edition; with 2 Plates. Fcp. 8vo. 5s. half-bound.

Harry Hieover.—The Pocket and the Stud; or, Practical Hints on the Management of the Stable. 3d Edition. Fcp. 8vo. with Portrait, 5s.

Harry Hieover.—The Stud, for Practical Purposes and Practical Men: Being a Guide to the Choice of a Horse. 2d Edition, with 2 Plates. Fcp. 5s.

Hartwig. — The Sea and its Living Wonders. By Dr. GEORGE HARTWIG. With numerous Wood Engravings, and a new series of Illustrations in Chromo-xylography from original designs by Henry Noel Humphreys. 8vo. 18s.

Hassall.—Adulterations Detected; or, Plain Instructions for the Discovery of Frauds in Food and Medicine. By ARTHUR HILL HASSALL, M.D. Lond., Analyst of *The Lancet* Sanitary Commission, and Author of the Reports of that Commission published under the title of *Food and its Adulterations* (which may also be had, in 8vo. price 28s.) With 225 Illustrations, engraved on Wood. Crown 8vo. 17s. 6d.

Dr. Hassall's History of the British Freshwater Algæ; Including Descriptions of the Desmideæ and Diatomaceæ. 2 vols. 8vo. with 103 Plates, £1. 15s.

Col. Hawker's Instructions to Young Sportsmen in all that relates to Guns and Shooting. 11th Edition, revised by the Author's Son, Major P. W. L. HAWKER. With Portrait, Plates, and Woodcuts. Sq. crown 8vo. 18s.

Haydn's Book of Dignities: Containing Rolls of the Official Personages of the British Empire, Civil, Ecclesiastical, Judicial, Military, Naval, and Municipal, from the Earliest Periods to the Present Time. Together with the Sovereigns of Europe, from the Foundation of their respective States; the Peerage and Nobility of Great Britain, &c. 8vo. 25s.

PUBLISHED BY LONGMAN, GREEN, AND CO.   11

Hayward. — Biographical and Critical Essays, reprinted from Reviews, with Additions and Corrections. By A. HAYWARD, Esq., Q.C. 2 vols. 8vo. 24s.

Hensman. — Handbook of the Constitution: Being a short account of the Rise, Progress, and Present State of the Laws of England. By ALFRED P. HENSMAN, Barrister-at-Law. Fcp. 8vo. 4s.

Sir John Herschel's Outlines of Astronomy. Fifth Edition, revised and corrected to the existing state of astronomical knowledge; with Plates and Woodcuts. 8vo. 18s.

Sir John Herschel's Essays from the *Edinburgh* and *Quarterly Reviews*, with Addresses and other Pieces. 8vo. 18s.

Hill. — Travels in Peru and Mexico. By S. S. HILL, Esq., Author of *Travels in Siberia*, &c. 2 vols. post 8vo. 21s.

Hinchliff. — Summer Months among the Alps: With the Ascent of Monte Rosa. By THOS. W. HINCHLIFF, Barrister-at-Law. Post 8vo. 10s. 6d.

Hind. — Narrative of the Cana- dian Red River and Assinniboine and Saskatchewan Exploring Expeditions: With a Description of the Physical Geography, Geology, and Climate of the Country traversed. By HENRY YOULE HIND, M.A., F.R.G.S., Professor of Chemistry and Geology in Trinity College, Toronto; in Charge of the Assinniboine and Saskatchewan Exploring Expedition. With Maps and numerous Illustrations. 2 vols. 8vo. [*Just ready.*]

Hints on Etiquette and the Usages of Society: With a Glance at Bad Habits. New Edition, revised (with Additions) by a Lady of Rank. Fcp. 8vo. 2s. 6d.

Hoare. — The Veracity of the Book of Genesis: With the Life and Character of the Inspired Historian. By the Rev. WILLIAM H. HOARE, M.A., late Fellow of St. John's College, Cambridge. 8vo. 9s. 6d.

Holland. — Medical Notes and Reflections. By Sir HENRY HOLLAND, M.D., F.R.S., &c., Physician in Ordinary to the Queen and Prince-Consort. Third Edition. 8vo. 18s.

Sir H. Holland's Chapters on Mental Physiology, founded chiefly on Chapters contained in *Medical Notes and Reflections*. Post 8vo. 8s. 6d.

Hooker's (Sir W. J.) Popular Guide to the Royal Botanic Gardens of Kew. With many Woodcuts. 16mo. 6d.

Hooker and Arnott's British Flora; comprising the Phænogamous or Flowering Plants, and the Ferns. Seventh Edition, with numerous Figures illustrative of the Umbelliferous Plants, the Composite Plants, the Grasses, and the Ferns. 12mo. with 12 Plates, 14s.; with the Plates coloured, price 21s.

Horne's Introduction to the Critical Study and Knowledge of the Holy Scriptures. *Tenth Edition*, revised, corrected, and brought down to the present time. Edited by the Rev. T. HARTWELL HORNE, B.D. (the Author); the Rev. JOHN AYRE; and S. PRIDEAUX TREGELLES, LL.D. With 4 Maps and 22 Vignettes and Facsimiles. 4 vols. 8vo. £3. 13s. 6d.

Horne. — A Compendious Intro- duction to the Study of the Bible. By the Rev. T. HARTWELL HORNE, B.D. New Edition, with Maps, &c. 12mo. 9s.

Hoskyns. — Talpa; or, the Chro- nicles of a Clay Farm: An Agricultural Fragment. By CHANDOS WREN HOSKYNS, Esq. Fourth Edition. With 24 Woodcuts from Designs by GEORGE CRUIKSHANK. 16mo. 5s. 6d.

Howard. — Athletic and Gym- nastic Exercises. With 64 Illustrations, and a Description of the requisite Apparatus. By JOHN H. HOWARD. 16mo. 7s. 6d.

Howitt. — The Children's Year. By MARY HOWITT. With Four Illustrations. Square 16mo. 5s.

Howitt. — Tallangetta, the Squatter's Home: A Story of Australian Life. By WILLIAM HOWITT. 2 vols. post 8vo. 18s.

Howitt. — Land, Labour, and Gold; or, Two Years in Victoria: With Visit to Sydney and Van Diemen's Land. By WILLIAM HOWITT. Second Edition, Two Volumes in One. Crown 8vo. 6s.

W. Howitt's Visits to Remarkable Places: Old Halls, Battle-Fields, and Scenes illustrative of Striking Passages in English History and Poetry. With about 80 Wood Engravings. *New Edition.* 2 vols. square crown 8vo. 25s.

William Howitt's Boy's Country Book: Being the Real Life of a Country Boy, written by himself; exhibiting all the Amusements, Pleasures, and Pursuits of Children in the Country. With 40 Woodcuts. Fcp. 8vo. 6s.

William Howitt's Rural Life of England. With Woodcuts by Bewick and Williams. Medium 8vo. 21s.

The Abbé Huc's Work on the Chinese Empire, founded on Fourteen Years' Travel and Residence in China. People's Edition, with 2 Woodcut Illustrations. Crown 8vo. 5s.

Hudson's Executor's Guide. New and improved Edition; with the Statutes enacted, and the Judicial Decisions pronounced since the last Edition, incorporated. Fcp. 8vo. 6s.

Hudson's Plain Directions for Making Wills in conformity with the Law. New Edition, corrected and revised by the Author; and practically illustrated by Specimens of Wills containing many varieties of Bequests, also Notes of Cases judicially decided since the Wills Act came into operation. Fcp. 8vo. 2s. 6d.

Hudson and Kennedy's Ascent of Mont Blanc by a New Route and Without Guides. *Second Edition,* with Plate and Map. Post 8vo. 5s. 6d.

Humboldt's Cosmos. Translated, with the Author's authority, by Mrs. SABINE. VOLS. I. and II. 16mo. Half-a-Crown each, sewed; 3s. 6d. each, cloth; or in post 8vo. 12s. each, cloth. VOL. III. post 8vo. 12s. 6d. cloth; or in 16mo. Part I. 2s. 6d. sewed, 3s. 6d. cloth; and Part II. 3s. sewed, 4s. cloth. VOL. IV. PART I. post 8vo. 15s. cloth; 16mo. 7s. 6d. cloth.

Humboldt's Aspects of Nature. Translated, with the Author's authority, by Mrs. SABINE. 16mo. price 6s.; or in 2 vols. 3s. 6d. each, cloth; 2s. 6d. each, sewed.

Humphreys.— Parables of Our Lord, illuminated and ornamented in the style of the Missals of the Renaissance by H. N. HUMPHREYS. Square fcp. 8vo. 21s. in massive carved covers; or 30s. bound in morocco, by Hayday.

Hunt's Researches on Light in its Chemical Relations; embracing a Consideration of all the Photographic Processes. 8vo. 10s. 6d.

Hunter. — Introduction to the *Writing of Précis or Digests,* as applicable to Narratives of Facts or Historical Events, Correspondence, Evidence, Official Documents, and General Composition: With numerous Examples and Exercises. By the Rev. JOHN HUNTER, M.A. 12mo. 2s.

KEY, 12mo. *just ready.*

Hutchinson's Impressions of Western Africa: With a Report on the Peculiarities of Trade up the Rivers in the Bight of Biafra. Post 8vo. 8s. 6d.

Idle's Hints on Shooting, Fishing, &c., both on Sea and Land, and in the Fresh-Water Lochs of Scotland. Fcp. 8vo. 5s.

Mrs. Jameson's Two Lectures on the Social Employments of Women, *Sisters of Charity* and the *Communion of Labour.* New Edition. Fcp. 2s.

Mrs. Jameson's Legends of the Saints and Martyrs, as represented in Christian Art. Third Edition; with 17 Etchings and upwards of 180 Woodcuts. 2 vols. square crown 8vo. 31s. 6d.

Mrs. Jameson's Legends of the Monastic Orders, as represented in Christian Art. Second Edition, enlarged; with 11 Etchings by the Author and 88 Woodcuts. Sq. crown 8vo. 28s.

Mrs. Jameson's Legends of the Madonna, as represented in Christian Art. Second Edition, corrected and enlarged; with 27 Etchings and 165 Wood Engravings. Square crown 8vo. 28s.

Mrs. Jameson's Commonplace-Book of Thoughts, Memories, and Fancies, Original and Selected. *Second Edition;* with Etchings and Woodcuts. Crown 8vo. price 18s.

Jaquemet's Chronology for Schools: Containing the most important Dates of General History, Political, Ecclesiastical, and Literary, from the Creation of the World to the end of the Year 1857. Fcp. 8vo. 3s. 6d.

Lord Jeffrey's Contributions to The Edinburgh Review. A New Edition, complete in One Volume, with Portrait and Vignette. Square crown 8vo. 21s. cloth; or 30s. calf.— Or in 3 vols. 8vo. price 42s.

PUBLISHED BY LONGMAN, GREEN, AND CO. 13

Bishop Jeremy Taylor's Entire Works: With Life by Bishop HEBER. Revised and corrected by the Rev. C. P. EDEN. Now complete in 10 vols. 8vo. price 10s. 6d. each.

Kane's Wanderings of an Artist among the Indians of North America; from Canada to Vancouver's Island and Oregon, through the Hudson's Bay Company's Territory, and back again. With Map, Illustrations in Colours, and Wood Engravings. 8vo. 21s.

Kemble. — The Saxons in England: A History of the English Commonwealth till the Conquest. By J. M. KEMBLE, M.A. 2 vols. 8vo. 28s.

Keith Johnston's Dictionary of Geography, Descriptive, Physical, Statistical, and Historical: Forming a complete General Gazetteer of the World. *Third Edition*, revised to April 1860. In 1 vol. of 1,360 pages, comprising about 50,000 Names of Places, 8vo. 30s. cloth; or half-bound in russia, 35s.

Kesteven. — A Manual of the Domestic Practice of Medicine. By W. B. KESTEVEN, F.R.C.S.E., &c. Square post 8vo. 7s. 6d.

Kirby and Spence's Introduction to Entomology; or, Elements of the Natural History of Insects: Comprising an Account of Noxious and Useful Insects, of their Metamorphoses, Food, Stratagems, Habitations, Societies, Motions, Noises, Hybernation, Instinct, &c. *Seventh Edition*, with an Appendix relative to the Origin and Progress of the work. Crown 8vo. 5s.

A Lady's Tour round Monte Rosa; with Visits to the Italian Valleys of Anzasca, Mastalone, Camasco, Sesia, Lys, Challant, Aosta, and Cogne. With Map, 4 Illustrations from Sketches by Mr. G. Barnard, and 8 Woodcuts. Post 8vo. 14s.

Lardner's Cabinet Cyclopædia of History, Biography, Literature, the Arts and Sciences, Natural History, and Manufactures. A Series of Original Works by EMINENT WRITERS. Complete in 132 vols. fcp. 8vo. with Vignette Titles, price £19. 19s. cloth lettered.

The Works *separately*, in single Volumes or Sets, price 3s. 6d. each Volume, cloth lettered.

Latham. — The English Language. By R. G. LATHAM, M.A., M.D., F.R.S., late Professor of the English Language in University College, London. Fourth Edition, 2 vols. 8vo. 28s.

Dr. Latham's Handbook of the English Language for the Use of Students of the Universities and Higher Classes of Schools. *Third Edition*. Post 8vo. 7s. 6d.

Mrs. R. Lee's Elements of Natural History; or, First Principles of Zoology: Comprising the Principles of Classification, interspersed with amusing and instructive Accounts of the most remarkable Animals. New Edition; Woodcuts. Fcp. 8vo. 7s. 6d.

L.E.L. — The Poetical Works of Letitia Elizabeth Landon; comprising the *Improvisatrice*, the *Venetian Bracelet*, the *Golden Violet*, the *Troubadour*, and Poetical Remains. 2 vols. 16mo. 10s. cloth; morocco, 21s.

Dr. John Lindley's Theory and Practice of Horticulture; or, an Attempt to explain the principal Operations of Gardening upon Physiological Grounds. With 98 Woodcuts. 8vo. 21s.

Dr. John Lindley's Introduction to Botany. New Edition, with corrections and copious Additions. 2 vols. 8vo. with Plates and Woodcuts, 24s.

Dr. Lindley's Synopsis of the British Flora arranged according to the Natural Orders; containing Vasculares or Flowering Plants. Fcp. 8vo. 6s.

Linwood's Anthologia Oxoniensis, sive Florilegium e Lusibus poeticis diversorum Oxoniensium Græcis et Latinis decerptum. 8vo. 14s.

Lorimer's Letters to a Young Master Mariner on some Subjects connected with his Calling. Fcp. 8vo. price 5s. 6d.

Loudon's Encyclopædia of Gardening: Comprising the Theory and Practice of Horticulture, Floriculture, Arboriculture, and Landscape Gardening. With 1,000 Woodcuts. 8vo. 31s. 6d.

Loudon's Encyclopædia of Trees and Shrubs, or *Arboretum et Fruticetum Britannicum* abridged: Containing the Hardy Trees and Shrubs of Great Britain, Native and Foreign, Scientifically and Popularly Described. With about 2,000 Woodcuts. 8vo. 50s.

Loudon's Encyclopædia of Agriculture: Comprising the Theory and Practice of the Valuation, Transfer, Laying-out, Improvement, and Management of Landed Property, and of the Cultivation and Economy of the Animal and Vegetable Productions of Agriculture. With 1,100 Woodcuts. 8vo. 31s. 6d.

Loudon's Encyclopædia of Plants: Comprising the Specific Character, Description, Culture, History, Application in the Arts, and every other desirable Particular respecting Plants found in Great Britain. With above 12,000 Woodcuts. 8vo. 73s. 6d.

Loudon's Encyclopædia of Cottage, Farm, and Villa Architecture and Furniture. New Edition, edited by Mrs. LOUDON; with more than 2,000 Woodcuts. 8vo. 63s.

Loudon's Hortus Britannicus; or, Catalogue of all the Plants found in Great Britain. New Edition, corrected by Mrs. LOUDON. 8vo. 31s. 6d.

Mrs. Loudon's Lady's Country Companion; or, How to Enjoy a Country Life Rationally. Fcp. 8vo. 5s.

Mrs. Loudon's Amateur Gardener's Calendar, or Monthly Guide to what should be avoided and done in a Garden. Crown 8vo. Woodcuts, 7s. 6d.

Love's Art of Cleaning, Dyeing, Scouring, and Finishing on the most approved English and French Methods: Being Practical Instructions in Dyeing *Silks, Woollens,* and *Cottons, Feathers, Chip, Straw,* &c.; Scouring and Cleaning *Bed* and *Window Curtains, Carpets, Rugs,* &c.; French and English Cleaning any Colour or Fabric of *Silk, Satin,* or *Damask.* Post 8vo. 7s. 6d.

Lowe. — Central India during the Rebellion of 1857 and 1858: A Narrative of Operations of the British Forces from the Suppression of Mutiny in Aurungabad to the Capture of Gwalior under Major-General Sir HUGH ROSE, G.C.B., &c., and Brigadier Sir C. STUART, K.C.B. By THOMAS LOWE, M.R.C.S.E. Post 8vo. with Map, price 9s. 6d.

Lowndes's Engineer's Handbook; explaining the Principles which should guide the young Engineer in the Construction of Machinery, with the necessary Rules, Proportions, and Tables. Post 8vo. 5s.

Lord Macaulay's Miscellaneous Writings; comprising his Contributions to *Knight's Quarterly Magazine*, Articles contributed to the Edinburgh Review not included in his *Critical and Historical Essays*, Biographies written for the *Encyclopædia Britannica*, Miscellaneous Poems and Inscriptions. 2 vols. 8vo. with Portrait, 21s.

Macaulay. — The History of England from the Accession of James II. By the Right Hon. Lord MACAULAY. New Edition. VOLS. I. and II. 8vo. 32s.; VOLS. III. and IV. 36s.

Lord Macaulay's History of England from the Accession of James II. New Edition of the first Four Volumes of the Octavo Edition, revised and corrected. 7 vols. post 8vo. 6s. each.

Lord Macaulay's Critical and Historical Essays contributed to The Edinburgh Review. Four Editions:—
1. A LIBRARY EDITION (the *Eighth*), in 3 vols. 8vo. price 36s.
2. Complete in ONE VOLUME, with Portrait and Vignette. Square crown 8vo. price 21s. cloth; or 30s. calf.
3. Another NEW EDITION, in 3 vols. fcp. 8vo. price 21s. cloth.
4. The PEOPLE'S EDITION, in 2 vols. crown 8vo. price 8s. cloth.

Lord Macaulay's Lays of Ancient Rome, with *Ivry* and the *Armada*. 16mo. price 4s. 6d. cloth; or 10s. 6d. bound in morocco.

Lord Macaulay's Lays of Ancient Rome. With Illustrations, Original and from the Antique, drawn on Wood by G. Scharf, jun. Fcp. 4to. 21s. boards; or 42s. bound in morocco.

Macaulay. — Speeches of the Right Hon. Lord MACAULAY. Corrected by HIMSELF. 8vo. 12s.

Mac Donald. — Poems. By George MAC DONALD, Author of *Within and Without*. Fcp. 8vo. 7s.

Mac Donald. — Within and Without: A Dramatic Poem. By GEORGE MAC DONALD. Fcp. 8vo. 4s. 6d.

Mac Dougall. — The Theory of War illustrated by numerous Examples from History. By Lieutenant-Colonel P. L. MAC DOUGALL, Commandant of the Staff College. *Second Edition*, revised. Post 8vo. with Plans, 10s. 6d.

Mac Dougall. — The Campaigns of Hannibal, arranged and critically considered, expressly for the use of Students of Military History. By Lt.-Col. P. L. MacDougall. Post 8vo. 7s. 6d.

Sir James Mackintosh's Miscellaneous Works; Including his Contributions to the Edinburgh Review. Square crown 8vo. 21s. cloth; or 30s. bound in calf: or in 3 vols. fcp. 8vo. 21s.

Sir James Mackintosh's History of England from the Earliest Times to the final Establishment of the Reformation. 2 vols. 8vo. 21s.

M'Culloch's Dictionary, Practical, Theoretical, and Historical, of Commerce, and Commercial Navigation. Illustrated with Maps and Plans. New Edition. 8vo. price 50s. cloth; or 55s. half-russia. SUPPLEMENT to the Edition published in 1859, containing the late Commercial Treaty with France, the New Indian Tariff, &c. price 2s. 6d.

M'Culloch's Dictionary, Geographical, Statistical, and Historical, of the various Countries, Places, and principal Natural Objects in the World. With 6 Maps. 2 vols. 8vo. 63s.

Maguire. — Rome; its Ruler and its Institutions. By JOHN FRANCIS MAGUIRE, M.P. Second Edition, enlarged. Post 8vo. 10s. 6d.

Mrs. Marcet's Conversations on Natural Philosophy, in which the Elements of that Science are familiarly explained. With 34 Plates. Fcp. 8vo. price 10s. 6d.

Mrs. Marcet's Conversations on Chemistry, in which the Elements of that Science are familiarly explained and illustrated. 2 vols. fcp. 8vo. 14s.

Marshman's Life of General Havelock.—Memoirs of Major-General Sir Henry Havelock, K.C.B. By JOHN CLARK MARSHMAN. With Portrait, Map, and 2 Plans. 8vo. 12s. 6d.

Marshman.—The Life and Times of Carey, Marshman, and Ward: Embracing the History of the Serampore Mission. By JOHN CLARK MARSHMAN. 2 vols. 8vo. 25s.

Martineau. — Studies of Christianity: A Series of Original Papers, now first collected, or New. By JAMES MARTINEAU. Crown 8vo. 7s. 6d.

Martineau. — Endeavours after the Christian Life: Discourses. By JAMES MARTINEAU. 2 vols. post 8vo. price 7s. 6d. each.

Martineau. — Hymns for the Christian Church and Home. Collected and edited by JAMES MARTINEAU. Eleventh Edition, 12mo. 3s. 6d. cloth, or 5s. calf; Fifth Edition, 32mo. 1s. 4d. cloth, or 1s. 8d. roan; an Edition in 18mo. price 2s. 10d. cloth.

Martineau.—Miscellanies: Comprising Essays chiefly religious and controversial. By JAMES MARTINEAU. Crown 8vo. 9s.

Maunder's Scientific and Literary Treasury: A new and popular Encyclopædia of Science and the Belles-Lettres; including all Branches of Science, and every subject connected with Literature and Art. Thoroughly revised Edition, with Corrections and Additions. Fcp. 8vo. 10s.

Maunder's Biographical Treasury; consisting of Memoirs, Sketches, and brief Notices of above 12,000 Eminent Persons of All Ages and Nations, from the Earliest Period of History: Forming a complete Dictionary of Universal Biography. Eleventh Edition, corrected and extended. Fcp. 8vo. 10s.

Maunder's Treasury of Knowledge and Library of Reference: Comprising an English Dictionary and Grammar, a Universal Gazetteer, a Classical Dictionary, a Chronology, a Law Dictionary, a Synopsis of the Peerage, numerous useful Tables, &c. New Edition, reconstructed by B. B. WOODWARD, B.A.; assisted by J. MORRIS, Solicitor, and W. HUGHES, F.R.G.S. Fcp. 8vo. 10s.

Maunder's Treasury of Natural History; or, a Popular Dictionary of Animated Nature: In which the Zoological Characteristics that distinguish the different Classes, Genera, and Species, are combined with a variety of interesting Information illustrative of the Habits, Instincts, and General Economy of the Animal Kingdom. With 900 Woodcuts. Fcp. 10s.

Maunder's Historical Treasury; comprising a General Introductory Outline of Universal History, Ancient and Modern, and a Series of Separate Histories of every principal Nation that exists; their Rise, Progress, and Present Condition, the Moral and Social Character of their respective Inhabitants, their Religion, Manners, and Customs, &c. New Edition, carefully revised throughout; with a new INDEX now first added. Fcp. 8vo. 10s.

Maunder's Treasury of Geography, Physical, Historical, Descriptive, and Political; containing a succinct Account of Every Country in the World: Preceded by an Introductory Outline of the History of Geography; a Familiar Inquiry into the Varieties of Race and Language exhibited by different Nations; and a View of the Relations of Geography to Astronomy and the Physical Sciences. New Edition, carefully revised throughout; with the Statistics throughout the volume brought, in every instance, up to the latest date of information. With 7 Maps and 16 Steel Plates. Fcp. 8vo. price 10s.

Merivale (Miss). — Christian Records: A Short History of Apostolic Age. By LOUISA A. MERIVALE. Fcp. 8vo. price 7s. 6d.

Merivale. — The Fall of the Roman Republic: A Short History of Last Century of the Commonwealth. By Rev. C. MERIVALE. 12mo. 7s. 6d.

Merivale. — A History of the Romans under the Empire. By the Rev. CHARLES MERIVALE, B.D., late Fellow of St. John's College, Cambridge. 8vo. with Maps :—

VOLS. I. and II. comprising the History to the Fall of *Julius Cæsar*. Second Edition, 28s.

VOL. III. to the Establishment of the Monarchy by *Augustus*. Second Edition......14s.

VOLS. IV. and V. from *Augustus* to *Claudius*, B.C. 27 to A.D. 54 ....32s.

VOL. VI. from the Reign of Nero, A.D. 54, to the Fall of Jerusalem, A.D. 70............16s.

Miles.—The Horse's Foot and How to Keep it Sound. *Eighth Edition;* with an Appendix on Shoeing in general, and Hunters in particular. 12 Plates and 12 Woodcuts. By W. MILES, Esq. Imperial 8vo. 12s. 6d.

Miles's Plain Treatise on Horse-Shoeing. With Plates and Woodcuts. Second Edition. Post 8vo. 2s.

Minturn. — From New York to Delhi by way of Rio de Janeiro, Australia, and China. By ROBERT B. MINTURN, Jun. With coloured Route-Map of India. Post 8vo. 7s. 6d.

Thomas Moore's Memoirs, Journal, and Correspondence. New Edition for the People, with 8 Portraits and 2 Vignettes on Steel. Edited and abridged from the First Edition by the Right Hon. LORD JOHN RUSSELL, M.P. Uniform with the *People's Edition of Moore's Poetical Works*. Square crown 8vo. 12s. 6d. cloth, gilt edges.

Thomas Moore's Poetical Works: Comprising the Author's Autobiographical Prefaces, latest Corrections, and Notes. Various Editions of the separate Poems and complete Poetical Works, as follows :—

	s.	d.
LALLA ROOKH, fcp. 4to. with Wood-cut Illustrations by TENNIEL.........	21	0
LALLA ROOKH, 32mo. ruby type	1	0
LALLA ROOKH, 16mo. Vignette	2	6
LALLA ROOKH, square crown 8vo. Plates	15	0
IRISH MELODIES, 32mo. ruby type..	1	0
IRISH MELODIES, 16mo. Vignette ..	2	6
IRISH MELODIES, square crown 8vo. Plates	21	0
IRISH MELODIES, illustrated by MACLISE, super-royal 8vo.................	31	6
SONGS, BALLADS, and SACRED SONGS, 32mo. ruby type	2	6
SONGS, BALLADS, and SACRED SONGS, 16mo. Vignette	5	0
POETICAL WORKS, People's Edition, 10 PARTS, each.......................	1	0
POETICAL WORKS, Cabinet Edition, 10 Vols. each..........................	3	6
POETICAL WORKS, Traveller's Edition, crown 8vo........................	12	6
POETICAL WORKS, Library Edition, medium 8vo............................	21	0
SELECTIONS, "POETRY and PICTURES from THOMAS MOORE," fcp. 4to. Wood Engravings	21	0
MOORE'S EPICUREAN, 16mo. Vignette..................................	5	0

Editions printed with the Music.

IRISH MELODIES, People's Edition, small 4to.	12	0
IRISH MELODIES, imperial 8vo. small music size	31	6
HARMONISED AIRS from IRISH MELODIES, imperial 8vo.	15	0
NATIONAL AIRS, People's Edition, small 4to.	12	0
NATIONAL AIRS, imperial 8vo. small music size	31	6
SACRED SONGS and SONGS from SCRIPTURE, imperial 8vo.	16	0

No Edition of Thomas Moore's Poetical Works can be published complete except by Messrs. LONGMAN and Co.

Mollhausen's Diary of a Journey from the Mississippi to the Coasts of the Pacific, with a United States Government Expedition. With an Introduction by Baron Humboldt; Map and Illustrations. 2 vols. 8vo. 30s.

Moore.—The Power of the Soul over the Body, considered in relation to Health and Morals. By GEORGE MOORE, M.D. Fcp. 8vo. 6s.

Moore.—The Use of the Body in relation to the Mind. By G. MOORE, M.D. Fcp. 8vo, 6s.

Moore.—Man and his Motives. By GEORGE MOORE, M.D. Fcp. 8vo. 6s.

James Montgomery's Poetical Works: Collective Edition; with the Author's Autobiographical Prefaces, complete in One Volume; with Portrait and Vignette. Square crown 8vo. 10s. 6d. cloth; morocco, 21s.—Or, in 4 vols. fcp. 8vo. with Plates, 14s.

Morell. — Elements of Psychology: PART I., containing the Analysis of the Intellectual Powers. By J. D. MORELL, M.A., One of Her Majesty's Inspectors of Schools. Post 8vo. 7s. 6d.

Morning Clouds. By the Author of *The Afternoon of Life*. Second Edition, revised throughout. Fcp. 8vo, 5s.

Morton's Agricultural Handbooks.—Handbook of Dairy Husbandry: Comprising Dairy Statistics; Food of the Cow; Milk; Butter; Cheese; General Management; Calendar of Daily Dairy Operations; Appendix on Cheese-making; and Index. By JOHN CHALMERS MORTON. 16mo. 1s. 6d.

HANDBOOK of FARM LABOUR, Steam, Horse, and Water Power, *nearly ready.*

Morton.—The Resources of Estates: A Treatise on the Agricultural Improvement and General Management of Landed Property. By JOHN LOCKHART MORTON. With 25 Lithographic Illustrations. Royal 8vo. 31s.6d.

Moseley.—Astro-Theology. By the Rev. HENRY MOSELEY, M.A., F.R.S., Chaplain in Ordinary to the Queen, &c. Fcp. 8vo. 4s. 6d.

Moseley's Mechanical Principles of Engineering and Architecture. Second Edition, enlarged; with numerous Woodcuts. 8vo. 21s.

Memoirs and Letters of the late Colonel ARMINE MOUNTAIN, Adjutant-General of H. M. Forces in India. Edited by Mrs. MOUNTAIN. Second Edition, Portrait. Fcp. 8vo. 6s.

Mure.—A Critical History of the Language and Literature of Ancient Greece. By WILLIAM MURE, of Caldwell. VOLS. I. to III. 8vo. price 36s.; VOL. IV. 15s.; and VOL. V. 18s.

Murray's Encyclopædia of Geography, comprising a complete Description of the Earth: Exhibiting its Relation to the Heavenly Bodies, its Physical Structure, the Natural History of each Country, and the Industry, Commerce, Political Institutions, and Civil and Social State of All Nations. Second Edition; with 82 Maps, and upwards of 1,000 other Woodcuts. 8vo. 60s.

Neale.—The Closing Scene; or, Christianity and Infidelity contrasted in the Last Hours of Remarkable Persons. By the Rev. ERSKINE NEALE, M.A. 2 vols. fcp. 8vo. 6s. each.

Newman.—The Scope and Nature of University Education. By JOHN HENRY NEWMAN, D.D., of the Oratory. Second Edition. Fcp. 8vo. 6s.

By the same Author, fcp. 8vo. 6s. each,

LECTURES and ESSAYS on UNIVERSITY SUBJECTS.

The OFFICE and WORK of UNIVERSITIES.

Ogilvie.—The Master-Builder's Plan; or, the Principles of Organic Architecture as indicated in the Typical Forms of Animals. By GEORGE OGILVIE, M.D. Post 8vo. with 72 Woodcuts, price 6s. 6d.

Osborn.—The Discovery of the North-West Passage by H.M.S. *Investigator*, Captain R. M'CLURE, 1850-1854. Edited by Captain SHERARD OSBORN, C.B. Third Edition; with Portrait, Chart, and Illustrations. 8vo. 15s.

Professor Owen's Lectures on the Comparative Anatomy and Physiology of the Invertebrate Animals. Second Edition, with 235 Woodcuts. 8vo. 21s.

Professor Owen's Lectures on the Comparative Anatomy and Physiology of the Vertebrate Animals. VOL. I. 8vo. 14s.

Palleske's Life of Schiller. Translated by LADY WALLACE. Dedicated by permission to Her Majesty the Queen. 2 vols. post 8vo. with 2 Portraits, 21s.

Memoirs of Admiral Parry, the Arctic Navigator. By his Son, the Rev. E. PARRY, M.A. Seventh Edition; with a Portrait and coloured Chart of the North-West Passage. Fcp. 8vo. 5s.

Peaks, Passes, and Glaciers: a Series of Excursions by Members of the Alpine Club. Edited by JOHN BALL, M.R.I.A., F.L.S., President. Traveller's Edition (the *Fifth*), comprising all the Mountain Expeditions and the Maps, printed in a condensed form for the Pocket or Knapsack. 16mo. 5s. 6d.

The Fourth Edition of *Peaks, Passes, and Glaciers*, with 8 coloured Illustrations and many Woodcuts, may still be had, price 21s. Also the EIGHT SWISS MAPS, accompanied by a Table of the HEIGHTS of MOUNTAINS, 3s. 6d.

Peel.—Sketch of the Life and Character of Sir Robert Peel, Bart. By the Right Hon. Sir LAWRENCE PEEL. Post 8vo. 8s. 6d.

Dr. Pereira's Elements of Materia Medica and Therapeutics. *Third Edition*, enlarged and improved from the Author's Materials by A. S. TAYLOR, M.D., and G. O. REES, M.D. Vol. I. 8vo. 28s.; Vol. II. Part I. 21s.; Vol. II. Part II. 26s.

Dr. Pereira's Lectures on Polarised Light, together with a Lecture on the Microscope. 2d Edition, enlarged from the Author's Materials by Rev. B. POWELL, M.A. Fcp. 8vo. Woodcuts, price 7s.

Peschel's Elements of Physics. Translated from the German, with Notes, by E. WEST. With Diagrams and Woodcuts. 3 vols. fcp. 8vo. 21s.

Phillips's Elementary Introduction to Mineralogy. A New Edition, with extensive Alterations and Additions, by H. J. BROOKE, F.R.S., F.G.S.; and W. H. MILLER, M.A., F.G.S. With numerous Woodcuts. Post 8vo. 18s.

Phillips.—A Guide to Geology. By JOHN PHILLIPS, M.A., F.R.S., F.G.S., &c. Fourth Edition, corrected; with 4 Plates. Fcp. 8vo. 5s.

Piesse's Laboratory of Chymical Wonders: A Scientific Mélange intended for the Instruction and Entertainment of Young People. Fcp. 8vo. with Illustrations. *[Just ready.*

Piesse's Chymical, Natural, and Physical Magic, for the Instruction and Entertainment of Juveniles during the Holiday Vacation: with 30 Woodcuts and Portrait. Fcp. 8vo. 3s. 6d.

Piesse's Art of Perfumery, and Methods of Obtaining the Odours of Plants; with Instructions for the Manufacture of Perfumes for the Handkerchief, Scented Powders, Odorous Vinegars, Dentifrices, Pomatums, Cosmétiques, Perfumed Soap, &c.; and an Appendix on the Colours of Flowers, Artificial Fruit Essences, &c. *Second Edition;* Woodcuts. Crown 8vo. 8s. 6d.

Piozzi.—Autobiography, Letters, and Literary Remains of Mrs. Piozzi (Thrale), Author of *Anecdotes of Dr. Johnson.* Edited, with Notes and some account of her Life and Writings, by A. HAYWARD, Esq., Q.C. With a Portrait of Mrs. Piozzi, and an engraving from a Picture by Hogarth.

Pitt.—How to Brew Good Beer: A complete Guide to the Art of Brewing Ale, Bitter Ale, Table Ale, Brown Stout, Porter, and Table Beer. To which are added Practical Instructions for Making Malt. By JOHN PITT. Fcp. 8vo. 4s. 6d.

Porter.—History of the Knights of Malta, or the Order of the Hospital of St. John of Jerusalem. By Major WHITWORTH PORTER, R.E. With 5 Illustrations. 2 vols. 8vo. 24s.

Powell.—Essays on the Spirit of the Inductive Philosophy, the Unity of Worlds, and the Philosophy of Creation. By the Rev. BADEN POWELL, M.A., &c. Crown 8vo. Woodcuts, 12s. 6d.

Powell. — Christianity without Judaism: A Second Series of Essays on the Unity of Worlds and of Nature. By the Rev. BADEN POWELL, M.A., &c. Crown 8vo. 7s. 6d.

Powell.—The Order of Nature
considered in reference to the Claims of
Revelation: A Third Series of Essays
on the Unity of Worlds and of Nature.
By the Rev. BADEN POWELL, M.A.
Crown 8vo. 12s.

Power. — Virginia's Hand: a
Poem. By MARGUERITE A. POWER.
Fcp. 8vo. 5s.

Pycroft.—The Collegian's Guide;
or, Recollections of College Days: Setting forth the Advantages and Temptations of a University Education. By
the Rev. J. PYCROFT, B.A. Fcp.8vo. 6s.

Pycroft's Course of English
Reading; or, How and What to Read:
Adapted to every taste and capacity.
With Literary Anecdotes. Fcp. 8vo. 5s.

Pycroft's Cricket-Field ; or, the
Science and History of the Game of
Cricket. Third Edition; Plates and
Woodcuts. Fcp. 8vo. 5s.

Quatrefages' Rambles of a Na-
turalist on the Coasts of France, Spain,
and Sicily. Translated by E. C. OTTÉ.
2 vols. post 8vo. 15s.

Thomas Raikes's Journal from
1831 to 1847: Comprising Reminiscences of Social and Political Life
in London and Paris during that period. New Edition, complete in 2 vols.
crown 8vo. price 12s.

Ramsay.—The Old Glaciers of
North Wales and Switzerland. By A.
C. RAMSAY, F.R.S. and G.S. With
Map and 11 Woodcuts. Fcp. 8vo.
price 4s. 6d.

Rich's Dictionary of Roman and
Greek Antiquities, with nearly 2,000
Woodcuts representing Objects from
the Antique. Forming an Illustrated
Companion to the Latin Dictionary and
Greek Lexicon. Second and cheaper
Edition. Post 8vo. 12s. 6d.

Horsemanship; or, the Art of
Riding and Managing a Horse, adapted
to the Guidance of Ladies and Gentlemen on the Road and in the Field :
With Instructions for Breaking-in Colts
and Young Horses. By Captain RICHARDSON, late of the 4th Light Dragoons.
With 5 Plates. Square crown 8vo. 14s.

Riddle's Household Prayers for
Four Weeks : With additional Prayers
for Special Occasions. To which is
appended a Course of Scripture Reading for Every Day in the Year. Second
Edition. Crown 8vo. 3s. 6d.

Riddle's Complete Latin-English
and English-Latin Dictionary, for the
use of Colleges and Schools. New Edition, revised and corrected. 8vo. 21s.

Riddle's Diamond Latin-English
Dictionary. A Guide to the Meaning,
Quality, and right Accentuation of
Latin Classical Words. Royal 32mo. 1s.

Riddle's Copious and Critical
Latin-English Lexicon, founded on the
German-Latin Dictionaries of Dr. William Freund. Post 4to. 31s. 6d.

Rivers's Rose-Amateur's Guide;
containing ample Descriptions of all
the fine leading variety of Roses, regularly classed in their respective Families; their History and Mode of Culture.
Sixth Edition. Fcp. 8vo. 3s. 6d.

Dr. E. Robinson's Greek and
English Lexicon to the Greek Testament. A New Edition, revised and in
great part re-written. 8vo. 18s.

Mr. Henry Rogers's Essays se-
lected from Contributions to the *Edinburgh Review*. Second Edition, with
Additions. 3 vols. fcp. 8vo. 21s.

Samuel Rogers's Recollections
of Personal and Conversational Intercourse with Fox, Burke, Grattan, Porson, Horne Tooke, Talleyrand, Erskine,
Scott, Lord Grenville, *and the Duke of*
Wellington. *Second Edition.* Fcp.
8vo. 5s.

Dr. Roget's Thesaurus of Eng-
lish Words and Phrases classified and
arranged so as to facilitate the Expression of Ideas and assist in Literary
Composition. Ninth Edition, revised
and improved. Crown 8vo. 10s. 6d.

Ronalds's Fly-Fisher's Entomo-
logy : With coloured Representation
of the Natural and Artificial Insects,
and a few Observations and Instructions on Trout and Grayling Fishing.
Fifth Edition ; with 20 new-coloured
Plates. 8vo. 14s.

Rowton's Debater: A Series of complete Debates, Outlines of Debates, and Questions for Discussion; with ample References to the best Sources of Information. Fcp. 8vo. 6s.

Dr. C. W. Russell's Life of Cardinal Mezzofanti: With an Introductory Memoir of eminent Linguists, Ancient and Modern. With Portrait and Facsimiles. 8vo. 12s.

SchimmelPenninck (Mrs.) — Life of Mary Anne Schimmel Penninck. Edited by her relation, CHRISTIANA C. HANKIN. Fourth Edition, carefully revised throughout; with a few Additions and a Portrait of Mrs. Schimmel-Penninck. Post 8vo. 10s. 6d.

SchimmelPenninck's (Mrs.) Select Memoirs of Port Royal. Fifth Edition, revised, &c. by C. C. HANKIN. 3 vols. post 8vo. 21s.

SchimmelPenninck's (Mrs.) Principles of Beauty; with an Essay on the Temperaments, and Thoughts on Grecian and Gothic Architecture. Edited by C. C. HANKIN. With 12 coloured Illustrations in Facsimile of Original Designs by Mrs. Schimmel Penninck. price 12s. 6d.

SchimmelPenninck's (Mrs.) Sacred Musings on Manifestations of God to the Soul of Man; with Thoughts on the Destiny of Woman, and other subjects. Edited by C. C. HANKIN; with Preface by the Rev. Dr. BAYLEE. Post 8vo. 10s. 6d.

Dr. L. Schmitz's History of Greece, mainly based upon Bishop Thirlwall's History. Fifth Edition, with Nine new Supplementary Chapters on the Civilisation, Religion, Literature, and Arts of the Ancient Greeks, contributed by C. H. WATSON, M.A. Trin. Coll. Camb.; also a Map of Athens and 137 Woodcuts designed by G. Scharf, jun., F.S.A. 12mo. 7s. 6d.

Scoffern (Dr.)—Projectile Weapons of War and Explosive Compounds. By J. SCOFFERN, M.B. Lond. 4th Edition. Post 8vo. Woodcuts, 9s. 6d.

Senior.—Journal kept in Turkey and Greece in the Autumn of 1857 and the beginning of 1858. By NASSAU W. SENIOR, Esq. With 2 Maps and 2 Views. Post 8vo. 12s.

Sewell (Miss).—New Edition of the Tales and Stories of the Author of Amy Herbert, in 9 vols. crown 8vo. price £1. 10s. cloth; or each work complete in one volume, separately, as follows:—

AMY HERBERT............ 2s. 6d.
GERTRUDE................ 2s. 6d.
The EARL'S DAUGHTER.. 2s. 6d.
The EXPERIENCE of LIFE.. 2s. 6d.
CLEVE HALL............. 3s. 6d.
IVORS, or the Two COUSINS 3s. 6d.
KATHARINE ASHTON.... 3s. 6d.
MARGARET PERCIVAL .. 5s. 0d.
LANETON PARSONAGE .. 4s. 6d.

Also by the Author of Amy Herbert.

Passing Thoughts on Religion. New Edition. Fcp. 8vo. 5s.

Ursula: A Tale of English Country Life. 2 vols. fcp. 8vo. 12s.

History of the Early Church: from the First Preaching of the Gospel to the Council of Nicea. 18mo. 4s. 6d.

Self-Examination before Confirmation: With Devotions and Directions for Confirmation-Day. 32mo, 1s. 6d.

Readings for a Month preparatory to Confirmation: Compiled from the Works of Writers of the Early and of the English Church. Fcp. 8vo. 4s.

Readings for every Day in Lent: Compiled from the Writings of Bishop JEREMY TAYLOR. Fcp. 8vo. 5s.

Bowdler's Family Shakspeare: In which nothing is *added* to the Original Text; but those words and expressions are *omitted* which cannot with propriety be read aloud. Illustrated with 36 Woodcut Vignettes. *Library Edition*, in One Volume, medium 8vo. price 21s.; *Pocket Edition*, in 6 vols. fcp. 8vo. price 5s. each; each *Play* separately, price 1s.

Sharp's New British Gazetteer, or Topographical Dictionary of the British Islands and narrow Seas: Comprising concise Descriptions of about 60,000 Places, Seats, Natural Features, and Objects of Note, founded on the best authorities. 2 vols. 8vo. £2. 16s.

Shee.—Life of Sir Martin Archer Shee, President of the Royal Academy, F.R.S., D.C.L. By his Son, MARTIN ARCHER SHEE, of the Middle Temple, Esq., Barrister-at-Law. 2 vols. 8vo. 21s.

Short Whist; its Rise, Progress, and Laws: With Observations to make any one a Whist-Player. Containing also the Laws of Piquet, Cassino, Ecarté, Cribbage, Backgammon. By Major A. New Edition; with Precepts for Tyros, by Mrs. B. Fcp. 8vo. 3s.

Simpkinson. — The Washingtons: a Tale of an English Country Parish in the Seventeenth Century. By the Rev. J. N. SIMPKINSON. Post 8vo. 10s. 6d.

Simpson.—Handbook of Dining; or, How to Dine, theoretically, philosophically, and historically considered: Based chiefly upon the *Physiologie du Goût* of Brillat-Savarin. By LEONARD FRANCIS SIMPSON, M.R.S.L. Fcp. 8vo. 5s.

Sir Roger De Coverley. From the Spectator. With Notes and Illustrations, by W. HENRY WILLS; and 12 Wood Engravings from Designs by F. TAYLER. Crown 8vo. 10s. 6d.; or 21s. in morocco by Hayday.

The Sketches: Three Tales. By the Authors of *Amy Herbert*, *The Old Man's Home*, and *Hawkstone*. Fcp. 8vo. price 4s. 6d.

Sleigh.—Personal Wrongs and Legal Remedies. By W. CAMPBELL SLEIGH, of the Middle Temple, Esq., Barrister-at-Law. Fcp. 8vo. 2s. 6d.

Smee's Elements of Electro-Metallurgy. Third Edition, revised; with Electrotypes and numerous Woodcuts. Post 8vo. 10s. 6d.

Smith (G.) — History of Wesleyan Methodism. By GEORGE SMITH, F.A.S., Author of *Sacred Annals*, &c. VOL. I. *Wesley and his Times;* VOL. II. *The Middle Age of Methodism*, from 1791 to 1816. Crown 8vo. 10s. 6d. each.

Smith (J.) — The Voyage and Shipwreck of St. Paul: With Dissertations on the Life and Writings of St. Luke, and the Ships and Navigation of the Ancients. By JAMES SMITH, F.R.S. With Charts, Views, and Woodcuts. Crown 8vo. 8s. 6d.

The Wit and Wisdom of the Rev. Sydney Smith: a Selection of the most memorable Passages in his Writings and Conversation. 16mo. 7s. 6d.

A Memoir of the Rev. Sydney Smith. By his Daughter, LADY HOLLAND. With a Selection from his Letters, edited by Mrs. AUSTIN. *New Edition.* 2 vols. 8vo. 28s.

The Rev. Sydney Smith's Miscellaneous Works: Including his Contributions to The Edinburgh Review. Four Editions:—
1. A LIBRARY EDITION (the *Fourth*), in 3 vols. 8vo. with Portrait, 36s.
2. Complete in ONE VOLUME, with Portrait and Vignette. Square crown 8vo. 21s. cloth; or 30s. bound in calf.
3. Another NEW EDITION, in 3 vols. fcp. 8vo. 21s.
4. The People's Edition, in 2 vols. crown 8vo. price 8s. cloth.

The Rev. Sydney Smith's Elementary Sketches of Moral Philosophy, delivered at the Royal Institution in the Years 1804 to 1806. Fcp. 8vo. 7s.

Snow.—Two Years' Cruise off Tierra del Fuego, the Falkland Islands, Patagonia, and in the River Plate: A Narrative of Life in the Southern Seas. By W. PARKER SNOW. With Charts and Illustrations. 2 vols. post 8vo. 21s.

Robert Southey's Complete Poetical Works; containing all the Author's last Introductions and Notes. Complete in One Volume, with Portrait and Vignette. Medium 8vo. 21s. cloth; 42s. bound in morocco. Or in 10 vols. fcp. 8vo. with Portrait and 19 Vignettes, 35s.

Southey's Doctor, complete in One Volume. Edited by the Rev. J. W. WARTER, B.D. With Portrait, Vignette, Bust, and coloured Plate. Square crown 8vo. 21s.

Southey's Life of Wesley; and Rise and Progress of Methodism. Fourth Edition, edited by Rev. C. C. SOUTHEY, M.A. 2 vols. crown 8vo. 12s.

Spencer.—Essays, Scientific, Political, and Speculative. By HERBERT SPENCER, Author of *Social Statics*. Reprinted chiefly from Quarterly Reviews. 8vo. 12s. cloth.

Spencer. — The Principles of Psychology. By HERBERT SPENCER, Author of *Social Statics*. 8vo. 16s.

Spitta.—Lyra Domestica: Christian Songs for Domestic Edification. Translated from the *Psaltery and Harp* of C. J. P. Spitta. By Richard Massie. Fcp. 8vo. with Portrait, price 4s. 6d.

Sir James Stephen's Essays in Ecclesiastical Biography. 4th Edition, complete in One Volume; with Biographical Notice of the Author by his Son. 8vo. 14s.

Sir J. Stephen's Lectures on the History of France. Third Edition. 2 vols. 8vo. 24s.

Stonehenge.—The Dog in Health and Disease: Comprising the various Modes of Breaking and using him for Hunting, Coursing, Shooting, &c.; and including the Points or Characteristics of Toy Dogs. By Stonehenge. With about 70 Illustrations engraved on Wood. Square crown 8vo. 15s.

Stonehenge's Work on the Greyhound: Being a Treatise on the Art of Breeding, Rearing, and Training Greyhounds for Public Running; their Diseases and Treatment: Containing also Rules for the Management of Coursing Meetings, and for the Decision of Courses. With Frontispiece and Woodcuts. Square crown 8vo. 21s.

Stow's Training System, Moral Training School, and Normal Seminary for preparing Schoolmasters and Governesses. Eleventh Edition; Plates and Woodcuts. Post 8vo. 6s. 6d.

Strickland.—Lives of the Queens of England. By Agnes Strickland. Dedicated, by express permission, to Her Majesty. Embellished with Portraits of every Queen, engraved from the most authentic sources. Complete in 8 vols. post 8vo. 7s. 6d. each.

Tate on the Strength of Materials; containing various original and useful Formulæ, specially applied to Tubular Bridges, Wrought Iron and Cast Iron Beams, &c. 8vo. 5s. 6d.

Tennent.—Ceylon: An Account of the Island, Physical, Historical, and Topographical: with Copious Notices of its Natural History, Antiquities, and Productions. Illustrated by 9 Maps, 17 Plans and Charts, and 90 Engravings on Wood. By Sir J. Emerson Tennent, K.C.S., LL.D., &c. Fifth Edition. 2 vols. 8vo. price 50s.

Bishop Thirlwall's History of Greece. Library Edition; with Maps. 8 vols. 8vo. £3.—An Edition in 8 vols. fcp. 8vo. with Vignette Titles, 28s.

Thomson's Seasons. Edited by Bolton Corney, Esq. Illustrated with 77 fine Wood Engravings from Designs by Members of the Etching Club. Square crown 8vo. 21s. cloth; or 36s. bound in morocco.

The Rev. Dr. Thomson's Outline of the Necessary Laws of Thought: A Treatise on Pure and Applied Logic. 5th Edition. Post 8vo. 5s. 6d.

Thomson's Tables of Interest, at Three, Four, Four-and-a-Half, and Five per Cent., from One Pound to Ten Thousand, and from 1 to 365 Days, in a regular progression of single Days; with Interest at all the above Rates, from One to Twelve Months, and from One to Ten Years. Also, numerous other Tables of Exchange, Time, and Discounts. 17th Edition, revised and stereotyped. 12mo. 3s. 6d.

The Thumb Bible; or, Verbum Sempiternum. By J. Taylor. Being an Epitome of the Old and New Testaments in English Verse. Reprinted from the Edition of 1693. 64mo. 1s. 6d.

Todd (Dr.)—The Cyclopædia of Anatomy and Physiology. Edited by Robert B. Todd, M.D., F.R.S., &c. Now complete in 5 vols. 8vo. pp. 5,350, with 2,853 Woodcuts, £6. 6s. cloth.

Tooke.—History of Prices, and of the State of the Circulation, during the Nine Years from 1848 to 1856 inclusive. Forming Vols. V. and VI. of Tooke's *History of Prices*; with full Index to the whole work. By Thomas Tooke, F.R.S. and William Newmarch. 2 vols. 8vo. 52s. 6d.

Trevelyan (Sir C.) — Original Papers illustrating the History of the Application of the Roman Alphabet to the Languages of India. Edited by Monier Williams, M.A. 8vo. 12s.

Trollope.—The Warden, a Novel. By Anthony Trollope. New and cheaper Edition. Crown 8vo. 3s. 6d.

Trollope's Barchester Towers, a Sequel to *The Warden*. New and cheaper Edition, complete in One Volume. Crown 8vo. 5s.

The Traveller's Library: A Collection of original Works well adapted for *Travellers* and *Emigrants*, for *School-room Libraries*, the *Libraries of Mechanics' Institutions*, *Young Men's Libraries*, the *Libraries of Ships*, and similar purposes. The separate volumes are suited for School Prizes, Presents to Young People, and for general instruction and entertainment. The Series comprises fourteen of the most popular of Lord Macaulay's *Essays*, and his *Speeches* on Parliamentary Reform. The department of Travels contains some account of eight of the principal countries of Europe, as well as travels in four districts of Africa, in four of America, and in three of Asia. Madame Pfeiffer's *First Journey round the World* is included; and a general account of the *Australian Colonies*. In Biography and History will be found Lord Macaulay's Biographical Sketches of *Warren Hastings, Clive, Pitt, Walpole, Bacon,* and others; besides Memoirs of *Wellington, Turenne, F. Arago,* &c.; an Essay on the Life and Genius of *Thomas Fuller*, with Selections from his Writings, by Mr. Henry Rogers; and a history of the *Leipsic Campaign*, by Mr. Gleig,—which is the only separate account of this remarkable campaign. Works of Fiction did not come within the plan of the TRAVELLER'S LIBRARY; but the *Confessions of a Working Man*, by Souvestre, which is indeed a fiction founded on fact, has been included, and has been read with unusual interest by many of the working classes, for whose use it is especially recommended. Dumas's story of the *Maitre-d'Armes*, though in form a work of fiction, gives a striking picture of an episode in the history of Russia. Amongst the works on Science and Natural Philosophy, a general view of Creation is embodied in Dr. Kemp's *Natural History of Creation*; and, in his *Indications of Instinct* remarkable facts in natural history are collected. Dr. Wilson has contributed a popular account of the *Electric Telegraph*. In the volumes on the *Coal-Fields*, and on the Tin and other Mining Districts of *Cornwall*, is given an account of the mineral wealth of England, the habits and manners of the miners, and the scenery of the surrounding country. It only remains to add, that among the Miscellaneous Works are a Selection of the best Writings of the Rev. Sydney Smith; Lord Carlisle's *Lectures and Addresses*; an account of *Mormonism*, by the Rev. W. J. Conybeare; an exposition of *Railway* management and mismanagement by Mr. Herbert Spencer; an account of the Origin and Practice of *Printing*, by Mr. Stark; and an account of *London*, by Mr. M'Culloch.—To be had, in *complete Sets* only, at £5. 5s. per Set, bound in cloth and lettered.

☞ *The Traveller's Library* may also be had as originally issued in 102 parts, 1s. each, forming 50 vols. 2s. 6d. each; or any separate parts or volumes.

Sharon Turner's History of the Anglo-Saxons, from the Earliest Period to the Norman Conquest. 3 vols. 36s.

Dr. Turton's Manual of the Land and Fresh-Water Shells of Great Britain: With Figures of each of the kinds. New Edition, with Additions by Dr. J. E. GRAY, F.R.S. Crown 8vo. with 12 coloured Plates, 15s.

Twisden. — Elementary Examples in Practical Mechanics, comprising copious Explanations and Proofs of the Fundamental Propositions. By the Rev. JOHN F. TWISDEN, M.A., Professor of Mathematics in the Staff College. Crown 8vo. 12s.

Dr. Ure's Dictionary of Arts, Manufactures, and Mines: Containing a clear Exposition of their Principles and Practice. New Edition, chiefly rewritten and greatly enlarged; with nearly 2,000 Woodcuts. Edited by ROBERT HUNT, F.R.S., F.S.S., Keeper of Mining Records. 3 vols. 8vo. £4.

Walford. — The Handybook of the Civil Service. By EDWARD WALFORD, M.A., late Scholar of Balliol College, Oxford. Fcp. 8vo. 4s. 6d.

"HERE is the very book which aspirants to Government situations are in search of. It explains the whole system from principles to details. One objection to it may be that it tends to open for the candidate a road rather too royal." ATHENÆUM.

Warburton. — Hunting Songs and Miscellaneous Verses. By R. E. EGERTON WARBURTON. Second Edition. Fcp. 8vo. 5s.

Waterton's Essays on Natural History, chiefly Ornithology: With Autobiography of the Author. THREE SERIES; with Portrait and 2 Vignettes. 3 vols. fcp. 8vo. price 16s.

Webb. — Celestial Objects for Common Telescopes. By the Rev. T. W. WEBB, M.A., F.R.A.S. With Map of the Moon, and Woodcuts. 16mo. 7s.

Webster and Parkes's Encyclopædia of Domestic Economy; comprising such subjects as are most immediately connected with Housekeeping: viz. The Construction of Domestic Edifices, with the Modes of Warming, Ventilating, and Lighting them—A description of the various Articles of Furniture, with the Nature of their Materials — Duties of Servants — &c. With nearly 1,000 Woodcuts. 8vo. 50s.

Weld.—Two Months in the Highlands, Orcadia, and Skye. By CHARLES RICHARD WELD, Barrister-at-Law. With 4 Illustrations in Chromo-lithography and 4 Woodcuts from Sketches by Mr. GEORGE BARNARD and the Author. Post 8vo. 12s. 6d.

Weld's Pyrenees, West and East. With 8 Illustrations in Chromoxylography. Post 8vo. 12s. 6d.

Weld's Vacation Tour in the United States and Canada. 10s. 6d.

Weld's Vacations in Ireland. Post 8vo. 10s. 6d.

Dr. Charles West's Lectures on the Diseases of Infancy and Childhood. Fourth Edition, carefully revised throughout; with numerous additional Cases, and a copious INDEX. 8vo. 14s.

Dr. Charles West on Nursing Sick Children: Containing Directions which may be found of service to all who have the Charge of the Young. Second Edition. Fcp. 8vo. 1s. 6d.

White and Riddle.—A Latin-English Dictionary. By the Rev. J. T. WHITE, M.A., of Corpus Christi College, Oxford; and the Rev. J. E. RIDDLE, M.A., of St. Edmund Hall, Oxford. Founded on the larger Dictionary of Freund, revised by himself. Royal 8vo. [Nearly ready.

Whiteside.—Italy in the Nineteenth Century. By the Right Hon. JAMES WHITESIDE, M.P., LL.D. Third Edition, abridged and revised; with a new Preface. Post 8vo. 12s. 6d.

Wilkins.—Political Ballads of the Seventeenth and Eighteenth Centuries, annotated. By W. WALKER WILKINS. 2 vols. post 8vo.

Willich's Popular Tables for ascertaining the Value of Lifehold, Leasehold, and Church Property, Renewal Fines, &c. With numerous additional Tables—Chemical, Astronomical, Trigonometrical, Common and Hyperbolic Logarithms; Constants, Squares, Cubes, Roots, Reciprocals, &c. Fourth Edition. Post 8vo. 10s.

Wills.—"The Eagle's Nest" in the Valley of Sixt; a Summer Home among the Alps: Together with some Excursions among the Great Glaciers. By ALFRED WILLS, of the Middle Temple, Esq. Barrister-at-Law. Second Edition, with 2 Maps and 12 Illustrations. Post 8vo. 12s. 6d.

Wilmot.—Lord Brougham's Law Reforms; or, an Analytical Review of Lord Brougham's Acts and Bills from 1811 to the Present Time. By Sir JOHN E. EARDLEY-WILMOT, Bart., Recorder of Warwick. Fcp. 8vo. 4s. 6d.

Wilmot's Abridgment of Blackstone's Commentaries on the Laws of England, in a series of Letters from a Father to his Daughter. 12mo. 6s. 6d.

Wilson's Bryologia Britannica: Containing the Mosses of Great Britain and Ireland systematically arranged and described according to the Method of *Bruch* and *Schimper*; with 61 illustrative Plates. Being a New Edition, enlarged and altered, of the *Muscologia Britannica* of Messrs. Hooker and Taylor. 8vo. 42s.; or, with the Plates coloured, price £4. 4s.

Yonge's New English-Greek Lexicon: Containing all the Greek Words used by Writers of good authority. Second Edition. Post 4to. 21s.

Yonge's New Latin Gradus: Containing Every Word used by the Poets of good authority. For the use of Eton, Westminster, Winchester, Harrow, and Rugby Schools; King's College, London; and Marlborough College. *Sixth Edition.* Post 8vo. 9s.; or, with APPENDIX of *Epithets*, 12s.

Youatt's Work on the Horse: With a Treatise on Draught. New Edition, revised and enlarged by E. N. GABRIEL, M.R.C.S., C.V.S. With numerous Woodcut Illustrations, chiefly from designs by W. Harvey. 8vo. Price 10s. 6d. cloth.

Youatt.—The Dog. By William Youatt. A New Edition; with numerous Engravings, from Designs by W. Harvey. 8vo. 6s.

Zumpt's Grammar of the Latin Language. Translated and adapted for the use of English Students by Dr. L. SCHMITZ, F.R.S.E.; With numerous Additions and Corrections by the Author and Translator. 8vo. 11s.

[*October* 1860.

www.ingramcontent.com/pod-product-compliance
Lightning Source LLC
Chambersburg PA
CBHW030748230426
43667CB00007B/884